MARINES AND HELICOPTERS
1946 - 1962

By
Lieutenant Colonel Eugene W. Rawlins, USMC

Edited by
Major William J. Sambito, USMC

HISTORY AND MUSEUMS DIVISION
HEADQUARTERS, U. S. MARINE CORPS
WASHINGTON, D. C.
1976

FOREWORD

This history, which traces the development of helicopters in the Marine Corps from 1946 to 1962, offers a tribute to the creative vision and planning of a handful of Marine officers who conceived of the vertical assault concept in amphibious operations at a time when suitable aircraft to make it work did not exist. The story of the subsequent struggle to procure and develop those aircraft, to refine a doctrine for their employment, and to familiarize the Marine Corps with their use is an interesting and vital part of modern Marine Corps history. The documentary basis for this monograph was primarily the official records of the Marine Corps and Navy Department, but considerable use was made of interviews and correspondence with key individuals involved in all phases of helicopter development.

The author, Lieutenant Colonel Eugene W. Rawlins, received his Bachelor of Arts degree in history from California State University at Fullerton. His experience in Marine Corps aviation includes tours in fighter, attack, transport, and helicopter aircraft. During a period of separation from the Marine Corps he was employed by Sikorsky Aircraft as a production test pilot and later flew for San Francisco and Oakland Helicopter Airlines. After returning to the Marine Corps, Lieutenant Colonel Rawlins served in Vietnam with HMM–361 and –364 in 1963–1964. Three years later he returned to Vietnam for a tour with HMH–463. In 1971 after an assignment as Commanding Officer, HMH–361 at Santa Ana, he came to the History and Museums Division where he remained until July 1973.

Comment copies of the manuscript were sent to many individuals involved with both the conceptual and operational aspects of Marine helicopter development. Major William J. Sambito incorporated these comments and edited the manuscript for printing. Major Sambito earned his Bachelor of Arts degree in psychology from Colby College, Maine, and is an experienced helicopter pilot who served with HMM–262 and –165 during the Vietnam War. After attending the Armed Forces Staff College in January 1975, he was assigned to the History and Museums Division.

The History and Museums Division welcomes any comments on the narrative and additional information or illustrations which might enhance a future edition.

Reviewed and approved:
31 December 1976

E. H. SIMMONS
Brigadier General, U.S. Marine Corps (Retired)
Director of Marine Corps History and Museums

PREFACE

. . . the evolution of a set of principles governing the helicopter employment cannot wait for the perfection of the craft itself, but must proceed concurrently with that development. . . .

COLONEL VICTOR H. KRULAK, USMC
1948

During the early stages of helicopter development, when helicopters were able to lift just slightly more than their own weight, the military services were eagerly seeking to obtain a variety of larger, more useful helicopters. The youthful helicopter industry expressed optimism, although at times unrealistic, in its ability to meet the military requirements.

The development of the helicopter program within the Marine Corps was sparked by the foresight and imagination of the officers of the period. While early helicopters provided stepping stones for an orderly progression of the program, the slowness of the technical advances and the periods of financial austerity after World War II and Korea prevented the Marine Corps from developing the vertical envelopment concept as rapidly as desired. The program gained interest and momentum, however, as a result of the success of helicopters in Korea. As Lieutenant General Gerald C. Thomas stated: "Indeed, the helicopter gave clear evidence, from its first tactical employment, that a major advance in combat was at hand."

The division owes a special debt of gratitude to those who commented on the manuscript and provided valuable insight and assistance. Particularly helpful were the responses of General Vernon E. Megee, USMC (Ret); Lieutenant Generals Edward A. Craig, USMC (Ret) and Victor H. Krulak, USMC (Ret); Major Generals Norman J. Anderson, USMC (Ret), George S. Bowman, Jr., USMC (Ret), Frank H. Lamson-Scribner, USMC (Ret), and Noah C. New, USMC; Colonel George W. Herring, USMC (Ret); and Mr. Robert L. Sherrod.

Appreciation is also extended to the many government and military historians and archivists who assisted in the collection of the reference material. An additional note of gratitude is extended to Mr. Benis M. Frank and Mr. Jack Shulimson of the Historical Branch for their help and encouragement.

The monograph was produced under the editorial direction of Mr. Henry I. Shaw, Jr., Chief Historian of the History and Museums Division. The manuscript was typed and indexed by Miss Cathy Stoll and prepared for publication by the Production Editor, Mr. Douglas Johnston. Most of the photographs used in this monograph are official Department of Defense (Marine Corps) photographs from the History and Museums Division. Other photographs were provided by the U.S. Naval Historical Center, Kamen Aircraft Corporation, and the U.S. National Archives.

WILLIAM J. SAMBITO
Major, U.S. Marine Corps

EUGENE W. RAWLINS
Lieutenant Colonel, U.S. Marine Corps

TABLE OF CONTENTS

INTRODUCTION

Early Helicopter Developments

The commissioning of Marine Helicopter Squadron 1 (HMX-1) in 1947 at Quantico, Virginia, is often cited as the official beginning of rotary-winged aviation within the Marine Corps. Interest by the Marine Corps in the capabilities and potentialities of rotary-winged machines, however, dates back some 15 years prior to the commissioning of HMX-1. It was in the early 1930s that the Marine Corps evaluated the Pitcairn OP-1 autogyro to determine its potential military value. Field tested in Nicaragua during 1932, the four-bladed, stubby-winged aircraft was found suitable only for liaison purposes and medical evacuation of the lightly wounded. Considered by those in Nicaragua as unsafe to fly when carrying loads in excess of 200 pounds, the OP-1 soon disappeared from active Marine Corps inventory. Three years later the Marine Corps tested another autogyro, the Kellett OP-2, a wingless version similar to the OP-1, and found it to be equally unsatisfactory due to its small payload capability. The epitaph of the autogyro as a useful Marine Corps rotor-winged aircraft was written in 1936 by Lieutenant Colonel Roy S. Geiger, an early pioneer in Marine aviation who had served as a pilot in World War I and in the ground forces in Nicaragua, the Philippines and China. In a memorandum for his brigade commander, Geiger said, in his position as Commanding Officer, Aircraft One, Fleet Marine Force, Quantico, Virginia, in relation to the autogyro:

> To date no type of autogyro has been demonstrated which will carry a reasonable fuel supply and military load and at the same time retain its peculiar characteristics of taking off and landing in a restricted area and hovering over a given spot. Until such time as this type aircraft can carry a satisfactory military load and retain its flying characteristics its use [by] the Marine Corps is not recommended.[1]

Although the autogyro contributed substantially to rotary-wing development, a useful configuration of a helicopter continued to elude designers and inventors. It was not until 1939 that Igor I. Sikorsky, a Russian-born aircraft designer and builder, successfully test flew the first practical

The Pitcairn Autogyro was the first rotary-winged Marine aircraft. Field tested in Nicaragua, it soon disappeared from the active inventory (Marine Corps Photo 515209).

helicopter in the Western Hemisphere.* This was the Vought-Sikorsky 300 (VS-300),** [2] a 28-foot, 3-bladed main rotor helicopter with an open cockpit and powered by a 4-cylinder, 75-horsepower engine.

The building of a rotary-winged machine and

---

* The world's first practical helicopter appeared in 1937 in Germany. This was the Focke-Achgeles 61a which had two main rotors mounted side-by-side on outriggers extending from an airplane-type fuselage. The FA-61 had good control; it was once flown inside a 100-by-300-foot exhibition hall in Berlin by a woman pilot, Henna Reitsch.

** In 1929 Sikorsky Aviation Corporation became a subsidiary of United Aircraft which in turn merged the Sikorsky and Chance Vought Divisions in 1939 to form Vought-Sikorsky. Still later, in 1942, Vought-Sikorsky was separated, with Chance Vought remaining in Stratford, Connecticut, and Sikorsky Aircraft Division moving a short distance away to Bridgeport.

subsequent success with the VS–300 were not surprising in view of Igor I. Sikorsky's previous experimentation in the field. As early as 1910, while still in Europe, he had designed and built a coaxial helicopter with a 25-horsepower engine driving two 16-foot contra-rotating rotors through a concentric shaft. Unfortunately, the machine could lift only its own weight. Consequently, Sikorsky turned his talents to designing fixed-wing aircraft.

In 1919, six years after building the world's first successful four-engine aircraft, Igor Sikorsky emigrated from Russia and settled in Connecticut where he continued to pursue the manufacturing of large land and seaplanes. Then, in 1938, he again turned his talent to the field of rotary-wing aircraft and began the most difficult construction of all helicopter designs—the single rotor. While his past experiments had been with the coaxial configuration, Sikorsky preferred the single lifting rotor with a small anti-torque tail rotor. He con-

sidered it to be the best rotor arrangement for a helicopter rather than the more popular side-by-side or tandem lifting rotors.

Realizing the potential value of Sikorsky's new helicopter, the U.S. Army Air Corps awarded a contract to Vought-Sikorsky * on 10 January 1941 for an experimental machine, the XR–4, which was to be built on an expanded scale of the VS–300. Exactly one year later the first R–4 flew at the Sikorsky plant, with subsequent improved versions, the R–5 and R–6, taking to the air in August and October of 1943.

Enlarged in size to suit a 450-horsepower engine, the R–5 eventually proved to be the most successful of the three types. The R–4 and R–6 were powered by 175- and 245-horsepower engines, respectively. Later, the two-passenger R–5 (HO2S–1) was further redesigned to meet civilian and mili-

---

* The Air Corps was acting under a 1939 interservice agreement which gave the Army the initial responsibility for the development of all U. S. helicopters.

The robot OP–1 never got past the testing stage (National Archives Photo 80–G–215856).

tary requirements and became, in August 1946, the first helicopter to be sold to a commercial operator. This three-passenger version of the R–5, while retaining its 450-horsepower engine, was designated by Sikorsky as the S–51 and by the Navy in 1946 as the HO3S–1.

While Sikorsky was the first designer to build a practical helicopter, other American designers soon produced successful and useful rotary-winged machines. In 1943, Frank N. Piasecki, a Pennsylvania engineer, founded the P-V * Engineering Forum at Sharon Hills, Pennsylvania. Piasecki started his company at age 21 with a wealth of knowledge gained by working on various designs of autogyros while employed by the Platt-LePage Aircraft Company in Eddystone, Pennsylvania. He built a small, 3-bladed, single-rotor helicopter, the PV–2, which made its first flight in April 1943. The 1,000-pound gross weight, single-place machine was the first helicopter to incorporate cyclic

---

* Piasecki-Venzi. In 1946 the company's name changed to Piasecki Helicopter Corporation, to Vertol Aircraft Corporation in 1956, in 1960 to Vertol Division, Boeing Company, and in 1972 to the Boeing Vertol Company, a division of the Boeing Company.

control and to have dynamically balanced blades. Both of these features were major advancements to the flight control system of a helicopter. Although the PV–2 was Piasecki's first helicopter to achieve flight, it was also the only single rotor design the company would build since advanced designs of other types were already on the company's drawing boards.

A third helicopter manufacturer appeared on the scene in the early 1940s, the Bell Aircraft Corporation, of Buffalo, New York. An established fixed-wing aircraft manufacturer, Bell began helicopter development early in 1942 in a garage located in Gardenville, New York. To the thousands of employees at the nearby fixed-wing plant in Buffalo, the secret project was known only as "Gyro Tests." The goal was to develop and construct a two-place helicopter. Within the next three years the independently operating group had successfully developed three single rotor helicopters. The first aircraft, designated Bell Model 30–1, was a 1,300-pound, single-place, cigar-shaped craft with an open cockpit. The second machine, Model 30–2, was a two-place, closed-cockpit design, with the

The Sikorsky HO3S-1 became operational in 1946 (Marine Corps Photo 529985).

Lieutenant General Roy S. Geiger, an early aviation pioneer (Marine Corps Photo 1 130 65).

third configuration, Model 30–3, having a three-place capacity.

The Model 30 proved to be so successful that the president, Larry D. Bell, who began his career in 1912 with the Martin Aircraft Company, approved production of a refined version of the third experimental machine. By 1946 Bell had constructed 10 helicopters of the new version and designated them as the Bell Model 47, one of which was issued a Type Certificate H–1 by the Civil Aeronautics Administration on 8 May 1946. This was the first commercial license to be issued to a helicopter.

These three manufacturers (Bell, Piasecki, and Sikorsky) most directly influenced the development of both the Navy's and Marine Corps' helicopter programs. Other manufacturers, though, were actively engaged in experimental helicopter design and construction. Few, however, would produce a model suitable for military use, and those not until the next decade.

Initial Procurements and Designs

As one observer stated, "before Igor Sikorsky flew the VS–300 there was no helicopter industry; after he flew it, there was." [3] Without military procurement of helicopters, prompted by World War

II, it is doubtful that the industry as a whole would have blossomed so rapidly. Navy procurements of Sikorsky helicopters followed closely those made by the Army Air Forces, and in some instances, joint procurement of the same machine was made by the two services. Both the R–4 and R–6 models were accepted by the Navy during World War II, with a significant number of R–5s under contract. With the end of the war, however, the Navy cancelled production of the R–5 except for two aircraft. By the end of 1946, the total number of helicopters in Navy inventory was 20: 7 R–4s (HNS), 9 R–6s (HOS), and 4 Sikorsky commercial Model S–51s (HO3S–1). [4] The four HO3S–1s were procured "off the shelf" in November and December of that year for use in the Antarctic on Operation HIGHJUMP. This low inventory figure was only temporary as the manufacturers were eagerly working on improved models designed to meet present and future military requirements.

HRP–1 Development

All the small Sikorsky helicopters and the Piasecki PV–2 lacked the lifting capacity necessary to perform a rescue mission involving the carrying of more than one person, but more lifting ability and passenger space meant a larger helicopter. One method of obtaining a larger design, was to take a "proven" configuration and multiply it by 1½ or 2 times its original size. At this time, however, the Navy's Bureau of Aeronautics (BuAer) wanted to stay within the scope of existing component development and eliminate as many unknown areas of design and construction as possible. [5] Therefore, BuAer decided to approve the design of a helicopter with two smaller lift rotors, each approximately 40 feet in diameter rather than attempt construction of a larger rotor system (60 to 70 feet in diameter) which was still in the early design stage. [6]

In May 1943, prior to the flight of the PV–2, Piasecki had discussed with BuAer a design for a helicopter with two main rotors in tandem, one forward and one aft. [7] The power plant would drive the two 37-foot diameter rotors through reduction gearing and shafting. It would carry a useful load * of about 1,800 pounds, [8] by far the best

---

* Useful load is defined as the difference between the empty weight of the aircraft and the overall gross (maximum) weight at take-off. Useful load includes the weight of the pilot, fuel, oil, any other special equipment, and the payload. Payload, however, is quite variable. It is not only a function of distance but also of many other factors including altitude of operation, fuel load, temperature, humidity, and wind conditions.

lifting capability of any helicopter to that date.

Piasecki's May 1943 proposal conformed somewhat to BuAer's desire, although there was considerable doubt as to whether a tandem machine could be made to fly—mainly because of the interference of the air-flow to the rear rotor and the problem of longitudinal control. After almost a year of negotiations and study, BuAer awarded Piasecki a contract in early 1944 for the tandem rotored machine, the XHRP-X. This was the Navy's first experimental helicopter, a design arrangement which never received serious attention by any of the leading helicopter manufacturers except Piasecki.[9]

Development of the XHRP-X into a final design acceptable for Navy use was slow. The policy of BuAer required the contractor to produce a full-sized flying model without Navy inspection or interference, with the idea that the contract would be cancelled if the model did not prove success-

ful.[10] The plan also required the test aircraft, XHRP-X, or "Dogship," to be flown by the contractor prior to commencing construction of the first production type HRP-1.

The "flying banana," as the HRP-1 was later nicknamed, and also referred to as the "sagging sausage," was designed to be powered by a 600-horsepower engine driving the two 41-foot rotors. With a full fuel load and a crew of two, it was to carry 900 pounds and cruise at 75 miles per hour. The cargo space could accommodate seats for 10 passengers and would measure 14 feet long and 5 feet wide.

Within one year after receiving the contract, Piasecki built and successfully flew the PV-3 (XHRP-X). The March 1945 flight of the "Dogship" paved the way for design and construction of the 6,400-pound gross weight HRP-1. Unfortunately, the first production aircraft would not be

The HRP-1 by Piasecki was also called the "flying banana" and became operational in 1948 (Marine Corps Photo A-55644).

Marines disembark from HRP–1 during a demonstration at Quantico, Va., on 30 November 1948 (Marine Corps Photo 528063)

The HRP–2 replaced the HRP–1 and provided greater payload and higher speed (Marine Corps Photo 529983).

delivered to the Navy for almost two years after BuAer approved the contract.

The HJP–1 Utility and Rescue Evaluation

Since the Army Air Forces was supporting the single main rotor configuration, the Navy turned to other types of rotor arrangements, not being sold on any one design in particular.[11] In an effort to obtain the best ship-based helicopter for spotting, rescue, and utility missions on board battleships and cruisers, the Navy, in 1946, contracted with both Sikorsky and Piasecki for two helicopters from each company. The competitive contract resulted in Piasecki developing the PD–14 (XHJP–1), the first overlapping tandem-rotor helicopter, while Sikorsky entered the S–53 (XHJS–1), a design using many components of the R–5 (HO2S–1). According to preliminary characteristics and design performance requirements, both machines were to be configured for a gross weight of less than 5,000 pounds including two passengers.

After comparative evaluation, the Navy selected the Piasecki XHJP–1 over the Sikorsky XHJS–1. One major reason for the selection of the XHJP–1 (later redesignated by the Navy as the HUP–1) was that the Sikorsky model required a ballast change in order to accommodate a change in the loading.[12] Sikorsky designed another helicopter to correct the ballast problem but was too late for entry into the utility evaluation. The HUP–1 was finally developed for the Navy with a 600-horsepower engine and seats for four passengers. The helicopter was restricted to a gross weight of 6,000 pounds and an air speed of 104 knots.

The HTL–1 Trainer

With Piasecki's XHRP–1 in production and the XHJP–1 in the design stage, the Navy took further steps to acquire a suitable trainer and settled upon the Bell Model 47. Late in 1946 Bell Aircraft Corporation was awarded a contract for the first of a long series of Navy HTLs, a slightly modified version of the Model 47.

Designs for the Future

As early as the summer of 1944, the Navy had awarded a contract to the McDonnell Aircraft Corporation, St. Louis, Missouri, for the world's first twin-engine helicopter to operate in the 10,000-pound gross weight class and to provide "greater insight into the problems of helicopter design." Variations of rotor diameter, roto-engine gear ratio, and control sensitivity were possible in the large helicopter. The Navy-designated XHJD–1, which first flew in August 1944, cruised over 100 miles per hour and carried a useful load of more than 3,000 pounds. The two 46-foot rotors which turned in opposite directions were arranged side-by-side and were powered by two 450-horsepower engines.

At the same time, another experimental model, the Piasecki-designed PV–15 (XH–16), was also being developed for the Army Air Forces as a long-range transport and rescue aircraft. This helicopter was to have a direct influence on the progress of the Marine Corps' forthcoming helicopter program. It appealed to all services because it had a gross weight of 46,000 pounds and a useful load capability of 14,000 pounds or 40 passengers. The tandem design XH–16, with two engines driving the two 82-foot diameter rotors, was the largest helicopter in the world. Although development of this gigantic helicopter was started by Piasecki in 1946, almost concurrent with the HJP–1, its first flight would not occur until more than seven years later.

Helicopter Applications

During the early part of World War II, the Navy Department initially visualized the helicopter as an aid in combating German submarines which were seriously menacing United States and Allied shipping. Original plans called for the helicopters, piloted by Coast Guard flyers, to accompany ocean convoys and operate as scout aircraft from platforms constructed on the merchant ships.[13] The Navy accepted delivery of its first helicopter, the R–4 (HNX–1), on 16 October 1943 and assigned it to the United States Coast Guard, Coast Guard Air Station, Floyd Bennett Field, Brooklyn, New York. Testing of the helicopter's suitability as an antisubmarine weapon began the following month. At first, the HNS–1 appeared promising, but open sea shipboard trials in January 1944 showed the helicopter to be too difficult to handle and the operation was deemed too hazardous with the present state of the helicopter's development.[14]

During the course of the trials, the Chief of Naval Operations (CNO) approved, on 18 Decem-

The extended rotor idea of the McDonnell XHJD–1 never proved workable as the aircraft was unstable (National Archives Photo 80–G–395920).

ber 1943, the Coast Guard Air Station at Floyd Bennett as a helicopter training base and assigned the Coast Guard the entire helicopter program.* The training portion was to be "under the supervision of the CNO's Aviation Training Division, Op-33," and the development program remained under the Bureau of Aeronautics.[15]

Helicopter operations continued at Floyd Bennett Field until March 1946 with the Coast Guard training its own pilots as well as Navy and Civil Aeronautics Administration personnel. A number of British pilots were also trained at the field during this period.

During the latter years of World War II, a few Sikorsky helicopters were used by the Navy in a utility role on board ships for shuttling very light loads between ships, from ships to shore stations, and occasionally for rescue work. Most operations though were confined to evaluating the helicopter at Floyd Bennett for possible future military application.

* On 1 November 1941, the United States Coast Guard by Executive Order 8929 was transferred from the Treasury Department to the Navy, where it operated during World War II as an integral part until 1 January 1946.

After the war, the Navy's first operational helicopter unit was formed for participation in the Bikini atomic bomb tests in July 1946. Four HOS–1s (R–6s) transferred personnel, recovered film records, and performed other utility missions.

Two months prior to the Bikini tests, a helicopter development program had been initiated by the Navy on 16 May 1946,[16] when the CNO directed the commissioning of Helicopter Development Squadron Three (VX–3). In his letter, the CNO stated that the Secretary of the Navy had approved a development program to provide for comprehensive service trials and experimentation with existing types of helicopters.[17] On 1 July, VX–3 was officially commissioned at Floyd Bennett Field. By this time, the Coast Guard had moved its helicopter operations from Floyd Bennett to Elizabeth City, North Carolina.

Assigned as operations officer of the Navy's new development squadron was World War II fighter pilot and Navy Cross winner, Marine Major Armond H. DeLalio.[18] Two years previously, Major DeLalio had received helicopter flight instruction from the Coast Guard[19] at Floyd Bennett and on 8 August 1946 he became the first Marine to be designated as a naval helicopter pilot.* [20] When VX–3 moved to Naval Air Station, Lakehurst, New Jersey, in September, Major DeLalio remained as operations officer of the squadron.

At Lakehurst, the unit functioned as the Navy's sole activity for helicopter training and development until its decommissioning in early 1948. During that short period, however, VX–3 became well known to future Marine helicopter pilots for it was through its training program, under the supervision of Major DeLalio,** [21] that many of the Marine Corps' pioneer helicopter pilots were introduced to the controls of a helicopter.

Early Outlook

Throughout this early period, rotary-wing manufacturers were enthusiastic about producing machines of larger gross weights than those already designed or flying. Igor I. Sikorsky, for example, gave his views on improvement of future helicopter designs and capabilities:

> The largest commercially successful helicopter built up to now [1946] has a gross weight of 5,000 to 6,000 pounds. Helicopters with a gross weight of 10,000 to 20,000 pounds can well be produced in the immediate future, on the basis of information already available and along any of the configurations that have already been tested. This gross weight could undoubtedly be doubled within the next five to ten years. There is no doubt that still larger helicopters could be produced in the more remote future. [22]

Sikorsky's predictions for the immediate future were overly optimistic, but it was this type of optimism that enticed the services, not only during the immediate postwar period but later, in the 1950s and 1960s, to contract for rotary-winged aircraft with performance characteristics considerably beyond the state-of-the-art. Yet, optimism on the part of the manufacturers was further bolstered by the eagerness of the services to obtain a variety of larger, more useful helicopters. Unfortunately, helicopters produced for the military in the late 1940s were far from an acceptable service aircraft —all Army and Navy test reports declared the machines to be unsatisfactory for load carrying purposes. [23] The HNX–1 (R–4) and HOS–1 (R–6) required the aid of ground effect * or a good wind before hovering was possible at the designed gross weight. [24] However, these early aircraft, limited as they were, proved to be the true stepping stones in an orderly, but slow, helicopter developmental program.

---

* Major DeLalio is listed number 16 on the chronological list of qualified helicopter pilots with the date of qualification as 8 August 1946.

** Lieutenant Colonel DeLalio was killed in 1952 at the Naval Air Test Center, Patuxent River, Maryland. As a test pilot, he was attempting to test the thrust augmentation of a 1000-pound jet-assisted take-off (JATO) rocket attached to an HO4S–1 helicopter when the rocket came detached from its mount and caused the helicopter to become uncontrollable.

* Ground effect, or ground cushion, is experienced when the helicopter is hovering within a height from the ground equal to or less than its rotor diameter. The maximum lifting capability of the helicopter is derived when hovering closest to the ground.

CHAPTER 1

THE ADVENT

The Quest For An Alternative

After the disappointing performance of the auto-gyro during the 1930s, Marine Corps interest in rotary-winged aircraft was not fully revived until 1943. During that year Marine officers from Division of Aviation (DivAvn), Headquarters Marine Corps (HQMC) sat as members of a joint Navy-Coast Guard-Marine Corps board to discuss formation of a program for the use of Sikorsky R–4 and R–6 helicopters.[1] It was not until June 1946, however, that the first official action to institute a Marine Corps helicopter program began when General Alexander A. Vandegrift, Commandant of the Marine Corps (CMC), established a billet for one officer and three enlisted men within his headquarters.[2] Although there was no mention in his letter to the CNO of forming a developmental helicopter squadron as the Navy had done, General

General Alexander A. Vandegrift, 18th Commandant (Marine Corps Photo A413197).

Vandegrift did state that the Marine Corps was particularly interested in the evaluation of the helicopter and requested that his staff be kept informed as to its application.

Nothing significant was accomplished by the Commandant's newly established program until September of that year when Lieutenant General Roy S. Geiger, Commanding General, Fleet Marine Forces, Pacific (CGFMFPac) viewed the atomic bomb tests at Bikini Lagoon as the Commandant's personal representative. During World War II, General Geiger had commanded the III Amphibious Corps which took part in operations on Bougainville, Guam, Peleliu, and Okinawa. He also became the first Marine to command a force on the army level when he led the Tenth Army to a successful conclusion of the Okinawa operation. In his report of 21 August, he expressed to the Commandant his opinion concerning the effects the atomic bomb might have on Marine Corps doctrine during the post-World War II period. General Geiger stated that "since our probable future enemy will be in possession of this weapon, it is my opinion that a complete review and study of our concept of amphibious operations will have to be made." General Geiger went on to say, "It is quite evident that a small number of atomic bombs could destroy an expeditionary force as now organized, embarked, and landed . . . I cannot visualize another landing such as was executed at Normandy or Okinawa." In his final paragraph he urged the Commandant to "consider this a very serious and urgent matter [and that the Marine Corps] use its most competent officers in finding a solution to develop the technique of conducting amphibious operations in the Atomic Age."[3]

The Commandant acted swiftly by referring General Geiger's letter to a special board composed of three major generals: Lemuel C. Shepherd, Jr., Oliver P. Smith, and Field Harris. General Shepherd had commanded the 1st Provisional Marine Brigade at Guam and the 6th Marine Division on Okinawa and in China. General Smith had been

General Lemuel C. Shepherd, Jr., 20th Commandant (Marine Corps Photo A46471).

the Assistant Division Commander of the 1st Marine Division in the Peleliu campaign and had served as Deputy Chief of Staff with the Tenth Army for the joint Army-Marine Corps Okinawa operation. General Harris served as Chief of Staff to the Commander, Aircraft, at Guadalcanal; as Commander, Aircraft, Northern Solomons; and as the Director of Marine Aviation. The Commandant's instructions to this special board, stressed that "general principles must be determined in order to orient the effort of the Marine Corps away from the last war and toward the next." The final paragraph gave specific instructions as to what the board was to accomplish:

> . . . the Special Board . . . is directed to propose, after thorough research and deliberation, the broad concepts and principles which the Marine Corps should follow, and the major steps which it should take, to fit it to wage successful amphibious warfare at some future date . . . .[4]

General Shepherd's special board was staffed with a Secretariat of three officers—Colonel Merrill B. Twining, Colonel Edward C. Dyer, and Lieutenant Colonel Samuel R. Shaw.* [5] All three were

---

* The name of Lieutenant Colonel Clair W. Shisler appears as the original third member of the Secretariat with Lieutenant Colonel Shaw assigned as his replacement when Lieutenant Colonel Shisler became ill. Shaw signed

then on duty at Marine Corps Schools, Quantico, Virginia and like the generals on the Commandant's board, had held responsible assignments during World War II and were well qualified to undertake their new task. Colonel Twining had served as the Assistant Chief of Staff, G–3, of the 1st Marine Division during the Guadalcanal campaign and later in the Solomons as Assistant Chief of Staff, G–3, I Marine Amphibious Corps. Colonel Dyer, a naval aviator, saw duty in the Pacific as operations officer of the Strategic Air Force, Pacific Ocean Areas, as Chief of Staff to the Commander, Air, Northern Solomons, and finally as commanding officer of Marine Aircraft Group 61 in the Philippines. Having taken part in the defense of Pearl Harbor on 7 December 1941 as Company Commander, Marine Barracks, Lieutenant Colonel Shaw saw combat as commanding officer of the 6th Pioneer Battalion, 6th Marine Division on Okinawa and later served as Assistant Chief of Staff, G–4, of the same division at Tsingtao, China.

Brigadier General Oliver P. Smith (Marine Corps Photo 94702).

---

the Secretariat's report as the third member after Colonels Twining and Dyer.

Brigadier General Edward C. Dyer (Marine Corps Photo A401815).

The three-member Secretariat agreed that the mass destructive capability of the atomic bomb and the vulnerability of a massed amphibious landing force made dispersion a necessity—but only at the risk of defeat through slow and piecemeal commitment of forces ashore. In order to disperse the landing force sufficiently and still, equally important, have a reconcentration of forces at the point of contact with the enemy, a new mode of assault was needed as a supplement to the existing amphibious landing craft.

To solve this problem, the committee considered a variety of means to achieve a rapid buildup of assault forces ashore including transport aircraft, gliders, and parachutists. Transport aircraft would require prepared airfields which, in most cases, would not be available within the objective area. Gliders likewise required a clear and flat area in which to land and discharge troops. Assault by employing parachutists was discarded because of the difficulty in maintaining unit integrity. The use of troop and cargo carrying submarines appeared to offer a better solution than any of the airborne methods previously mentioned. The Secretariat also considered the employment of the helicopter which, appearing to be superior in its characteristics to all other assault vehicles, offered a practical means of overcoming the effects of dispersion while con-

currently reducing exposure of the amphibious task force. The Secretariat members knew that the performance of the helicopter was discouraging, but the relative primitive state of helicopter development did not deter their enthusiasm for its application.

Before committing themselves to the employment of the helicopter as a vehicle for a new method of assault, the Secretariat acquainted themselves first-hand with the capabilities of the helicopter. Colonel Dyer visited Sikorsky Aircraft Company and discussed with Mr. Sikorsky the Secretariat's concept. Colonel Dyer stated that the Marine Corps was thinking along the lines of lifting 5,000 pounds by helicopter, with Mr. Sikorsky replying that the plan "was a magnificent idea and that there was no problem, that we [Sikorsky] can do that now, this is within our present knowledge. We can build an airplane [helicopter] that will carry 5,000 pounds. We can build an airplane that will carry much more than that. We know how to do it. Take my word for it." [6] After receiving the rather optimistic report from Mr. Sikorsky, Colonels Dyer and Twining visited the Piasecki Aircraft Corporation on 14 November 1946 where Mr. Piasecki again expressed his opinion that there was "no problem" [7] in constructing a helicopter capable of lifting a 5,000-pound payload.

After their return to Quantico, the members of the Secretariat corresponded frequently with the two helicopter manufacturers.[8] Sikorsky Aircraft presented its developmental ideas and Piasecki pointed out the possibilities of the 10-passenger HRP–1 transport, and the giant 40-passenger XH–16 rescue and transport helicopter as ample evidence of its capability to fulfill the requirements of the Marine Corps for an assault transport helicopter. Colonel Dyer related that the helicopter:

. . . seemed to be our source of action, but we didn't do much. It sort of died. We went off on other [related] projects, until one day [Lieutenant Colonel] Marion [E.] Carl,* a test pilot at Patuxent, flew a helicopter to Marine Corps Schools to demonstrate it to the students. I'll never forget—he hoisted [Lieutenant Colonel Victor H.] Brute Krulak on a hoist and pulled him off the ground about 15 feet and pulled him into the cockpit. Twining and I were standing by the window and watching, and I said, 'Bill, lets go with this thing [helicopter] and quit fooling around.' He said 'Okay . . . so he wrote the theory . . . principles . . . background . . . reasoning . . . and I wrote a program.[9]

---

* Lieutenant Colonel Marion E. Carl was a World War II ace with 18 Japanese planes to his credit. He was on duty at NAS, Patuxent River, Maryland, where as a test pilot, he had taught himself to fly a helicopter.

The idea of using large assault transport seaplanes also received considerable attention by the Secretariat—a sort of "flying LST." But like the helicopter, a seaplane of the size needed for carrying troops and their equipment was not in existence. The Secretariat, nevertheless, concluded that a mixture of these large flying boats and helicopters would be the most promising combination, with the helicopter appearing to be the real "answer to the amphibious prayer." [10]

In early December 1946, the study had progressed to the point where the principal recommendations could be foreseen and the Secretariat sent their report to the Special Board for approval. The Special Board submitted to the Commandant on 16 December an advanced report, recommending that "two parallel programs be initiated which would provide for the development of both the transport seaplane and a transport helicopter." Organization of a Marine helicopter experimental squadron was also recommended at the "earliest practical date for the training of pilots and mechanics and for the practical development of helicopter tactics and techniques for a ship-to-shore operation." Finally, it was suggested that the "Marine Corps Schools be directed to submit a tentative doctrine for helicopter employment." [11]

General Vandegrift concurred with the board's recommendations and on 19 December 1946, only three days after the report arrived at HQMC, it was endorsed and sent to the Marine Corps Schools (MCS) with a statement by General Vandegrift directing that steps be taken to implement the development programs outlined therein.

Concurrently, General Vandegrift sent a letter to the CNO with the Special Board's report as an enclosure. His letter was the first in a long series of correspondence between the two services on the subject of future amphibious operations and was the first service document known to propose the use of helicopters as a tactical vehicle for the transportation of combat troops from a naval vessel to a landing area ashore. General Vandegrift briefly defined the Marine Corps' plan for what later became known as the Vertical Assault Concept for Amphibious Operations and the premises upon which it was based. "Carrier-based transport helicopters," the Commandant stated:

> . . . offer all the advantages of the conventional airborne operation but few of the disadvantages. They can be operated from aircraft carriers now in existence with cover and preparatory fires on landing areas provided by their aircraft from the same force. [12]

General Vandegrift continued:

> With a relatively unlimited choice of landing areas, troops can be landed in combat formations and under full control of the flanks or rear of a hostile position. The helicopter's speed makes transport dispersion at sea a matter of no disadvantage and introduces a time-space factor that will avoid presenting at any one time a remunerative atomic target. It should be noted also that transport helicopters offer a means for rapid evacuation of casualties, for the movement of supplies directly from ship to dump and for subsequent movement of troops and supplies in continuing operations ashore. [13]

A Helicopter Program for 1947

In order to give the new program its initial impetus, the Commandant recommended to the CNO that implementation begin immediately on the two programs recommended in the Special Board's report. He also urged that the corresponding development of tactics, techniques, and organization be given the same consideration so that all areas would be developed concurrently.

The Bureau of Aeronautics was tasked by United States Naval Regulations for the design, development, testing, procurement, and production of Marine Corps Aircraft. Therefore, in aircraft related matters the Commandant had to submit his recommendations to the CNO for his approval.

A series of five recommendations were made to the CNO for the helicopter program in 1947 and three for the following year. During 1947, the Commandant recommended that the Marine Corps organize one developmental aircraft squadron equipped with 12 helicopters of the first available type, with the second recommendation that the Marine Corps study the employment of helicopters in amphibious operations, and the third that it establish the military characteristics of such an aircraft. He also recommended that the Navy begin procuring 48 HRP–1 helicopters for delivery to the Marine Corps in 1948, the Navy accelerate the development of transport helicopters, and the Navy and Marine Corps conduct a token ship-to-shore operation by helicopter at the earliest practicable date. The plan for 1948 contained recommendations to organize one additional developmental helicopter squadron, for the Navy to initiate procurement of a suitable transport helicopter for delivery in 1949 and 1950, and finally, that the Navy and Marine Corps conduct a small-scale ship-to-shore exercise employing helicopters during fleet maneuvers.

Overall approval of the Commandant's program was not immediately forthcoming as various departments within the office of the CNO were required to comment upon the new proposals. The recommendations by General Vandegrift were considered, in general, to be sound and practical although certain phases of the time schedule appeared to be optimistic. On 17 March the CNO's Air Planning Group determined that it was "impracticable to set aside funds in the budget years 1947 and 1948 for the procurement of helicopters for the Marine Corps"; however, it was agreed to "include requirements for Marine Corps helicopters in the 1949 budget." The group "approved tentatively that Piasecki helicopters (HRPs) would be furnished to the Marine Corps for development of techniques and tactics for employment of such aircraft" and to "permit familiarization of Marine pilots with the Piasecki helicopter by sending them to VX–3 at Lakehurst for helicopter training." [14] "Formation of a helicopter developmental squadron and initial design studies of a large transport type helicopter" were approved with "procurement of an assault transport helicopter to be dependent upon results of the developmental squadron's evaluation" of the new technique.[15]

The Chief of the Bureau of Aeronautics, Rear Admiral Harold B. Sallada, commented primarily on the technical aspects of the plan. He mentioned that various helicopter designs were under development and due to a lack of established requirements there was no large transport helicopter included in the Navy's program. Development of a large helicopter by the Army Air Forces, the XH–16, was being followed closely by his bureau. An assault helicopter could be developed, upon receipt of the required characteristics, commensurate with the assigned priority and budgetary considerations. The speed of the program would depend not only on the funds available, but also on the unproven ability of design personnel in the new field; therefore, no assurance was given that an acceptable military requirement could be met by any specified date. "The procurement of 48 additional HRP-1 helicopters for delivery in 1948," the letter read, "would involve the expenditure of approximately $11,000,000. These funds can only be obtained by reducing or eliminating aircraft procurement programs now planned." [16]

Assault Helicopter Characteristics and Design Problems

Meanwhile, at Marine Corps Schools, the Committee of the Academic Board headed by Colonel Robert E. Hogaboom submitted its first report on 10 March 1947 on the desired characteristics for an assault transport helicopter in response to the Commandant's directive of 19 December. Colonel Hogaboom had taken part in combat during World War II on such Central Pacific islands as Makin, Kwajalein, Saipan, Tinian, Guam, and Iwo Jima. During the Saipan and Tinian operations he served as the Assistant Chief of Staff, G–3, Northern Troops and Landing Force, and later, on Iwo Jima, he was Chief of Staff, 3d Marine Division. Entitled "Military Requirements of Helicopter for Ship-to-Shore Movement of Troops and Cargo," Colonel Hogaboom's report stated:

> On the premise that the helicopter offers a valuable means of accelerating and dispersing the ship-to-shore movement, it is recognized that the complete replacement of all existing ship-to-shore conveyances may at some future date be desirable. Under such conditions, it would appear necessary that there be designed a relatively small type helicopter for transportation of assault troops, as well as large type helicopter capable of lifting all divisional loads. However, examination of current technical developments indicates that the latter type may not be practical for some time to come. Accordingly, it is considered more realistic to approach the problem in increments, establishing initially the characteristics for a purely assault conveyance . . . .[17]

It is apparent that the board was considering a helicopter similar to Piasecki's XH–16, which was still on the drawing board, as the large helicopter for lifting the divisional loads. As for the small assault helicopter, its requirements were in consonance with the stated abilities of the helicopter industry, but yet not entirely so, for the board was basing the desired capacity on a tactical consideration—maintaining integrity in the basic infantry combat unit. The report stated:

> Such a machine should provide seating space for 15 and a maximum of 20 infantrymen suitably armed and equipped to initiate combat. The lower figure, considered to be a practical minimum, will permit the transportation, as a unit, of the basic rifle squad plus two additional individuals from platoon or company headquarters. The maximum figure, considered to be far more desirable, will permit the transportation as a unit of the basic rifle squad, plus a skeletonized machine-gun squad or 60mm mortar squad, along with several individuals from platoon or company headquarters. A capacity in excess of 20 men is not desirable in an assault helicopter since the craft will undoubtedly be extremely vulnerable.[18]

"The ideal payload of 5,000 was a desirable optimum," the report stated, with 3,500 pounds quoted as the minimum acceptable load. The 5,000-pound capability would greatly improve the value of the assault helicopter during the ship-to-shore movement of light artillery. Other specifications included a range of 200 to 300 nautical miles (500 miles with an auxiliary fuel tank), a cruise speed of 100 knots, a hovering ceiling of 4,000 feet, an external hook and hoist, and self-sealing fuel cells. One of the most critical considerations was vaguely addressed—the aircraft's dimensions— the report stating only:

> . . . the craft should be designed to meet the limiting dimensions of the hangar deck and elevators [of the CVE or CVL aircraft carrier].* However, if these restricting factors should cause a material reduction in payload or optimum dimensions of the helicopter, it is believed that steps should be taken to investigate possible structural modifications in the CVE.[19]

The Commandant reiterated the Academic Board's recommendations in a letter to the CNO on 24 March. He believed the Marine Corps Schools' report to be an excellent basis for direction of future developments in the helicopter program.

The Deputy Chief of Naval Operations (Air), (DCNO(Air)), Vice Admiral Donald B. Duncan, commented that the 20 combat troop and 5,000 pound requirements were considered feasible while only minor modifications were necessary in the airspeed and range specifications. The big obstacle rested in the limitations imposed by CVE and CVL elevators and hangar deck dimensions and "modification of CVE-CVL types to handle such an aircraft is considered to be a project of major proportions."[20] The DCNO (Air) was also concerned that "actual construction of such an aircraft could not be reasonably expected prior to 1951 and the imposition of the CVE-CVL restrictions would make the meeting of the minimum requirements [of the Marine Corps] very doubtful." In conclusion, it was stated that until the type of aircraft carrier to be used for helicopter operations was officially determined, further work on a design study which had begun in April in the Bureau of Aeronautics was being stopped.[21]

The DCNO (Operations), Vice Admiral Forrest P. Sherman, in a memorandum to DCNO (Air), recommended on 6 May that a two-step study be undertaken to determine exactly which size helicopter should initially be designed for the Marine Corps. In the memo, Admiral Sherman gave no

assurance that a larger type aircraft carrier than a CVE or CVL could be assigned for an amphibious operation employing helicopters as one of the assault elements; therefore, he recommended that the DCNO (Air) investigate the practicability of alterations to hangars and elevators of either CVE or CVL types to handle the helicopter of 5,000 pounds capacity. "If this appears possible without excessive cost and loss of other characteristics of the type," the memo read, "proceed with the design and procurement of the 5,000 pound capacity helicopter."[22] The second recommended step was almost identical to the first, only the weight of the helicopter was changed to read 3,500 pounds in lieu of 5,000 pounds.

By 3 June 1947, Admiral Duncan had concluded the studies as recommended in the 6 May memorandum from Admiral Sherman. "It appears that the 5,000 pound helicopter would be of such dimensions both in length and height as to preclude modifying the CVE or CVL carriers except at exorbitant cost." Admiral Duncan continued:

> By overlapping the rotors in future designs it appears possible to . . . permit stowage of a 3,500 pound helicopter in the CVE–CVL class carriers without modification of the ship or elevators. . . . [therefore] the Chief of the Bureau of Aeronautics is being requested to obtain design proposals for a 3,500 pound payload helicopter.[23]

While the office of the Chief of Naval Operations was making every effort possible to resolve the CVL and helicopter compatibility issue, the Commandant was busily revising his original helicopter development program. The new program was in compliance with a request contained in the CNO's reply to the Commandant's letter written on 19 December 1946. The CNO reiterated Rear Admiral Sallada's (Chief of the Bureau of Aeronautics) contention that procurement of 48 additional HRPs for delivery in 1948 would involve approximately $11,000,000 which could only be obtained at the expense of programs already planned. "Therefore," he commented, "it is estimated that 1948 deliveries of HRP-1 helicopters to the Marine Corps will be sufficient only to bring the experimental squadron up to strength (12 aircraft). Additional procurement will depend on experience gained with this type."[24] The CNO concurred in general with the Commandant's recommendations but pointed out certain factors affecting the outlined time schedule and asked the Commandant for revised recommendations on his helicopter program.[25]

The revised program submitted by General Vandegrift on 4 June eliminated completely the

---

* CVE, Escort Aircraft Carrier; CVL, Light Aircraft Carrier. As an example, specifications are given here for the Casablanca Class CVE (*Thetis Bay*, CVE-90) and the Independence Class CVL (*Monterey*, CVL-26):

	Tons	Length	Beam	Draft	Speed.
Casablanca	7,800	512 ft.	108 ft.	22 ft.	19 kts.
Independence	11,000	622 ft.	109 ft.	26 ft.	32 kts.

request for the 48 HRP-1s and the additional developmental helicopter squadron. Accordingly the Marine Corps program for 1947 was changed to contain three elements: 1) A developmental squadron with as many helicopters as possible be provided; 2) A study of the techniques and tactics of ship-to-shore helicopter operations be conducted; and 3) A request be made to the Navy to accelerate the development of transport helicopters. The new 1948 recommendations sought to keep the one developmental squadron at full strength and to continue experimentation to determine the suitability of the type helicopter being used, while determining the additional specifications and characteristics of the helicopter desired for ship-to-shore movement. Based upon the results of the experimentation, the Navy was to initiate procurement of suitable transport helicopters for delivery in 1949 and 1950. A small-scale ship-to-shore exercise employing helicopters during fleet exercises was further recommended for 1948.[26] In the last paragraph of his letter to the CNO, General Vandegrift mentioned that the 12 HRP-1s proposed for the Marine developmental squadron would permit only a token exercise with a maximum of two platoons. "It is considered," he stated, "that this action will provide much desired information on the problems of tactics and logistics involved. Expansion of this operating force should be undertaken as soon as an improved helicopter is available." The Commandant concluded by "recommending that all remaining available funds be used to accelerate development of a service type helicopter."[27]

General Vandegrift recognized the HRP-1 as only a transition helicopter for experimental use and for the development of the ship-to-shore techniques and not suitable except for those purposes. The aircraft were very expensive and funds for helicopter development were limited. He considered the procurement of HRPs beyond the original 12, now authorized by the CNO for use in the developmental squadron, as undesirable and that the funds should be used in accelerating the development of a new assault helicopter.[28]

On 9 July the Commandant made another important change relating to the helicopter's characteristics by specifying only one size helicopter of a 5,000-pound minimum payload capability. It eliminated the requirement for the helicopter to be accommodated by the ship's elevator and stowed on the hangar deck and listed the overall dimensions as "small as possible." The cancellation of the design proposal for a 3,500-pound helicopter, as requested by the DCNO (Air) on 3 June, was

not mentioned, although it is assumed that it was discontinued.

The elimination of the elevator and hangar deck requirement was initiated by the Chief of Military Requirements Section of DCNO (Air). A memorandum dated 3 June to the Assistant Chief of Naval Operations (Marine Aviation), (ACNO (Marine Aviation)), Major General Field Harris, recommended that the Commandant eliminate the stowage requirements for the assault helicopter as it imposed many undesirable design factors—the most pertinent one being "that a rotor overlap * of approximately 75 percent to 80 percent would be necessary in order to meet the elevator dimensions." The only helicopter closely meeting that criteria at the time was the small Piasecki XHJP-1 which was still in the design stage and, in addition, had a useful load of only 1,024 pounds, almost 4,000 pounds less than the required minimum. The Military Requirements Section memorandum further mentioned that rotor overlap of such magnitude imposed "a heavy unknown factor on the design." The requirement for the helicopter to be serviced (stowed, repaired, and checked) on the hangar deck of a carrier imposed the undesirable design factor thereby jeopardizing the success of entire proposal. In order to meet the optimum requirement for a 5,000-pound payload the memorandum mentioned flight deck servicing should be accepted in lieu of hangar deck "and many marginal design factors and difficult design limitations would be eliminated."[29] In addition, the Commandant specified to the CNO a tactical reason for the change:

> In order that the early landing may be provided with necessary continuity, it is necessary that communications vehicles, recoilless weapons, and initial resupply be provided at an early hour and, ideally, that these should be followed by artillery. This requires a payload of approximately 5,000 pounds.[30]

With the Commandant's 9 July revision to his original requirement of 24 March, the specifications for the design of the assault helicopter were temporarily settled. Following that, the CNO stated in a letter to BuAer on 4 November that the Navy's New Development Program for 1949 assigned a priority 3 to the Navy's antisubmarine warfare (ASW) helicopter development and a priority 2 to the Marine's assault helicopter. "In view of the limited funds available for helicopter development during fiscal 1949," the memorandum read, "it is requested that all [fiscal] 1949 funds

---

* A term used for a tandem-type helicopter to denote the percentage of overlap which occurs when the rear rotor blade passes over the lower forward rotor blade.

be concentrated on meeting the requirements of the assault helicopter as set forth in [my letter of 24 July]." [31] The redirection of funds in favor of the assault helicopter was taken to support the Marine Corps' helicopter program at a time when the Navy was eagerly seeking a suitable helicopter for ASW operations, and when both procurement and research and development funds were exceptionally low.

In spite of Admiral Sherman's directive concentrating funds on the Marine Corps' assault helicopter, progress in its development was doomed to be slow. The Chief of the Bureau of Aeronautics cast the assault helicopter transport program into the development doldrums by linking it with the Air Force's XH–16 program. The CNO was informed by BuAer on 24 December 1947 that additional studies indicated the development of a large helicopter meeting the requirements of the Marine Corps was feasible, but it would involve a four-

or five-year program and require considerably more funds than could be obtained in view of the continuing budget curtailments. "It now appears," the Bureau Chief stated:

> . . . that the assault helicopter characteristics are very similar to those of the XH–16 helicopter contemplated by the Air Force . . . and insofar as the basic helicopter is concerned, are almost identical. In view of this fact, effort on the assault helicopter will be undertaken on the basis of joint Air Force/Navy development of the XH–16. [32]

The result of BuAer's action to combine the two projects, an economic necessity on the part of the Navy, delayed the development of a suitable assault transport helicopter and made the Commandant's program fall far short of its goal. Two and one half years later, essentially the same helicopter requirements would be presented to the CNO, and at that time, action would prove to be more responsive to the Marine Corps' request.

CHAPTER 2

CONCEPT DEVELOPMENT

Commissioning and Operations of HMX–1

While progress on the design of the Marine Corps assault transport helicopter was under way, Colonel Dyer also had been busy at Quantico preparing for the eventual organization of the new developmental squadron. The Commandant had appointed him to command the future squadron and concurrently relieved him of his assignment on the Secretariat.

As the prospective commanding officer, Colonel Dyer first had to find a suitable location. The air station at Quantico was chosen as the most advantageous site as it was relatively close to both helicopter manufacturers, Sikorsky and Piasecki, and was literally next door to the Marine Corps Schools. At the same time it was far enough away from FMF operations at Camp Lejeune and Marine Corps Air Station (MCAS), Cherry Point, to permit the squadron to work on purely experimental projects without being encumbered with the operational problems so common to the fleet units.[1]

For selection of personnel, Colonel Dyer turned to the student body of Marine Corps Schools. Addressing members of the Junior Course in session during early 1947, he briefed them on the helicopter and plans for its future employment in the Marine Corps. To the 60 officers present, Colonel Dyer displayed drawings of helicopters of the future, and charts depicting the speeds and payloads which helicopters were expected to achieve. Colonel Dyer later remarked about the results of the briefing:

> I described what our squadron hoped to accomplish and how we hoped to go about it. Then I said, "Now there is a large body of opinion in the Marine Corps that figures that helicopters aren't going any place, so if you are interested stay here, and I'll get your names. If you are not, don't waste your time or mine, just shove off right now!" At that I'd say about two-thirds of everybody there got up and left.[2]

Although still more dropped out later, the majority of the interested officers who stayed constituted the nucleus of Dyer's new squadron.

Plans for the commissioning of Marine Helicopter Squadron 1 (HMX–1) (often incorrectly referred to as Marine Helicopter Experimental Squadron One or Marine Helicopter Development Squadron One) were published in the CNO's Aviation Plan No. 57 on 23 June 1947. This plan tentatively scheduled the commissioning of HMX–1 for 1 July.[3] Unfortunately, at that early date, there was an insufficient number of helicopters available for assignment to HMX–1 and arrangements had not been made for helicopter pilot training, so the commissioning date was delayed. Then on 10 September, the CNO informed BuAer that plans had been made to form HMX–1 on approximately 1 January 1948. He additionally declared that the Navy had recently purchased 22 HO3S–1s from the Sikorsky Aircraft Company with the 9th, 12th, and 13th aircraft of the total package designated for delivery to HMX–1. The CNO further stated that the aircraft scheduled for HMX–1 would be retained and operated by VX–3 at NAS Lakehurst until HMX–1 was commissioned.[4] Two days later, the CNO proclaimed that the Navy was purchasing 20 HRP–1s from the Piasecki Helicopter Corporation with the 5th, 6th, and 7th HRPs going to HMX–1, and like the HO3Ss, these would be sent to VX–3 until HMX-1 was formed.[5] In view of this news, General Harris, ACNO (Marine Aviation),* proposed to the DCNO (Air) that HMX–1 be commissioned on 15 November. This would permit the Marine Corps to assemble the necessary personnel, establish administrative and supply channels, and have hangar space and area assigned so that the squadron would be capable of immediate operations upon receipt of the aircraft.[6] It was not until 22 November 1947, however, that the CNO directed the Commandant

---

* The Director of the Division of Aviation/Assistant Commandant of the Marine Corps (Air) concurrently held an additional position within the CNO's office as Assistant Chief of Naval Operations (Marine Aviation).

to form and commission Marine Helicopter Squadron 1 on 1 December 1947.[7]

In a related action two days later, the DCNO (Air) approved a plan for the decommissioning of VX–3 at NAS Lakehurst in April of 1948 and the concurrent formation of two fleet units, Helicopter Utility Squadron 1 (HU–1) and Helicopter Utility Squadron 2 (HU–2), with the latter assuming the training mission of VX–3. In the same plan, supplement No. 2 to CNO's Aviation Plan No. 57, it was explained that helicopter deliveries above VX–3's training requirements would be apportioned among the three prospective squadrons, including HMX–1.[8] This action by CNO essentially established a rotating basis upon which HMX–1 would receive its first group of aircraft.

Accordingly, HMX–1 was commissioned on 1 December 1947 at MCAS Quantico, Virginia, with Colonel Dyer as the commanding officer and sole member.[9] On 3 December six pilots joined Colonel Dyer's squadron: Major Russell R. Riley; Captains Paul J. Flynn, Charles D. Barber, and Robert A. Strieby; First Lieutenants Roy L. Anderson and Robert A. Longstaff. All officers except

Captain Flynn and Lieutenant Longstaff had completed helicopter training on 11 November at Lakehurst and were designated Naval Helicopter Pilots.[10] Colonel Dyer was likewise a qualified helicopter pilot having earlier, in September and October, completed 40 hours of flight instruction at the Sikorsky plant in Stratford, Connecticut, under the guidance of Dimitry D. (Jimmy) Viner, Sikorsky's chief test pilot.[11] By 6 December, three enlisted men had arrived bringing the total complement of the squadron to 10 officers and enlisted men.

Three days after commissioning, HQMC published the squadron's missions and tasks. As originally issued, the two-fold mission was to: "Develop techniques and tactics in connection with the movement of assault troops in amphibious operations," and secondly, "Evaluate a small helicopter as a replacement for the present OY aircraft in gunfire spotting, observation, and liaison missions in connection with amphibious operations."[12] The six tasks assigned to the development squadron under the two general missions were to:

Igor Sikorsky visits with officers of HMX–1, MCAS, Quantico, Va., in 1948. The aircraft is a Sikorsky HO3S–1 (Marine Corps Photo A322389).

1. Develop a doctrine for the aviation tactics and techniques in the employment of the helicopter in amphibious operations as outlined in [the general missions].

2. Assist the Marine Corps Schools in the development of a doctrine covering the tactics and techniques of the employment of helicopters in amphibious operations.

3. Study the operations and maintenance of assigned aircraft.

4. Develop the flight proficiency of pilots and crewmen.

5. Develop and maintain the technical proficiency of mechanics.

6. Submit recommendations for tables of organization, equipment allowances, and related data for future helicopter squadrons.[13]

The squadron now had to prepare for the arrival of its first aircraft which were scheduled for delivery in January. The ultimate complement of aircraft had been established by the CNO on 28 November at 6 HO3S-1s and 12 HRP-1s, with 5 of each type expected to be assigned to the squadron by 1 June 1948.[14] Although the Marine Corps was hopeful of having helicopters operating in HMX-1 in January 1948, the first two Sikorsky HO3S-1s did not arrive from VX-3 until 9 February. Three more reached the squadron by the end of the month having been ferried directly from the Stratford plant. As indicated in the CNO's Aviation Plan No. 57, Supplement No. 3, the full complement of six HO3S-1s was not expected to be reached until 1 July 1949.[15] In the same aviation plan dated 6 April, it was indicated that only six HRPs were to be in the squadron's inventory by the same date. This announcement brought great disappointment to Marine Corps planners as they were expecting to have the complete complement of 12 transport helicopters by the July 1949 date.

Before HMX-1 received the HO3S-1, the Navy had used its first four, purchased from Sikorsky, on Operation HIGHJUMP during the winter of 1946. Later, as more were accepted, the HO3Ss were evaluated by the Navy for plane guard duty, mail delivery, personnel transfer, and also as training aircraft. The helicopter was a minor modification of the Sikorsky commercial model S-51, which was, in turn, a larger modification of the Navy's HO2S-1—a version in itself of the Air Force's R-5. A Wasp Jr. R-985-AN-5 450-horsepower engine turned a single three-bladed main rotor and torque compensating tail rotor. The aircraft could be equipped with dual controls and had accommodations for a pilot and three passengers. Originally, the helicopter weighed 3,788 pounds empty with a maximum take-off weight limited to 4,988 pounds. The model had a tricycle landing gear and differed from the standard commercial model by having an oil dilution system—needed for operation in cold weather—installed in addition to provisions for one 50-gallon fuel tank and a 300-pound capacity rescue hoist. Because of the limited instrumentation in the HO3S, the aircraft was restricted to day flying, visual flight rules (VFR), and a maxium airspeed of 90 knots.[16]

The Marines' new HO3Ss were primarily intended for utility use; however, the squadron at Quantico was not too concerned with the official mission description listed in the BuAer publications. The aircraft were first put to use in the training of the pilots and mechanics as an additional four officers and nine enlisted men had joined the squadron during January. The first mission of an operational nature, exclusive of training, was on 24 February when an HO3S was used to lead a salvage party to an amphibious jeep ("Weasel") that had become mired in a creek.

Improvement of pilot techniques continued through the month of March, and in addition, various flights were made to determine the value of helicopters for aerial photography, artillery spotting, reconnaissance, and wire laying. Many indoctrination flights were also given to ground officers for the purpose of familiarizing them with the helicopter's characteristics.[17]

In early April 1948, a Bell Aircraft representative and test pilot visited HMX-1 to demonstrate the company's new 47-D helicopter. Besides the demonstration, the Bell test pilot gave the squadron pilots some very helpful and eagerly sought after advanced flight instruction. The Bell team also demonstrated the 47-D, the equivalent of the Navy's new HTL-2, to members of the staff of MCS, Fleet Marine Force, Atlantic, and 2d Marine Division audiences.

Initial Request for an Observation Helicopter

Until 1948 there was not a helicopter specifically designed for military observation in actual production. In existence, however, was the Bell model 47E in flight test at the Bell factory and the one Sikorsky S-52, which had already completed flight test; both of which, it was believed, could easily be converted for military observation use. At the time though, the Navy's HTL-2, an improved version of the HTL–1 which incorporated a larger engine and bubble canopy, was being produced in quantity for the Navy as a trainer and represented a close approximation to the final configuration of what could be expected in future observation helicopters. But until such time as either the experimental Bell or Sikorsky observation helicopters became operational and were available in quantity, considerable operational experience could be gained through operating a small number of the Navy's HTL–2s. With this thought in mind, and with a desire to comply with the squadron's second mission of evaluating a helicopter as a replacement for the OY fixed-wing aircraft, Colonel Dyer recommended, on 28 April 1948, that the Marine Corps procure three HTL–2 trainers.[18] The new Commandant, General Clifton B. Cates, who had relieved General Vandegrift on 1 January 1948, requested on 13 May that the CNO provide HMX–1 with the three HTL–2s.

General Cates, as well as his predecessor, appreciated the potential value of the helicopter as it applied to amphibious assault techniques. During World War II, he had commanded the 1st Marines in the 1942 Guadalcanal campaign and in 1944 was the commanding general of the 4th Marine Division in the Saipan, Tinian, and Iwo

Bell HTL-2s on board the USS Valley Forge *in the early 1950s (National Archives Photo 80-G-424772).*

Jima campaigns. In the period between 1942 and 1944, General Cates was Commandant, Marine Corps Schools. Returning to Quantico in 1945, he became president of the Marine Corps Equipment Board for six months before being named as the Commanding General, Marine Barracks, Quantico, and ultimately, Commandant in 1948. On 23 May the CNO replied to General Cates' letter concurring with its content, but reduced the number allotted to two aircraft.[19]

Approximately 10 weeks later, on 9 August, the squadron received the first HTL–2 from NAS Lakehurst, New Jersey. The Bell helicopter was two-place, dual controlled, and powered by a 178-horsepower engine driving a two-bladed main rotor. The cruising speed, similar to the HO3S, was 80 knots but unlike the HO3Ss, the gross weight was only 2,200 pounds.[20]

Since most of the pilots had received a minimum of 15 hours in the HTL–1 while undergoing training at HU–2, a familiarization syllabus was not necessary. Tests were immediately begun to compare the HTL–2 with the OY aircraft in artillery spotting, liaison, and aerial photography work. The results of the preliminary evaluations indicated that the HTL was superior in all respects to the OY, except that the OY's cruising speed was higher.[21]

By November the evaluation had been completed and the results sent to the Commandant by Colonel Dyer. Based upon Colonel Dyer's letter, on 24 November General Cates asked permission of the CNO to change the complement of a Marine observation squadron from its previously authorized eight OY aircraft to four OY and four helicopters. The Commandant stated that all of the helicopters observed and tested as replacements for the OY aircraft, the latest model Bell HTL–3 and the Sikorsky S–52 closely met the Marine

General Clifton B. Cates, 19th Commandant (Marine Corps Photo 306430-A).

Corps' requirements of size, configuration, and gross weight, with the S–52 rated as the most desirable of all models.[22]

The Sikorsky S–52 was a two-place, three-bladed single-rotor-system utility helicopter built completely at Sikorsky's expense and concurrently with the larger and now practically defunct XHJS–1. The 2,100-pound gross weight of the S–52 permitted the aircraft to carry a useful load of approximately 1,000 pounds at a maximum airspeed of 91 knots. The HTL–3 trainer was similar in general configuration to the HTL–2 except that a 200-horsepower engine had been installed in place of the HTL–2s 178-horsepower engine which increased the useful load to approximately 706 pounds.

As an interim measure, therefore, the Commandant recommended that 12 HTL–3s or S–52s be procured for the Marine Corps to implement the change in the VMO's aircraft complement. As a long-range recommendation, he requested that the design and procurement of a light helicopter be initiated to meet specifically the requirements for a military observation helicopter.[23] At this point the Commandant's request for the interim helicopters "struck a snag when BuAer replied that the new machines of the desired type were not available"—for assignment to the Marine Corps.[24]

It was not until the next year that the CNO's Aviation Plan Number 21–49, dated 7 April 1949, outlined the plans for outfitting the VMO squadrons. The plan specified that the HTLs were considered satisfactory for Marine observation requirements and that as the HTL helicopters became available they would replace half the observation aircraft in existing VMO squadrons.[25]

Approximately three months after the 1949 aviation plan appeared, the Commandant submitted to the CNO the Marine Corps' specific requirements for the desired type of observation helicopter. The letter, dated 1 July 1949, mentioned that HMX–1 had conducted extensive evaluation of helicopters as replacements for the OY type aircraft for VMO squadrons and determined that some specific requirements were necessary if the aircraft were to be suitable for observation work. Generally, the specifications required that the helicopter carry a useful load of between 800 to 1,000 pounds, have dual controls, be capable of flight at maximum gross weight for a duration of four hours, and carry a pilot, observer, and one additional passenger. The requirements listing the maximum air speed and dimensions were omitted.[26]

One requirement which had been a problem in single-main-rotor helicopters was the need to shift the ballast inside the aircraft either fore or aft. This was necessary to keep the helicopter within its designed flight control parameters—for, should

The Bell HTL–3 was an improved version of the HTL–2 (Marine Corps Photo 529989).

the center of gravity change excessively, the helicopter would become uncontrollable in the air. In
tandem-configured helicopters a change in the
center of gravity was less critical due to the location of the lifting rotors. Therefore, the tandem
rotor helicopter permitted a less stringent loading
requirement—a feature which appealed to the
helicopter pilots and loading crews. In this relationship, the new observation helicopter requirement stipulated that the aircraft should be capable
of operations within allowable center of gravity
limits at minimum and maximum loading conditions without having to resort to shifts in ballast,
or equipment, to stay within operating center of
gravity limits. In relation to size, the aircraft was
to be small enough to lend itself to ease of con-
cealment and transportability on a widely varied
number of vehicles, and to be able to operate from
small areas in the field.[27]

Published later, on 16 August 1949, was CNO's
Operational Requirement AO-17503 (Liaison helicopter) which defined, in further detail, the requirements desired for such an observation helicopter. Seven such specifications were listed:

   1. Maximum visibility.
   2. Extreme maneuverability.
   3. High rate of climb.
   4. Performance and internal space sufficient to
carry two litters or a limited amount of cargo.
   5. Capability of sustained flight with all or part of
one rotor blade missing.
   6. Interchangeable and foldable rotor blade for
simplicity of maintenance and stowage of aircraft.
   7. Provisions for quick (five minutes or less) installation of television and electronic reconnaissance
equipment.[28]

As a result of the favorable flight evaluation of
the Sikorsky S-52, BuAer initiated a contract with
Sikorsky for the S-52-2, a version of the original
S-52 (Navy designation HO5S-1). When further
modified and later delivered to the Marine Corps,
it would be a four-place, 245-horsepower, three-
bladed machine with a quadricycle landing gear.
Official missions descriptions were listed as obser-
vation-liaison, reconnaissance, gunfire adjustment,
evacuation of wounded, transportation of personnel,
and general utility. As a medical evacuation aircraft, the copilot's seat could be removed and two
litter patients carried internally, in addition to the
pilot and attendant. An unusual feature, one which
would later amount to a great impairment in its
use, was that its take-off weight was limited to
2,769 pounds. With a pilot and observer, and a
full fuel load of 222 pounds, the 245-horsepower
engine would allow for a skimpy 157 pounds of

payload![29] The delivery date for the first aircraft
was scheduled for September 1951.* [30]

Operation PACKARD II

By the end of April 1948, HMX-1 had 12 officers and 32 enlisted men on duty with an additional four officers and eight enlisted men temporarily attached while undergoing pilot and
mechanical training. Although the squadron had
been operating helicopters for only three months,
sufficient progress had been made by this date in
both the operational and maintenance sections to
the point where Colonel Dyer was receptive to a
suggestion from Lieutenant Colonel Victor H.
Krulak, Assistant Director of the Senior School,
that HMX-1 participate in the MCS forthcoming
training exercise, Operation PACKARD II.

The MCS amphibious command post exercises
were held annually by joint Navy and Marine
Corps forces to simulate a ship-to-shore assault
landing against an enemy-defended beach. Operation PACKARD II represented an ideal opportunity for HMX-1 to implement one of the helicopter program objectives for 1948 and would
present the first test in the movement of troops
by helicopters in a ship-to-shore operation.

Lieutenant Colonel Krulak was extremely knowl-
edgeable on the subject of amphibious operations.
During World War II he commanded the diver-
sionary landing at Choiseul to cover the Bougainville invasion and had served as Assistant Chief
of Staff, G-3 for the 6th Marine Division then
under the command of Major General Lemuel C.
Shepherd Jr. Lieutenant Colonel Krulak earned
the Legion of Merit for his part in the planning
and execution of the Okinawa campaign. Colonel
Dyer later remarked about the conversation he had
with Krulak: "No one could ever characterize a
flight of five helicopters carrying three Marines
apiece as an overwhelming force, but Krulak felt
—and I agreed—that we [HMX-1] should go on
board ship and . . . make . . . a landing." [31] It
was also planned that because of the many unknown factors involved, that only a minimum
satisfactory performance should be sought rather
than a maximum endeavor which might develop

---

* The Sikorsky S-52 would be the first production
helicopter to have all-metal rotor blades. In view of the
climatic effects and sand abrasion on wood and fabric
rotor blades, this represented a basic improvement in dura-
bility and lifetime. During April 1949, the S-52 established
a world's speed record at Cleveland, Ohio, of 129.55 miles
per hour.

unforeseen difficulties and thereby jeopardize the operation.[32]

The squadron was given a list of objectives for PACKARD II, three of which were:

> 1. To take a positive step forward in the development program by making an actual landing of troops by carrier-based helicopters.
> 2. To gain experience in operating helicopters on board an aircraft carrier and experience in helicopter landing operations upon which a sound doctrine for these operations could be written.
> 3. To determine probable military requirements for landing force helicopters of the future.[33, 34] *

As finally developed, and later executed, the operational plan, prepared by the MCS student staff, provided for an element of the landing force, the staff of a regimental combat team (RCT), and HMX-1 to be embarked in escort aircraft carriers (CVEs). For problem purposes, the regimental staff planned in full, and theoretically executed, the ship-to-shore movement of a constructive regimental combat team using a problem force of 250 HRP-1 helicopters operating from four CVEs. This movement and subsequent employment of the helicopter-borne force was part of, and integrated with, the overall attack plan of the naval attack force and landing force. The RCT staff also planned the actual ship-to-shore movement of the regimental headquarters and this was executed in reality by five HO3S-1 helicopters, consistent as far as practicable with the theoretical plan.[35] The squadron spent the early part of May 1948 making plans and preparations for PACKARD II and on 18 May departed Quantico for Norfolk, Virginia, where it flew on board the USS *Palau* (CVE-122).

As the operation began on 23 May at 0930, the five HO3S-1s took off from the USS *Palau*, anchored off Onslow Beach at Camp Lejeune, North Carolina, and proceeded in formation to the designated landing zone a few miles inland. The troops of the first flight were landed precisely at 1000. Thereafter, continuous flights were made until all troops, less a small logistical group, were landed. Following the landing of the troops, a number of flights were made simulating the movement of cargo loads requested by the regiment ashore. During the day's operations, a total of 66 Marines and a considerable amount of communications equipment were transported to the beach by heli-

copter. A total of 35 flights was made between the *Palau* and the landing zone.[36]

The squadron concluded from its participation in PACKARD II that "transport helicopters capable of carrying at least eight troops were urgently needed if combat troops were to be landed expeditiously and in battle formation." Also, that "in order to use the space available in a CVE to full advantage, it would be necessary that embarked helicopters be capable of movement up or down on the ship's flight deck elevators," and in order to do this expeditiously, it was stressed "that automatic blade folding devices must be developed." Two of the five recommendations made at the termination of the exercise stressed "that the helicopter objectives be extended in a similar operation in 1949" and "that every effort be made to equip HMX-1 with at least five HRP-1 helicopters prior to December 1948."[37]

Again, from the standpoint of HMX-1, this was the first test to determine the value of the helicopter in the movement of assault troops in an amphibious operation. Although there was no attempt made to exploit the capabilities of rotary-wing aircraft, the operation was entirely successful in achieving its limited objectives. Neither theoretical nor actual insurmountable obstacles which could prevent future operations of massed landings of troops by helicopter were experienced. The success of PACKARD II proved that the helicopter could achieve the desired troop build-up ashore. As a result, Marine Corps planners became more firmly committed to the new technique of vertical assault in amphibious warfare. This was truly the beginning.

Publication of the New Concept—PHIB-31

In response to the Commandant's directive of December 1946, officers of the MCS were busily engaged in developing a concept covering the tactics and techniques of the employment of helicopters in an amphibious operation and by November 1948 the school had published the world's first printed textbook on the subject entitled *Amphibious Operations—Employment of Helicopters (Tentative)*. It was originally printed in mimeograph form in 1947 as an instructional guide for use within the school and later was used for the planning of Operation PACKARD II. The booklet was numbered 31 in a series of publications on amphibious operations and was written jointly with representatives from HMX-1, but under the

---

* General Krulak states that "although unwritten, the greatest and by far the most important objective of the Packard II helicopter element was *to create a state of mind* among students, instructors, the Navy and observers, as to the dramatic tactical horizons of the helicopter."

overall supervision of the Senior School's Director and senior member of the Helicopter and Transport Seaplane Board,* Colonel Robert E. Hogaboom.

Phib-31 provided the basis of doctrine governing helicopter landing operations. The preface defined its purpose:

> The advent of troop carrying helicopters and its establishment as standard equipment within the Marine Corps gives rise to a variety of questions related to the employment of such conveyances in the conduct of amphibious operations. It is the purpose of this pamphlet to explore the various aspects of helicopter employment, discerning the manner in which the characteristics of the vehicle can best be exploited to enhance the effectiveness of the amphibious attack.[38]

The publication spelled out the many advantages of the helicopter to the new amphibious concept:

> As a military conveyance, [it] possesses certain distinctive characteristics which, if exploited, can enhance greatly the speed and flexibility of the amphibious assault, while at the same time permitting a desirable increase in the dispersion of the attacking Naval forces. The ability of the helicopter to rise and descend vertically, to hover, and to move rapidly at varying altitudes all qualify it admirably as a supplement or substitute for the slower, more inflexible craft now employed in the ship-to-shore movement. Furthermore its ability to circumvent powerful beach defenses, and to land assault forces accurately and at any desired altitude, on tactical localities farther inland endow helicopter operations with many of the desirable characteristics of the conventional airborne attack while avoiding the undesirable dispersal of forces which often accompany such operations. The helicopter, furthermore, when transported to the scene of operations in aircraft carriers, makes operations possible at ranges which have not yet been achieved by the existing conventional troop carrier types.[39]

These words which appeared in the introduction to *Phib-31* were written by Lieutenant Colonel Krulak. In later years General Krulak had this to say about the book, "I wrote the words [to the introduction but] Dyer was unhappy with them, and properly so, because no helicopters of that era could do these things, or even approach them." As for preface, and the rest of the book, it "was written jointly by Dyer and me [with the help of eight board members]. We had so little to go on; no data: just conviction."[40, 41] ##

---

* This particular board had been formed for the purpose of devising a concept for the employment of both the transport helicopter and the assault seaplane transport (AST). *Phib-31* was the first product of the board.

Phib-31 was truly pioneering and it is significant to observe that it was copied in all its essential elements by the U. S. Army in its first helicopter manual.

A final statement in the introduction expressed, in a way, the attitude that prevailed among most officers at the MCS responsible for the new conceptual document. As an indication of their conviction and dedication in keeping the developmental pace of the concept ahead of the advances in helicopter construction, it said:

> . . . the evolution of a set of principles governing the helicopter employment cannot await the perfection of the craft itself, but must proceed concurrently with that development. Certain of these principles are now apparent, and a concept of employment based thereon is presented in the sections to follow.[42]

Throughout its 52 pages, *Phib-31* discussed, in eight separate sections, such features of helicopter employment as: organization and command, tactical considerations, embarkation, and the ship-to-shore movement. Also included within the text were such subjects as fire support, logistics, communications, and detailed lists of characteristics on the HRP-1 and the HO3S-1. *Phib-31* was published by the MCS as a tentative guide for instructional purposes and served as the guidebook for amphibious helicopter employment.

As General Krulak remarked years later, "the best we could do was to rationalize the operational principles, praying they would turn out to be valid, since we had no real experience."[43]

Other Significant Demonstrations and Operations by HMX–1

By early April 1949, HMX–1 was operating nine Piasecki HRP–1s, having received the first HRP–1 on 19 August 1948. The development of the amphibious assault by helicopter had advanced sufficiently by that time to publicly demonstrate the technique. On 9 May, the squadron, in conjunction with Marine air and ground forces, gave a two-part demonstration to members of the 81st Congress and senior Defense Department officials. The first phase of the show started with the guests witnessing the actual assault preparations and takeoff of eight HRPs with 56 fully-equipped combat Marines from a simulated carrier deck painted on the runway at MCAS Quantico. The helicopters took off, rendezvoused, and in formation flew past the visitors. Then later in the day, the officials were taken to a combat area for the landing phase where they saw the helicopters speed inbound toward the landing zone under the cover of fighter aircraft, which were strafing and laying smoke screens. The HRPs landed in the rough terrain, discharged their troops, and took off in approximately 25 seconds. Following the landing of the troops, a second wave of HRPs flew into the same zone transporting 75mm pack howitzers dangling from each helicopter's hook. After the guns were placed into position the crews readied them for firing. Other type helicopters gave demonstrations in laying communication wire, spotting for artillery, and evacuating casualties.[44]

Following the Congressional demonstration, the squadron took part in Operation PACKARD III which was the MCS amphibious command post exercise of 1949. The operation was held again at Camp Lejeune, North Carolina, and was basically the same as PACKARD II in which the squadron had participated the previous year.

The squadron had several objectives for PACKARD III. First, the squadron was to make a "definite advance in the employment of rotary-winged aircraft in amphibious warfare by operating, for the first time, transport helicopters in the ship-to-shore movement." In doing so, HMX–1 was to contribute to the "formulation of tactical doctrines and operating procedures by gaining practical experience and stimulating thought in operating large helicopters from aircraft carriers." As a final objective, the squadron was to "evaluate the operations of a small observation helicopter from an LST (Landing Ship, Tank) for artillery and infantry observation and liaison missions."[45]

For PACKARD III, the squadron's aircraft were divided into three separate sections. The main echelon consisted of eight HRP–1s based on board the USS *Palau* and, for problem purposes, represented a full helicopter aircraft group of 184 HRPs operating from six CVEs for the lifting of a complete regimental combat team. The second group was three HO3Ss land-based with the mission of search and rescue. The last group was assigned on board LST-155 with the squadron's HTL–2 for the observation mission and shipboard evaluation.[46]

A rehearsal was held at Naval Amphibious Base, Little Creek, Virginia, after which the ships moved into position off the coast of North Carolina. A two-day invasion was held beginning on 22 May with landing boats storming Onslow Beach while the HMX–1 helicopters transported troops inland to a point approximately six miles up the New River inlet. They landed and discharged their troops at a strategic road position. High winds and rough seas encountered during the entire operation swamped many landing boats as they approached the beach and upon their return they experienced great difficulty in tying up to their respective attack cargo ships (AKAs). The heli-

copter operations from the *Palau* were routine as their efficiency was not impaired by these elements. Each HRP helicopter carried six fully-equipped combat troops from the carrier for approximately 10 miles under a heavy cover of fighter aircraft which were simulating smoke and strafing runs on the defending forces. A total of 230 passengers were carried in addition to 14,000 pounds of cargo.[47]

During the exercise, the HTL–2 proved to be totally successful during its evaluation. The small helicopter operated for naval gunfire spotting and observation from the LST while the ship was both underway and at anchor. Although at times the LST pitched and rolled in the choppy seas, the HTL proved that small helicopters could work successfully from that type of vessel.[48]

The search and rescue group, which was based at Peterfield Point, North Carolina, later renamed MCAS, New River, was on station over the fleet for the entire daylight operation. The three HO3Ss had no cause to be used in their primary role, but were called upon for message drops and ship-to-shore transportation of personnel.

Operation PACKARD III was the most ambitious attempt to advance this type of helicopter operation. Although the squadron used only eight transport helicopters, it was convinced that a complete regimental combat team could have been hauled successfully in a helicopter amphibious assault.[49] The operation confirmed the previous conclusions derived from Operation PACKARD II and offered an excellent contribution to the Marine Corps' assigned function of developing amphibious tactics and techniques. The existing concept for the employment of helicopters in the amphibious assault, derived by MCS and HMX–1, was tested through the medium of this problem and proved "to be sound and workable in all respects."[50]

With the completion of PACKARD III, the squadron returned to Quantico and for the following 12 months participated in a variety of projects. Emphasis was placed first on pilot training during June in order to qualify more pilots to fly the HRP–1 and to train the newer pilots who had recently rejoined the squadron after their initial helicopter training at HU–2. The training activity was necessary as by 30 June 1949 the personnel strength had risen to 22 officers and 69 enlisted men, as compared with an authorized level of 21 officers and 89 enlisted.[51] The squadron also had an increase in the number of helicopters which now totaled 14; 9 HRPs, 4 HO3Ss, and 1 HTL–2. The CNO's Aircraft Complement and Allowance List, dated 15 June, had fixed the number of aircraft at 10 HRPs, 3 HO3Ss, and 2 HTLs.[52]

At the end of June, Colonel Dyer turned command of the squadron over to Lieutenant Colonel John F. Carey, who during World War II earned the Navy Cross at Midway, then subsequently served in an air mission in Peru. The change of command ceremony was a sad occasion for Colonel Dyer, but two months later he was to assume yet another challenging assignment as Commanding Officer, Marine Aircraft Group 12 (MAG-12).

Lieutenant Colonel Carey continued the agressive pace of helicopter demonstrations and evaluations carried on by Colonel Dyer and immediately began contributing many of his own ideas to the advancement of the new technique. During September, under Carey's leadership, HMX-1 sent four HRPs to the Cleveland air races to demonstrate publicly the employment of the helicopter as a troop and cargo transport.

Between 25 November 1949 and 5 April 1950, operations with the HRP were halted as all aircraft of that model were grounded for mechanical reasons. Nevertheless, during December, Carey's squadron experimented for the first time in night flying with the HO3S. For the evaluation, each pilot was given two 45-minute periods of local flying during which a portion of the time was spent in making landings in an area marked by flare pots. As a result of the night flying experiment, a request was sent to BuAer for landing lights and instruments adequate for night flying. These items were considered essential by the squadron before any large-scale night helicopter operations could be undertaken.[53]

As HRPs were still not available during February 1950, the squadron sent four HO3S-1s and the one HLT-2 as a detachment to the Naval Air Facility (NAF), Roosevelt Roads, Puerto Rico on the 11th of the month to participate in the Fleet Marine Force, Atlantic (FMFLant) Fleet Exercise, 1950. Later, on the nearby island of Vieques, during the amphibious landing, an HO3S directed the landing boats during their movement toward the beach by means of an externally mounted speaker system.[54] Other than this novel experiment, all aspects of the amphibious operation were routine.

The HRPs returned to operational status in April after the long grounding period due to a problem with the mid-transmission oil pump. During that month, for the Sixth Joint Civilian Orientation Conference at Quantico, and for Operation CROSSOVER, a 2d Marine Division maneuver held at Camp Lejeune, HMX-1 performed similar missions of delivering infantry troops and 75mm pack howitzers into specified landing areas. Also demonstrated by the helicopters were the techniques of wire laying, resupply, and the evacuation of the "wounded." [55]

The high point of May 1950 for HMX-1 was Operation PACKARD IV, which took place during the final week of the month. Six HRP-1s and two HO3S-1 helicopters landed on board the USS *Mindoro* (CVE-120) at Norfolk, Virginia, after which the ship sailed south to a point 15 miles off the coast of Camp Lejeune. The operation lasted only two days during which five HRPs and two HO3Ss carried ashore a total of 120 troops and over 20,000 pounds of cargo. As was the case in Operation CROSSOVER, the exercise afforded good training for the squadron although there were no new techniques of the amphibious assault exhibited.[56]

On 15 June 1950, HMX-1 was given an opportunity to demonstrate to President Harry S Truman and the Joint Chiefs of Staff the many tasks which Marine helicopters were now able to perform. A simulated amphibious assault was staged for the guests as the helicopters were "put through their paces" in presenting a complete amphibious demonstration similar to the Congressional exhibition given the previous year. The next day a parade and review was staged at Quantico in honor of Lieutenant General Lemuel C. Shepherd, Jr., the outgoing Commandant of the MCS, a position he had held since April 1948. At the close of the ceremony, six HRP-1s, six HO3S-1s, and the HTL-2 made a "Fly-by" in formation. This was believed to have been the largest group of helicopters to fly in formation to date.[57]

Reviewing the progress made by HMX-1 since its commissioning date to June 1950, the squadron performed practically all aspects of its assigned missions and tasks. Evidence indicated that the operations of HMX-1 had been completely satisfactory. Although the Commandant's time-table for the helicopter program had slipped, HMX-1 had used every conceivable opportunity to ensure that fulfillment of the program had been met to the best of its capability.

Development of tactics and techniques in connection with the movement of assault troops had been accomplished by participation in the PACKARD operations. The evaluation of a small helicopter for observation purposes had been completed and specifications submitted for its characteristics. Compliance with the last task assigned had also been completed when a proposed table of organization was submitted for a typical Marine helicopter squadron.

Although the squadron did not possess 18 aircraft as the original planners had envisioned and CNO had approved, by the end of June, HMX-1 was one aircraft in excess of the authorized level. The latest allowance list, dated 15 June 1950, established the maximum number of aircraft at 6 HRP-1s, 7 HO3Ss, and 2 HTL-2s. This com-

pared with an actual on hand accounting of 6 HRP-1s, 9 HO3Ss, and 1 HTL-3.[58] An HTL-3 had replaced the HTL-2 after it had sustained severe damage in a crash during April 1950.

Personnel strength at the end of June was likewise near the authorized level. It had been readjusted in April 1950 to 20 officers and 90 enlisted men with the squadron reporting a total of 23 officers and 86 enlisted.[59]

CHAPTER 3

A REVITALIZED HELICOPTER PROGRAM

The Marine Corps Board

While HMX–1 was engaged in testing, evaluating, and demonstrating the new amphibious technique from the operational point of view, Marine Corps Schools was developing the concept from the academic standpoint. Back in June 1949, a major impetus had been injected into the Marine Corps' helicopter program when the schools presented to the Commandant the most broad and intensive plan for expansion since the program's initial submission in December 1946.

The Marine Corps Board, MCS, headed by Major General Oliver P. Smith, the Assistant Commandant and Chief of Staff, HQMC, had been instructed by the Commandant in late 1948 to undertake a new study. General Smith was directed to look into the matters concerning the "measures which the Marine Corps should take in order to fulfill its obligations in maintaining its position as the agency primarily responsible for the development of landing force tactics, techniques, and equipment." In compliance with its instructions, the board during the early part of 1949, examined reports of Fleet Marine Force postwar maneuvers and found "little if any advancement or improvement was being made in landing force tactics and techniques. The postwar maneuvers had tended to become stereotyped with the execution falling into mechanical patterns." The practices "which had been developed to such a high degree during World War II were more or less standard procedures and were employed without variation." [1]

In searching for a means to develop new concepts and techniques for FMF maneuvers, the Smith Board reasoned that the "lack of flexibility and originality in the FMF was due at least in part to limitations imposed by the equipment being employed." It was considered that "until some quantum advance was made in equipment, little new could be expected in the way of advanced tactics and techniques." [2]

The board had observed with great interest the employment of HMX–1 in support of the MCS landing exercises at Onslow Beach in Operations PACKARD II and III and felt that "those exercises had successfully demonstrated that the helicopter offered the most promising possibilities of being the quantum advance for which the Marine Corps had been searching." It was believed that "the time was rapidly approaching when operating helicopter squadrons should be organized and placed in support of FMF maneuvers." The board was convinced that in this way "a means would be provided for putting new life into the amphibious problems and thereby take it out of the stereotyped forms toward which it was tending." [3]

Four basic problem areas were cited by General Smith's board, all of which had to be solved before helicopter squadrons could be placed in support of FMF maneuvers. Allocation of necessary funds in the budget was listed first with procurement of a suitable type helicopter seen as a second obstacle. The third and fourth problems were provisions for a helicopter squadron in the CNO's operational plan and organization and training of operational helicopter squadrons. [4]

It was obvious that a carefully prepared and vigorously executed program extending over several years would be necessary before the realization of operational helicopter squadrons could be achieved. The first step in such a program was to obtain the allocation of the necessary funds in the budget. Since the preparation of the 1951 budget had already begun, the earliest fiscal year in which funds could be allocated was 1952. Therefore, the board stated, studies should be undertaken immediately by the Division of Aviation, HQMC, with the view in mind toward obtaining the necessary funds in fiscal year 1952." [5]

In relation to the second problem, the board's report explained:

> An entirely satisfactory transport helicopter does not yet exist. However, types which can be in production by 1952 have acceptable characteristics for initiating work with the FMF. The Board believes that this program should not be delayed until the ideal military requirements for a transport helicopter are met. The type which, in fiscal 1952, comes the closest

to meeting our requirements should be procured at that time.[6]

Since procurement of aviation materiel was a function of BuAer, the report mentioned that early studies should be undertaken by the Division of Aviation in conjunction with BuAer "to determine the most effective means by which provisions for the requisite helicopter squadron could be made in operation force plans." While this problem was purely an administrative one, it nevertheless was difficult and complicated. "The creation of operational transport helicopter squadrons will" the report continued, "require decisions as to what effect the activation of these squadrons will have on presently activated Marine Corps squadrons and what effect, if any, it will have on the ratio of aviation to ground strengths."[7]

It was estimated that a period of eight months to a year would be required for the organization and training of a transport helicopter squadron before it could be prepared to participate with the FMF in maneuvers. To ease the training load, and also because it was estimated that the production rate of new helicopters would be slow, it was considered more feasible that new "squadrons should be activated successively rather than simultaneously." General Smith's report terminated with only one formal recommendation: "that a transport helicopter program with the objective of activating one 12-plane squadron [on each coast] in 1953 and one such squadron in 1954 be initiated immediately."[8]

The Second Attempt to Procure a 3,000-Pound Payload Helicopter

General Smith's report was circulated at HQMC between two main action agencies: the Divisions of Aviation, and Plans and Policy. Meanwhile, Colonel Dyer initiated a request from HMX–1 to the Commandant stating that the "squadron's recent participation on Operation PACKARD III had proved that helicopter operations were highly successful within the limitations of the HRP–1, and therefore, development of a carrier-based transport was now justified."[9] He understood that the Navy and Air Force were developing jointly the Piasecki XH–16 and, since it would undoubtedly be of military usefulness, felt the project should be continued. Because of the time required to perfect fully such a large helicopter, and its doubtful ability to operate from small

aircraft carriers, Colonel Dyer stressed that "it appears advantageous to proceed with an additional project for the development of a small helicopter which will meet our minimum requirements, which will be suitable for carrier operations, and might well be more easily and quickly obtained."[10]

In general terms, it was pointed out by Dyer that "such a helicopter should be designed for carrier-based operations . . . , capable of carrying a payload of about 3,000 pounds, (15 combat-equipped Marines)" and have "sufficient fuel for an operating radius of about 100 miles." He noted that "the specifications should meet the Marine Corps' immediate military requirements and present a reasonable goal for technical developments [of the helicopter]." The requirement specified that the helicopter be of a weight and size "to permit movement on the smallest flight deck elevators and of an overall height which would not prohibit storage on aircraft carrier hangar decks"[11]—a mandatory requirement if large numbers of helicopters were to operate from aircraft carriers.

Colonel Dyer's letter, dated 25 June 1949, his last to the Commandant on this subject as commanding officer of HMX–1, was endorsed by General Lemuel C. Shepherd, Jr., Commandant of Marine Corps Schools, who concurred with Dyer's recommendation and considered that "the development of such a helicopter should be in addition to the development now in progress on the XH–16."[12]

By 5 August Brigadier General Edwin A. Pollock, Director, Division of Plans and Policies (DivP&P) and Major General William J. Wallace, Director, Division of Aviation (DivAvn) agreed to form a joint study group at HQMC "to implement the execution of the program,"[13] as recommended in General Smith's report. General Pollock had served, since 1945, successively as Commanding Officer of the Basic School; Executive Officer of the MCS; and Chief of Staff of the Marine Barracks, Quantico. In June 1948 he was ordered to HQMC as the Military Secretary to the Commandant, and when promoted to brigadier general, became Director, Division of Plans and Policies in July 1949. General Wallace, prior to assuming the post of Director, Division of Aviation/Assistant Commandant of the Marine Corps (Air) in 1948, was Commanding General, Aircraft, FMFLant and Commanding General, 2d MAW. Earlier he had been Commanding General, Aircraft, FMFPac/Deputy Commander FMFPac.

The Commandant, General Clifton B. Cates, appointed Lieutenant Colonel George S. Bowman,

DivAvn, as senior member of a seven-man study group. The membership was directed to convene "as soon as may be practicable to study and report on a program for the activation of transport helicopter squadrons within the Marine Corps" [14] and to determine the most effective means of complying with the four problem areas of concern outlined in General Smith's report of 3 June.

While Lieutenant Colonel Bowman's board was meeting, the Commandant responded on 19 August to Colonel Dyer's letter of 25 June. Colonel Frank H. Lamson-Scribner, a veteran of Attu, Tarawa, and operations in the Marshall and Gilbert Islands during World War II, and who had been most recently assigned to the DivAvn after serving as commander Marine Air WestPac in China, prepared the Commandant's reply. It stressed that time was not available to design and construct the proposed 3,000-pound payload helicopter prior to the estimated completion date of the first XH–16 in 1952. It explained that the Marine Corps was also investigating the feasibility of transporting troops from friendly bases to hostile beaches by assault seaplane transports, in addition to the ship-to-shore movement of troops by helicopter, and that the assault seaplane concept had resulted in an engineering study contract being awarded for a "flying LST" to the Consolidated Vultee Corporation, San Diego, California. It was considered that any new programs could not be approved at that time for it would require the expenditure of additional money when the Navy was still faced with a cut-back in funds for new aircraft procurement. However, in spite of the financial situation, it was explained to Colonel Dyer that a board was in session at the time at HQMC to study and submit recommendations on a transport helicopter program. The board was to consider, among other factors, the specific type of helicopter most suitable for Marine Corps use. [15]

The final paragraph was most important as it initiated action to consolidate Marine Corps support firmly behind one type of air assault vehicle. It was evident that this action was the proper course to pursue if the Marine Corps desired a suitable helicopter in production prior to the 1952 date established in General Smith's report. The paragraph directed:

> If the 3,000-pound pay-load helicopter is considered more desirable than the XH–16 or the AST (Assault Support Transport) or both, recommendations should be made to this Headquarters relative to the reassigning of priorities for these projects. [16]

Lieutenant Colonel Carey, continuing in the footsteps of Colonel Dyer, regarded the reassigning of priorities of the program, as mentioned by General Cates, as a matter that could best be accomplished by a joint conference where all pertinent information could be available. He suggested representatives should come from HQMC agencies, DivAvn, Military Requirements Section of CNO, BuAer, and members from his own squadron. In addition to proposing the joint conference, Carey elaborated further on Colonel Dyer's reasons for establishing a 3,000-pound payload transport helicopter program. He commented that such a helicopter appeared to be the most feasible model for operating from escort aircraft carriers, whereas the XH–16's size would make it doubtful. Additionally, the XH–16 represented a large step forward in helicopter technology and would require extensive component and flight testing after the anticipated completion date of the first test aircraft in 1952. This would preclude the construction of production models for an appreciable length of time since only two experimental aircraft were being built.

Carey contended that sufficient information was available to support further a new helicopter design. Modifying an existing helicopter was one course of action suggested while making a model based upon "proven" and existing configurations was the alternate proposal. It was considered that extensive expenditures of funds for research and development would not be necessary in the "growth" version since a large part of the basic design and engineering was already completed. Procurement dates provided by the helicopter contractors indicated that such helicopters could be produced in quantity by 1952, the proposed delivery date of the first XH–16 flight test article. [17]

The specific models of helicopters suitable for modification were omitted from Carey's letter. Again, Piasecki, an organization devoted exclusively to the design and production of military transport helicopters, had in the advanced stages of construction its PD–22 (Air Force YH–21), a "beefed-up" version of the HRP. Although the overall dimensions of the YH–21 and the HRP were almost identical and somewhat similar in appearance, the YH–21 weighed twice as much empty (9,148 pounds), and had three times the horsepower (1,425) and useful load carrying capability (5,556 pounds), while retaining approximately the same air speed. The Piasecki Helicopter Corporation, its new name since 1946, was developing the YH–21 as an Arctic rescue helicopter for the Air Force. Three other helicopter manufacturers were competing in the Air Force evaluation with the initial testing of each company's entry to begin in November.

On 13 October 1949, General Cates approved Carey's recommendation for a joint conference. "The cognizant agencies have indicated their desire to attend the conference" the Commandant's letter stated, "which will be held as soon as practicable after the current Transport Helicopter Board has submitted its recommendations." [18]

The joint conference was not delayed by Bowman's board as General Cates received its report the following day. In considering the items before it, the board first determined the general requirements for a transport helicopter which could be procured in 1952–1953 and which would most nearly meet Marine Corps requirements. Based upon specifications submitted over the last two years the assumed general specifications were:

Range: 250 nautical miles
Payload: 3,000 to 3,500 pounds
Capacity: 13 to 15 combat troops @ 225 pounds
  2 pilots @ 200 pounds
Stowage: To fit the elevator of a CVE-105-class aircraft carrier and be capable of being stowed and moved about the hangar deck.
Date Required: 1952-1953 [19]

The board studied characteristics of existing helicopters and formed an opinion that none of the current models would be of sufficient improvement over the Piasecki HRP–1 to justify procurement, nor would they even approximate the board's assumed required general specifications. Further investigation by the board disclosed that only one —the YH–21 Air Force Arctic Rescue model— had the potential of closely approximating the desired specifications. The main variation, though, existing between Air Force and Marine Corps requirements, was that the former had a greater range demand where the latter had a requirement for larger troop capacity. It was felt that favorable results of the forthcoming Air Force evaluation would have a direct bearing on the Marine Corps' ability to procure a suitable production model in the 1952–1953 period. It also appeared that the most effective means of obtaining money would be to select an existing type helicopter which could be modified with production funds— since the availability of research and development funds was extremely critical. Other significant opinions reached by the board were: 1. That "the XH–16 did not meet the restrictions imposed by operations from escort carriers [CVEs and CVLs] and would not be procurable in 1952–1953." 2. "That the minimum requirement for the Marine Corps is two assault transport helicopter squadrons,

each capable of lifting one reinforced rifle company," [20] an opinion appearing for the first time in any helicopter study.

Other recommendations contained in Bowman's report urged the Commandant to request that the CNO examine the feasibility of modifying an existing helicopter and that the aircraft meet the general characteristics specified in his report. In addition, he stated, the CNO should "provide for two assault transport helicopter squadrons in 1953–1954 without reduction of Marine squadrons then in existence." Finally, that HMX–1 "be directed to prepare and submit [to HQMC] a tentative table of organization for the future assault transport helicopter squadron." [21]

The First Six Months of 1950

A vast amount of work remained for the Marine Corps at the beginning of 1950 if the prospects for continued advancement of the helicopter program were to be realized. Complete fulfillment of the original goal was impossible to achieve. The helicopter program was already two years behind the 1948 date established in 1946 for the commissioning of the first tactical helicopter squadron, and it was drifting even further behind schedule with the 1953–1954 dates proposed by General Smith's board. The pace had to be quickened. But how was the Marine Corps to accomplish this infusion of helicopter units into its aircraft wings while at the same time it was carrying out a schedule for a reduction in other areas of its wing forces? For example, during the past two years the Marine Corps had been required to decrease the number of its active combat squadrons from a July 1948 strength of 23 to 12 aircraft units by 1 July 1950—a reduction made necessary due to a lack of appropriations. [22] Research and development funds, production funds, as well as operational money for fleet squadrons had all been equally hard hit by the paucity of money. The complete spectrum of naval aviation, which includes Marine aviation, had felt the pinch, and the idea of forming new combat helicopter squadrons caught aviation planners at a time when they were being forced to think in terms of reducing strengths and expenditures rather than increasing them. Nevertheless, with no end in sight to the unfavorable fiscal trend, the Marine Corps continued with tenacity to pursue for its fleet forces the one new type of aircraft which it knew would be the key to success in maintaining world superiority in the field of amphibious operations.*

On 12 January 1950, the Commandant made a request for the 13- to 15-man assault helicopter. General Cates asked that the CNO procure for the Marine Corps a helicopter with the characteristics identical to those drawn up by the Bowman Board. He pointed out that employment of helicopters from the CVE–105 class carriers was entirely feasible and practical. It was a rigid requirement that the aircraft not only be capable of operating on the flight deck, but also be able to move to the hangar deck for storage and maintenance. General Cates made it known that the "helicopters employed by HMX-1 [the HRPs, HO3Ss, and the HTL] did not possess the required minimum range, payload, and troop capacity for Marine Corps employment as assault helicopters." The XH–16's lengthy development period was seen as seriously retarding the Marine Corps helicopter program and although it was not desired to divert funds for its support, "emphasis should be placed on allocation of funds toward the proposed helicopter . . . and given number one priority." In respect to the number of aircraft assigned to assault squadrons, the Commandant increased the number in each of the two squadrons from 12 to 15 aircraft and urged that the squadrons "be provided for in addition to other Marine squadrons then in existence." [24]

Admiral Sherman acknowledged the Commandant's letter on 2 February with a short statement: "The importance of the assault helicopter program to the Marine Corps is recognized. Consideration of this problem by various OpNav Divisions and BuAer Branches is necessary and is being undertaken." [25]

The informal conference, as recommended by Carey, was held on 28 March 1950. Fourteen members were present from key CNO offices and Marine Corps agencies to determine the best approach to satisfy the requirements presented in the Commandant's letter of 12 January for the 13- to 15-man helicopter. The BuAer representative, Navy Captain Paul H. Ramsey, presented what the conferees apparently felt was the logical course of action. His opinion was that the Air

Force's Arctic Rescue helicopter would be an unsatisfactory assault helicopter * and believed that the helicopter industry could now produce a helicopter capable of carrying 20 to 26 troops, go below decks of the CVE–CVL class carrier, and meet the other requirements established by the Marine Corps. The solution, as presented by Captain Ramsey, for obtaining the new assault helicopter for the Marine Corps involved five separate steps which at the time were the normal aircraft procurement procedures and represented nothing new nor expedited the procurement process. They were:

1. Establish an operational requirement for a 20-man helicopter.
2. Provide research and development funds for the procurement of experimental flying articles.
3. Solicit proposals from industry on a competitive basis.
4. Obtain and test the experimental assault helicopters.
5. Award a production contract to the manufacturer of the winning entry. [26]

It was his opinion that the time saved by obtaining the Arctic Rescue helicopter on the end of the Air Force contract would amount to about four months less than his proposed solution. It was also estimated that the first production aircraft, under this proposal, would be delivered sometime in 1954. The representatives concurred that the Marine Corps would benefit from the short delay by ultimately having a helicopter specifically designed and tested for the assault mission. His recommendation was accepted at the conference as the best solution for the helicopter program, but apparently no thought was given to meeting the requirements of the helicopter program during the intervening four years. It was pointed out, however, that before BuAer could proceed with the proposal, the Commandant would have to withdraw his previously submitted requirement for the 13- to 15-man helicopter as well as his support for the XH–16, both of which were seen as receiving favorable consideration. In matters of financing, the diversion of the remaining XH–16 Navy research and development funds was also viewed as meeting with CNO approval provided the Navy could be persuaded to terminate its support of the XH–16 project. [27]

The following week, the Navy's Air Readiness Division revised the operational requirements for an assault helicopter of the type specified in Gen-

* There is no evidence in the official records to indicate why Captain Ramsey supported this point of view, but as Colonel Harold J. Mitchener recalls, size and compatability with the carriers were his primary concerns.

eral Cates' letter of 12 January to reflect the recommendation of the conference of 28 March and transmitted it to BuAer for action. The specifications were contained in the Navy Research and Development Plan, Operational Requirement Number AO–17501 (Rotary Wing Assault Helicopter). The listed requirements were: "develop a rotary wing assault craft capable of transporting combat equipped troops (or the equivalent in combat equipment) from transport vessels to beachheads in support of landing operations . . ." and "that 20 combat equipped troops be transported with the weight of each man computed at 225 pounds." The assigned functions in AO–17501 for the helicopter were to "operate from a CVE or larger carrier, or between carriers and suitable equipped transport ships, carrying assault troops with their initial requirements in supply, communications and organic weapons . . . ." [28] Two of the main features listed were that it be multi-engine equipped and of an overall dimension compatible with movement on the elevator of the CVE–105 class carrier. Although the operational requirement did not assign a model designation, the twin-engine assault helicopter would subsequently bear the Sikorsky S–56 trademark and the Navy designation of XHR2S–1.*

Further Action by the Marine Corps Board

Still disenchanted with the progress of the helicopter program, the Marine Corps Board at Quantico submitted yet another report to the Commandant on 27 April 1950. This was the second report on the same subject in less than 10 months and was again signed by Major General Oliver P. Smith, the Assistant Commandant, as Chairman. The board reviewed the progress made since the helicopter program was initiated in 1946–1947 and was concerned about the trend of events that had taken place over the past years, and, in particular, the last year. Cited as a typical example of the delays encountered in the helicopter program was the recommendation made by the recent joint helicopter conference to "revert to the drawing board" for an assault helicopter rather than recommending procurement of an existing type which would come closest to meeting Marine Corps requirements. In summary, it was stated

that the Marine Corps transport helicopter program faced two distinct problems. First, "a lack of availability or even prospects of availability in the immediate future of a new and modern helicopter with increased operating capabilities." Secondly, an ever increasing maintenance and availability problem with existing [aging] helicopters" in HMX–1. In stating the recommendations for solving the primary problem, the board stressed "the standard approach to this problem of implementing the transport helicopter program has failed. It is apparent that drastic action on the part of the Marine Corps is the only remaining recourse available." General Smith's report went on to say that "strong representation must be made to the CNO to obtain sufficient funds to implement this program. Unless these funds are made available now and a new helicopter is developed soon, 1953–1954 will arrive finding the Marine Corps again without operational transport helicopter squadrons." [29]

As a solution to solving temporarily the second problem, the board recommended, as an interim measure, that "an urgent effort be made to obtain all HRP–1s now in existence for the Marine Corps. With these additional helicopters it is felt that HMX–1 can continue its efforts towards the practical development of air tactics and techniques . . ." while awaiting the new assault transport helicopter. [30]

General Smith's report received immediate action and formed the basis for a letter from General Cates to the CNO, Admiral Sherman. The letter, written on 12 May 1950, stressed the urgency of obtaining new and adequate equipment for the Marine Corps to cope with the manifest threat of the atomic bomb to the conventional ship-to-shore movement. "The HRP," the Commandant said, "has never been considered as a service type helicopter, but rather a means to develop the techniques and tactics of this new art. The Marine Corps is now at the crossroads. It possesses the knowledge but not the means to apply this knowledge. If the art of amphibious warfare is to be pursued, adequate means must be provided." To stress his point further, General Cates said, "The Marine Corps is effectively curtailed from performing this new concept in amphibious assault by one factor—the lack of suitable helicopters." Finally, Admiral Sherman was requested to take urgent action on these points, primarily to: raise the priority for the XHR2S–1 from its presently CNO-assigned status of 1C to 1B, and additionally, "to see that experimental helicopters be procured and evaluated with a view to procuring

* Operational Requirement Number AO–17501 (Rotary Wing Assault Helicopter) may be referred to hereafter in the text as the XHR2S–1.

two 15-plane assault squadrons . . . as soon as possible." [31]

In order to find a method by which the Marine Corps could further expedite and improve upon the new assault concept during the period 1950 to 1954, and also, to be able to find a solution to the ever-increasing maintenance problems of the aging HRPs, another joint helicopter conference was held on 22 May 1950. Attending were members from: BuAer, DCNO (Air) Aviation Plans, DCNO (Air) Readiness, and HQMC. The Marine representatives were Major General Wallace (DivAvn) and Brigadier General Pollock (Plans and Policies).

After a discussion of the problem by the conference members, it was determined that the helicopter program of the future should be composed of two parts. First, and as the longer-range solution, the Marine Corps should continue with the program to obtain a carrier-based assault helicopter which would meet the requirements of AO–17501 (XHR2S–1), as was recommended by the March helicopter conference, and simultaneously attempt to persuade the Army and Air Force to cancel the XH–16 project and join with the Marine Corps in developing the XHR2S–1. [32]

Secondly, and the one related to immediate Marine Corps needs, was the proposal to procure an interim assault helicopter from the best design currently available. General Wallace's conference proposed that the most practical and expeditious way to obtain an interim helicopter, and accelerate the program's pace, was to establish a board to make a survey of all current designs and production helicopters which gave promise of meeting Marine Corps requirements. The survey board would examine the production capability of each helicopter manufacturer. The capability of a manufacturer to produce the required number of assault helicopters would be one of the prime considerations in the choice of design. Dependent upon CNO approval of the aviation plan calling for two Marine assault helicopter squadrons in 1953–1954, a production contract would be let for 40 off-the-shelf interim assault helicopters; 16 for each of the squadrons, and eight for support. [33]

The Marine Corps planners were also concerned that an attempt should be made to increase the number of total aircraft allowed in Marine aviation so that no cut-back in current fixed-wing aircraft would result from this program. However, it was agreed by Generals Wallace and Pollock "that if the numerical ceiling for Marine Corps aircraft could not be increased, they would accept a reduction in other type aircraft in order to

have sufficient aircraft billets to provide for the two assault helicopter squadrons." [34]

Nine days after the conference, General Cates signed a letter addressed to the CNO outlining the two-step helicopter program as proposed by General Wallace. Admiral Sherman was advised that the delay involved in research and development for the XHR2S–1, while unavoidable, would prevent the delivery of an operational helicopter for about five years. The Commandant explained that it was necessary to provide "both Fleet Marine Forces with the means for training combat units in assault helicopter operations," and also necessary to provide the helicopters in order to "increase the combat readiness of the Marine Corps." The letter continued: "implementation of this program is considered to be of vital importance," and even though the "Army and Air Force are to be invited to join in the support of this project [XHR2S–1] . . . with or without their assistance, it is necessary to proceed concurrently with the procurement of the interim model." [35]

During June, the CNO replied to the Commandant's letter and in essence gave the Marine Corps a substantial sense of satisfaction. The response, originated by Vice Admiral John H. Cassady, DCNO (Air), outlined a specific program similar to the one suggested by General Cates. Cassady's letter specified that priority of AO–17501 would be evaluated by a special review board (within CNO offices) in relation to all existing priorities. Also, if agreement could be reached with the Air Force to discontinue support of the XH–16 project, the $200,000 remaining in the Fiscal Year 1951 funds would be applied to AO–17501 and design competition would be initiated for the XHR2S–1. It was reiterated that it would take five years before a production helicopter could be produced which would meet the requirements of AO–17501. Admiral Cassady stated that agreement had been reached within his offices to investigate the possibility of procuring an interim helicopter as requested by the Commandant, one which could be delivered in about 33 months. The Bureau of Aeronautics had also agreed to survey industry for the most suitable helicopter which could be modified to obtain the closest approximation of the XHR2S–1, and to secure the necessary information so as to award a contract prior to September 1950—only three months away. Finally, Cassady mentioned that the CNO had approved an aviation plan authorizing the two 15-plane squadrons with HMX–1 being redesignated as one of the future operational squadrons. [36] This redesignation of HMX-1 did not set well with Marine Corps planners as they had hoped to retain the experimental squadron as well as gain the two proposed operational units.

During the first half of 1950, visible progress had been made toward accelerating the helicopter program. Events during the following six months, however, not only saw the two-step plan implemented, but expanded to an extent far beyond all expectations.

Initial Interest in the Kaman Helicopter

While the assault transport helicopter program was being worked out, and prior to its expansion, another development had been taking place which in the future would have an effect upon the Marine Corps observation squadrons. Only one month after CNO had published his 1949 aviation plan designating the Bell HTL as the observation helicopter for the Marine Corps, the BuAer's daily publication, *BuAer Log*, announced that the Kaman Aircraft Corporation, Windsor Locks, Connecticut, desired to show its new Model K-190 observation helicopter. The demonstration would be held at National Airport, Washington, D. C., where BuAer and Division of Aviation personnel would be given the opportunity to view and, if desired, fly in the helicopter. Later it was to be demonstrated at MCAS, Quantico, for members of the air station and HMX-1.

Charles H. Kaman, president of the company, had begun experiments in 1945 to develop a new type of closely intermeshed twin two-bladed rotors which he developed on a test rig made from a chassis of a 1933 Pontiac automobile. A novel feature was that the control of the rotor blades was executed through an aerodynamic servo flap which twisted the rotor blade as it passed through the air. In flight, the close proximity of the twin intermeshing contra-rotating rotors made the helicopter appear as a single rotored helicopter. The K-190, powered by a 190-horsepower engine, was capable of transporting three passengers. The aircraft was certified for its first flight by the Civil Aeronautics Administration on 15 April 1949.[37]

Since the Kaman machine possessed some advanced, unique, and desirable features not incorporated in the helicopters at HMX-1, on 14 September 1949, the Commandant directed that MCS and HMX-1 submit recommendations as to the desirability of adding another experimental

The Kaman K-190 featured twin, intermeshed, two-bladed rotors. Only one model was purchased by the Marine Corps (Kaman Aerospace Corp. photo).

type of helicopter to those then under consideration. It was made clear by the Commandant that procurement of the K-190 would be in addition to any procurement scheduled for types already under test.[38]

BuAer had evinced interest in further development of the K-190 and was purchasing one for future technical tests. The bureau indicated that funds might possibly be made available for purchase of a second machine to be assigned to the Marine Corps, provided the Marine Corps was interested.[39]

On 6 October, the Commandant submitted a request for one Kaman K-190 to the CNO. "It was felt," the Commandant said, "that the Kaman 190 helicopter would prove to be of value to the Marine Helicopter Development Program." Although "it is not desired if it is to interfere with our present program by replacing any other type helicopter now scheduled for procurement and assigned to the Marine Corps."[40]

BuAer was directed by the CNO to provide the Navy's one K-190 to HMX-1 upon completion of the bureau's evaluation. In this case it was reasoned that the second K–190 would not be needed.[41] The Chief of the Bureau of Aeronautics, Rear Admiral Alfred M. Pride, responded to the CNO directive on 23 December 1949. He indicated that the overall evaluation program of the Kaman servo system (a major component of the flight control system) justified the purchase of an additional helicopter and that the bureau would initiate action for the procurement of one additional K–190 for the Marine Corps with delivery, unfortunately, not possible for some months to come.[42]

The Beginning in Retrospect

As the decade of the 1940s ended, it was obvious that the Marine Corps helicopter program was beginning to forge ahead. For 3½ years the Marine Corps had struggled to change the character of its World War II style of amphibious operation by introducing a new element of assault troop mobility, one which would eliminate the massing of ships closely off the coast and practically, if not entirely, eliminate the engagement of the adversary at the most vulnerable point of contact—the water's edge. The helicopter, with its ability to land troops and supplies inland in good order from ships to any relatively flat and clear terrain, provided the method to achieve the new three-dimensional concept. The change to "vertical envelopment," as it was also termed, had not been easy, nor had it been as swift as the planners and operators desired.

By the end of 1947, the new Marine program appeared to have a sense of direction and momentum. Organizationally, the first helicopter squadron had been formed in December for the purpose of determining the operational feasibility of the vertical envelopment concept. Plans for execution of the concept in terms of aircraft were based upon the eventual acquisition of a very large helicopter—the Piasecki XH–16. In preparation of a concept, the special group designated as the Helicopter and Transport Seaplane Board had been formed to develop a tentative doctrine for the employment of helicopters in amphibious operations.

Unfortunately, two years later, the whole process had reached a developmental plateau which jeopardized the entire helicopter program. Lack of continued progress could be attributed to the inability to realize that the helicopter manufacturers were unable to comply with their own predictions for meeting the specifications and

requirements which they had so willingly accepted. Additionally, an exceptionally long developmental period was required once the decision on the type of helicopter was made and the money budgeted to coincide with its development.

In spite of the delays, and in reviewing the complete spectrum of progress for all the services during 1947 to 1950, the Marine Corps had certainly not been relegated to a second rate competitor in the helicopter field, but, rather, was the leader. Each service desired the helicopter for performing missions peculiar to its own needs. The development of amphibious vertical assault techniques made the Marine Corps the leader in its own area of endeavor, as the vertical envelopment operation entailed practically all aspects of helicopter applications.

The main interest of the Navy, as it had been since 1943, was in obtaining a helicopter with sufficient hovering capability to perform antisubmarine warfare missions. Of secondary importance to the Navy was the need for the utility helicopter, which for the time was being filled by the Piasecki HUP–1.

The Army Field Forces had used small helicopters since 1947. Army helicopters were used for tasks similar to those performed by the "jeep." The Army too saw the advantages of larger lift helicopters for use in the movement of heavy artillery pieces, bridging material, and the tactical movement of combat troops.[43]

After the Armed Services Unification Act of 1947, Air Force interest in helicopters was limited to the pursuit of a helicopter suitable for search and rescue services. Like the Air Force, the Coast Guard was also interested in a search and rescue helicopter and would most likely adopt one of the Navy's designs to meet its requirement.

Throughout this period each service was required to settle for far less lift performance from helicopters than planners desired. The list of experimental helicopters on both the drawing boards and in the various stages of development was exceptionally long, with most of the experimental machines supposedly capable of satisfying the most demanding specification of the military planners. In the interlude, though, this meant that the existing helicopters had to fill roles for which they were not designed. They served as an "interim" machine for rescue, ASW, assault, liaison, observation, or for whatever tasks were necessary and could be performed.

Credit for energizing the helicopter program in early 1950 can be attributed to the crusading zeal of the Marine Corps Board and the sub-

The Piasecki HUP–1, shown practicing a rescue lift, was one of the last helicopters introduced in the 1940s and was the first of the multipurpose helicopters (Marine Corps Photo 529604).

sequent actions by the Division of Aviation. The five-year waiting period for the ideal assault helicopter could not be reduced. On the other hand, the Marine Corps realized that the vacuum had to be filled during that period by an additional program which meant that a less-than-optimum assault helicopter had to be adopted to keep the concept and program viable.

CHAPTER 4

KOREAN WAR EXPANSION

Plans for an Accelerated Helicopter Program

United States military assistance to the Government of South Korea against invading Communist North Korean forces forced a change in Marine Corps helicopter development plans. The planned formation in 1953 and 1954 of two assault transport helicopter squadrons as authorized by the CNO was now unrealistic in view of the war. Before that timetable could be revised to an earlier date, however, a suitable helicopter would have to be selected and be available in definite quantities within a reasonably short period of time.

The Division of Aviation took the initial action for accelerating the pace. On 21 July 1950, General Wallace addressed a memorandum to the CNO's Air Readiness Division requesting that "necessary steps be taken to immediately procure 40 [interim] transport helicopters, preferably of the Sikorsky HO4S–1 type." [1] Admiral Cassady, DCNO(Air), acted promptly on the request, forwarding it to BuAer. The admiral's directive instructed the Bureau of Aeronautics to procure 40 HO4S–1 for equipping the two 15-plane squadrons. "The HO4S–1," Admiral Cassady erroneously indicated, "is capable of transporting 10 troops (225 [pounds] per man) for a distance of 150 miles. . . . Procurement is predicated on delivery commencing in six months after notification to the company." [2] In addition to the Marine Corps' immediate needs, Cassady stressed the point that the time-table should be rearranged and accelerated for future procurement of the 20- to 26-man ultimate assault transport helicopter defined in operational requirement AO–17501.[3] "The program," he said, "should be aimed at production commencing in 18 to 24 months from its initiation." He urged further that immediate action be taken by BuAer to initiate the program, which meant the solicitation of design proposals from the manufacturers. The initial purchase of no less than 40 new helicopters was considered to

be minimum by the CNO after the design had been selected.[4]

The HO4S–1 was the Navy's designation for the Sikorsky commercial Model S–55. The helicopter was built by Sikorsky without the aid of government funds and first flown in November 1949. It had been designed originally to compete against Piasecki's PD–22 (H–21) for use as the Air Force's Arctic Rescue helicopter. In May 1950, after the Air Force had chosen the H–21, the Navy purchased 10 S–55s for use in an evaluation project to determine its value as an interim ASW helicopter.

The transport version of the HO4S–1 was redesignated as the HRS–1. Its design features included one Pratt and Whitney R–1340–57 600-horsepower engine installed behind clam-shell doors in front of the helicopter. Brigadier General Noah C. New in recalling this helicopter, states: "Placing the engine in the nose of the HRS–1, where it was easily accessible, was ingenious. It not only had tremendous advantages in servicing the aircraft, but it completely eliminated the critical center of gravity problems previously encountered by placing the payload directly below the rotor hub." [5] A drive shaft transmitted engine power to the three-bladed main rotor through the center rear section of the cockpit. The cabin, which had foldable seats for 10 passengers, was situated directly beneath the main rotor. The HRS's empty weight was 4,462 pounds with its gross weight originally predicted and listed as 8,070 pounds. The maximum forward airspeed was 90 knots. Other features included all metal main and tail rotor blades, instruments suitable for night VFR flight, and an external cargo sling and hook situated underneath the fuselage. The aircraft stood 14 feet high, had a rotor blade diameter of 53 feet, and measured approximately 42 feet long with its blades folded.[6] It was built upon similar, but enlarged, mechanical components of the HO3S–1. In appearance it was entirely different although it retained the typical Sikorsky single main rotor design.

The reason for the Marine Corps' choice of the

The HO5S–1 was used for observation in Korea (Marine Corps Photo A346328).

The Sikorsky HRS–1, also known as the HO4S–1, at Quantico, Va. (Marine Corps Photo 530002).

Sikorsky S–55 was readily apparent. Since Sikorsky had not received the contract for the Arctic rescue model, the company could commence production immediately on a first-come, first-serve basis with delivery of the first aircraft in six months. Piasecki, on the other hand, also had the capability of building an assault version of its H–21, the PD–22C, although delivery could not be made until approximately September 1951, a difference of eight months. The PD–22C's specification appeared somewhat similar to the HRS–1 as the model was predicted to have the capability to carry 15 combat troops or 3,400 pounds over a short radius of 50 miles. A three-months additional wait beyond the September date would have provided Piasecki with sufficient time to construct its proposed PD–22D; a version similar to the PD–22C except for the incorporation of a much larger engine. According to Piasecki, it would have been able to carry a load of 20 combat troops, or the equivalent weight in cargo, over an operating radius of 70 miles.[7] Time was of the essence to the Marine Corps, however, and the most readily available model was chosen, the HRS–1.

Meanwhile, the Marine Corps had activated the 1st Provisional Marine Brigade at Camp Pendle-ton, California shortly after the outbreak of the Korean War. The brigade was formed under the command of Brigadier General Edward A. Craig, a World War II veteran of Bougainville, Guam, and Iwo Jima. The new organization consisted of the 5th Marines and Marine Aircraft Group 33 (MAG–33). Commanding the MAG was Brigadier General Thomas J. Cushman who had recently been Commanding General, Aircraft, Fleet Marine Force, Pacific. General Cushman's MAG was composed of three Marine fighter squadrons and VMO–6.

The observation squadron, VMO–6, had been operating with eight OY–2 fixed-wing aircraft at Camp Pendleton, California, but was expanded in early July for deployment as a composite squadron by the addition of four HO3S–1s. Along with the four helicopters came seven officers and 30 enlisted men from HMX–1. Taking command of the newly reorganized squadron was Major Vincent J. Gottschalk. With the addition of the helicopters, VMO–6 became the first squadron of its kind. The squadron sailed from San Diego, on 14 July on board the USS *Badoeng Strait* (CVE–116) bound for Korea.

Within a month of its departure from the West Coast, the 1st Provisional Brigade plunged into the

The HRS–1 with its front-mounted engine was a breakthrough in helicopter design. These aircraft from HMR–161 land 4.5-inch rocket launchers at Panjong-ni, Korea, in 1952 (Marine Corps Photo A163934).

desperate battles of the Pusan Perimeter, reinforcing U. S. Army and South Korean United Nations troops. The brigade, maneuvering rapidly, repeatedly counterattacked the North Korean penetrations of the perimeter. In this series of improvised mobile operations, the helicopters of VMO-6 more than proved their worth. As General Craig put it:

> Marine Helicopters have proven invaluable . . . They have been used for every conceivable type of mission. The Brigade utilized helicopters for liaison, reconnaissance, evacuation of wounded, rescue of Marine flyers downed in enemy territory, observation, messenger service, guard mail at sea, posting and supplying of outguards on dominating terrain features and the re-supplying of small units by air.[8]

Colonel Gottschalk recalled another significant use of helicopters by the brigade. He declared:

> . . . perhaps the most important use of the helicopter in the early months of the Korean War concerned command and control. The flexibility provided the Brigade Commander to control his forces, change direction of movement, give personal instructions to subordinate commanders, and observe the resultant battlefield movement in a dynamic fast moving situation provided a new dimension to tactical control of the battlefield in a difficult terrain setting.[9]

The usefulness of the helicopters of VMO-6 led General Craig to call for more. He recommended that "a transport type helicopter squadron, equipped with Sikorsky 55 type aircraft" be sent to Korea or at least that "eight liaison and two transport type helicopters be added to the observation squadron for employment by Marine Divisions." Anticipating on a limited scale later airmobile tactics, he pointed out:

> . . . The mountainous terrain of Korea presents a difficult problem for security of flanks and rear and of bivouac areas. The troop carrier type of helicopter would be ideal for use . . . to post patrols on high, dominating terrain which it would take hours to climb and which quickly exhausts the troops. . . . It is believed their use would materially contribute to the effectiveness and security of our operations and insure the earlier defeat of the enemy. . . .[10]

Lieutenant General Lemuel C. Shepherd, Jr. Commanding General, FMFPac, after an inspection trip to the war zone during which he was briefed on and viewed the operations of the brigade and of VMO-6, echoed General Craig's praise of helicopters and repeated his call for more of them:

> There are no superlatives adequate to describe the general reaction to the helicopter. Almost any individual questioned could offer some personal story to emphasize the valuable part played by the five HO3S

planes available.* Reconnaissance, liaison, visual flank security, movement of security patrols from one key locality to the next, posting and supply of security detachments and many more. There is no doubt that the enthusiasm voiced by the brigade is entirely warranted. Moreover the usefulness of the helicopter is not by any means confined to a situation such as encountered in Korea. No effort should be spared to get helicopters—larger than the HO3S-1s if possible —but helicopters in any form, to the theater at once —and on a priority higher than any other weapon.[11]

In view of General Shepherd's statement pertaining to the helicopter in Korea, Brigadier General Clayton C. Jerome, who relieved Major General Wallace as the Director of Aviation on 1 September 1950, sent a memorandum to Admiral Cassady in which he included General Shepherd's statement. General Jerome said "this emphasizes the [remark] I made the other day in connection with the requirements for helicopters, more helicopters, and more helicopters in the Korea Area." [12] Major General Lamson-Scribner recalled the period:

> Just prior to the receipt of General Shepherd's letter, General Jerome and I attended a conference [at] which Admiral Cassady, was chairman of the Navy Aircraft Procurement Program for Fiscal 51. The program was for only a relatively few helicopters. We insisted that we needed more than programed for purchase. Admiral Mel Pride, Chief of BuAir, remarked in essence 'If you know as little about helicopters as we do you would not get into one.' Admiral Cassady said, 'Mel, the Marines want them. Make some changes in the program to provide more helicopters for the Marines.' [13]

General Jerome's memo was only the latest of many attempts to convince the Department of the Navy to increase the Marine Corps' inventory of aircraft for the Korean buildup. On 19 July, General Cates submitted a request to the Secretary of the Navy for an additional four Marine fighter squadrons in an effort to increase the total to 12. Then, a month later, on 23 August 1950, General Cates made a further request to the CNO on behalf of the helicopter program. The Commandant explained the value of the helicopter to the Marine Corps in carrying out amphibious and land warfare. He quoted an excerpt from a letter written by General Craig which indicated the "incalculable value of the helicopter as an implement of present and future armed conflict" and further: [14]

> VMO-6 was flown to Pusan from Japan. These aircraft have been invaluable in reconnaissance and the helicopters are a Godsend in this type of terrain, not only for reconnaissance but for supporting of

---

* VMO-6 had received an additional HO3S after it had arrived in Korea.

Brigadier General Edward A. Craig, Commanding General, 1st Provisional Marine Brigade, in Korea (Marine Corps Photo A-1309).

combat patrols in mountainous terrain; for supply of food, water, ammunition; but also for the evacuation of casualties. . . . By separate dispatch to you . . . a request has been made to bring out elements of the Helicopter Transport Squadron. It is believed that this innovation will meet with outstanding results in combat in this mountainous terrain for the landing of patrols on top of mountain ranges. . . . The helicopters presently available have been invaluable beyond expression . . . [However] I feel they will not be able to sustain all the demands.[15]

The Commandant also reiterated that BuAer, by production contract number 51–075, dated 17 August, had obligated the Navy to purchase 40 HRS helicopters for the Marine Corps and that Sikorsky anticipated delivering the first production aircraft sometime during February 1951. "In view of the extremely urgent need for helicopters," General Cates urged, "every effort should be made by BuAer and the Sikorsky Division to deliver the HRS (interim assault) helicopter as soon as possible." Moreover, the Commandant said ". . . [helicopters] are of such urgent nature that it is requested that BuAer be directed to authorize the Sikorsky Aircraft Division to increase deliveries to the maximum."[16]

Vice Admiral Cassady acted on General Cates'

letter by requesting BuAer to contact all manufacturers who held, or whom BuAer contemplated holding, helicopter contracts to ascertain the kind of delivery rate which could be obtained by: "Increasing present contracts numberwise by 50 per cent . . . and by 100 per cent."[17]

Emphasis was also placed upon procuring observation helicopters as well as transport helicopters. The first contract of this sort provided for 12 Sikorsky HO5S–1s; four for each of the two VMO squadrons and four as replacements for the HO3S–1s in HMX–1. Delivery was expected to be at a rate of not less than three per month beginning in March 1951.[18] During July the number was raised from 12 to 22 aircraft[19] and shortly thereafter was again enlarged to 42.[20] This demand for observation helicopters was based on planning which called for replacing all OY fixed-wing aircraft in VMO squadrons with the helicopter. In addition, the number of aircraft per squadron was raised again to 12 from the original number of eight due to the activation of two force artillery battalions—which increased the requirement for observation missions.[21]

So far, the action taken by HQMC to procure more aircraft did not solve the immediate problem of providing additional helicopters to the 1st Provisional Brigade. Something had to be done to fill the gap until such time as the HRSs and the HO5Ss became available. Although the HO3S–1s were performing a valuable service and were practically indispensible to the brigade, the fact remained that they were not a suitable military helicopter due to their deficiencies in payload, range, flight instrumentation, and communication equipment. As a temporary measure to solve the problem, the Division of Aviation, as recommended in a letter from the Commanding Officer of HMX–1, initiated a plan which proposed the assignment of 10 Navy Bell-manufactured HTL–4s to the Marine Corps. The CNO subsequently approved the plan with the first three to be made available in October 1950 and the last one before the end of December. The Navy had only recently purchased 16 of the new models for training aircraft, but due to the urgency created by the Korean situation it was tentatively willing to release 10 of the 16. The HTLs were to be used in VMO–6 until production deliveries of the Sikorsky HO5Ss began.[22]

The HTL–4 was similar to the previous Bell models except for a few added refinements. Two features affecting its appearance were the removal of the tail boom covering aft of the cabin, which

The HTL–4 saw action as a medevac and observation aircraft in Korea (Marine Corps Photo 529982).

made the helicopter 156 pounds lighter, and the substitution of a skid type landing gear in lieu of its wheels. The cabin could accommodate two passengers besides the pilot, whereas all previous HTL models could carry only one passenger. The aircraft came equipped with provisions for carrying two external litters, each mounted parallel with the cabin across the top of the skid. The empty weight was 1,546 pounds with a maximum take-off weight of 2,350 pounds. Sea level air speed was restricted to 80 knots, almost identical to that of the HTL–3s.[23]

Although the Marine Corps was fortunate in its ability to procure the HTL for use by VMO–6, it was only beginning to view progress in obtaining the most sought-after of all helicopters—the ultimate assault transport.

A Bell HTL-5 demonstrates wire laying at Quantico (Marine Corps Photo KVI-4173).

Awarding of the First
Assault Transport Helicopter
Contract

Late in 1950, in response to BuAer's request, the helicopter manufacturers competing for the assault transport helicopter presented their proposals. Thereafter, in March 1951, the bureau selected two aircraft companies to build the helicopter, McDonnell and Sikorsky.

McDonnell Aircraft received a contract for two experimental models of an extremely advanced design. It incorporated the conventional single main rotor configuration; however, the power was to be provided by jet burners located in each rotor blade tip. Also unique in the McDonnell design, and a feature which made it a compound helicopter, was the installation of twin gas turbine propeller engines mounted externally in wings.[24] The compound helicopter was designated as the XHRH–1 (H-helicopter, R-transport, H-heavy) and was estimated to carry a useful load of 13,000 pounds at a cruising speed of 150 to 200 knots. The empty weight was estimated at a little over 26,000 pounds.[25] The flight technique for the HRH envisioned the machine taking off as a conventional helicopter, then as its airspeed increased it would convert to fixed-wing flight; with the reverse procedure for executing the landing phase.

Sikorsky Aircraft Company submitted two different designs. One, a basic helicopter referred to as XHRS–A, and a second design, a compound helicopter somewhat similar to McDonnell's although the propulsion for the main rotor was "conventional" wherein it did not propose the use of rotor blade tip burners.* The compound design was designated by Sikorsky as the XHRS–B.[26]

The proposed XHRS–A had twin engines located in wing-mounted external nacelles which transmitted their power to a single main transmission. The design called for a main rotor with five blades and a torque-compensating tail rotor of four blades; both rotors were of all-metal construction. Sikorsky claimed that the XHRS–A could carry 36 combat-equipped troops or an alternate amount of cargo in the 1,250-cubic-foot cabin. Loading and unloading of vehicles the size of jeeps could take place through clamshell doors which opened in the nose. This feature, however, restricted the helicopter's performance since it could not be flown with the doors open which delayed the loading/ unloading operation, thus extending the time on the ground. Other features were: automatic blade folding, retractable landing gear, and a form of automatic pilot (automatic stabilization). The helicopter measured almost 88 feet in length and 20 feet high with the blades spread. Cruising speed was listed at 140 knots.[27]

The XHRS–B had essentially the same fuselage design with identical engines and transmission facilities. Increased performance over the XHRS–A was proposed by the addition of foldable outer wing panels extending beyond the engine nacelles and the incorporation of standard propellers on the front of the engines. These additional features of the HRS–B were proposed as a logical future development of the XHRS–A basic helicopter. Both the basic and compound designs could be powered by reciprocating or gas turbine engines, depending upon BuAer's desires. The first HRS–A aircraft was estimated to be available within 18 to 20 months from date of contract.[28]

The straightforward "pure" helicopter, the XHRS–A, was a much less complicated aircraft. It appeared to involve fewer problems of development, logistics, and maintenance in the field and was one which could be built in the shortest time. Therefore, BuAer awarded Sikorsky a contract for five experimental aircraft realizing that even with the simplest design there would be unforeseen problems and delays in the program.[29]

The awarding of dual contracts for the same operational requirement (AO–17501) appeared justified in view of the complexities involved in both McDonnell's and Sikorsky's proposals. The two-phase program was established in order to provide the Marine Corps with maximum protection in the event one of the designs failed to materialize. In this case, progress in the development of the assault transport helicopter was planned to provide two helicopters in logical sequence with the XHRH going beyond existing requirements. The procurement provided for the development of equipment to satisfy future requirements by taking advantage of technological progress beyond that incorporated in the HRS–A.[30]

Completion dates for Sikorsky's five experimental models were established; however, in McDonnell's case, the original contract did not specify such a date nor did the CNO assign a priority number. Later, on 9 April 1952, the CNO assigned a priority of 1C to the XHRH,[31] and subsequently BuAer published a proposed first flight date of December 1955.[32] The first HRS–A (later designated by Sikorsky as its S–56, and by the Navy as the XHR2S–1) had been given a priority

---

* This method of propulsion is also referred to as the "pressure jet principle." To produce thrust, compressed air is routed to each rotor blade tip where it is then mixed with fuel and ignited.

The HR2S-1 was the first large, cargo/assault helicopter used by the Marines. The first aircraft was received in September 1956 (Marine Corps Photo 529980).

of 1B and was predicted to make its initial flight during May 1953,[33] after which a period of experimentation would follow before a production contract would be granted.

Related Events to the Expanded Helicopter Program

Since the CNO had approved BuAer contracting for 40 HRS-1s as interim assault transport helicopters, the Marine Corps had to make plans for commissioning, locating, and manning the squadrons to which the helicopters would eventually be assigned. The first planning effort for the expanded program took place at a conference at HQMC in early September 1950. Representatives from the HQMC General Staff, (G–1, G–3, G–4), and Division of Aviation devised a comprehensive plan for implementing an enlarged helicopter program, initially as a basis for discussion with CNO, DCNO, and BuAer representatives.[34] After a slight modification and eventual approval by the Commandant, it was sent to the CNO on 19 October. The plan provided for the commissioning of two assault helicopter squadrons, referred to as HMR–1 and HMR–2, and the redesignation and conversion of Marine observation squadrons (VMO) to Marine helicopter observation squadrons (HMO) all during Fiscal Year 1951. Commissioning dates for the two HMR squadrons were set at 15 January and 1 April 1951 with the first unit to be formed on the West Coast and the second on the East Coast. A cadre of personnel was to remain at Quantico in order to accept, test, and ready the aircraft for delivery to the squadrons. It

was also considered necessary that the units be commissioned on the coast where their operation and training was to be conducted. It was anticipated that the commissioning date established for each squadron would be approximately one month prior to the receipt of its first aircraft.[35]

To supply personnel for the additional squadrons, the Marine Corps improvised new training organizations. Until October 1950, the U. S. Navy had trained Marine helicopter pilots at Lakehurst, New Jersey, but the requirements of the Korean expansion exceeded the Navy's training capabilities. The Marine Corps, therefore, pressed its helicopter squadron, HMX–1, into service as a training command. The squadron, commanded from late 1950 to 1952 by Lieutenant Colonel Keith B. McCutcheon, trained the nucleus of pilots and mechanics for the first Marine Helicopter Transport Squadron (HMR) 161.* In turn, HMR–161 and the FMF squadrons that followed took over most of the development of tactics, for which they were better equipped than was HMX–1. Eventually, the Marine Corps planned to have all helicopter training conducted by the Naval Air Training Command at Pensacola so that the experimental and operational squadrons could concentrate on their primary missions.[36]

The new plan further anticipated that during Fiscal Year 1952, two additional squadrons, HMR–3, and HMR–4, would be formed on 1 July and 1 September 1951. All HMRs, 1 through 4, would be equipped initially with 15 HRSs. When the ultimate HR2S-1 assault helicopter became operational, HMR–5 and HMR–6 would be formed

---

* The designation HMR represents: H, helicopter, M, Marine, R, Transport.

with 15 aircraft each with commissioning anticipated sometime during the Spring of 1953. Eventually as the HR2Ss became more plentiful, they
would phase out all the HRSs. According to the
plan, therefore, by 1954 the Marine Corps expected
to have an inventory of 148 helicopters: 90
HR2S–1s, 40 HO5S–1s, and a mixture of 18 experimental and operational helicopters in
HMX–1.[37]

Marine Corps Air Station, El Toro, near Santa
Ana, California, was selected as the location for
the first HMR with MCAS Cherry Point, North
Carolina, as the location for forming HMR–2. The
pattern of alternating the commissioning site between the two coastal air stations was to be continued as each new unit was formed.

This completed the plans for expansion except
for a third VMO squadron. Since VMO–1 and
VMO–6 were already functioning squadrons, the
formation of HMO–2 was to be delayed until
January 1952. The redesignation of all the VMOs
to HMOs was to become effective upon receipt of
the HO5S–1s by the squadrons.[38] In respect to
HMX–1's redesignation to an operational squadron, nothing further was mentioned in the plan.

In responding to the helicopter plan, the CNO
approved the proposal for Fiscal Year 1951 in
which the first two squadrons were to be formed.
Approval of the program for Fiscal Years 1952
through 1954 was withheld pending further designation of forces for that period. Tentative plans,
however, for Fiscal Year 1952 were indicated in
the CNO's reply and fortunately coincided with
those which the Commandant had requested for
that period.[39]

By way of informing the Director of Plans and
Policy as to the number designation and title of
the helicopter squadrons, General Jerome stated
that the first squadron to be commissioned on the
West Coast would be designated "Marine Assault
Helicopter Squadron 161," short designation
"HMR–161" and the second squadron commissioned on the East Coast would be HMR–261. He
explained that the "numerals were selected in an
extension of the current numbering system of
Marine aviation units. The highest digit previously
used for Marine Aircraft Groups designation being
5 (MAG–15, 25, etc.), it is logical to use 6 as the
group designator of the future HMR Groups."
General Jerome concluded by explaining that "the
first HMR organized in the First Marine Aircraft
Wing becomes 161, and the first HMR in the
Second Marine Aircraft Wing becomes 261."[40]

Coincidentally, however, as the Aviation Section
of the Educational Center at the Marine Corps

Schools was reviewing a related study on Marine
aviation, it noticed that when reference was made
to helicopter squadrons they were continually referred to as "Assault Helicopter Squadrons." It
was pointed out in its comments on the study that
the designation should be changed to "Helicopter
Transport Squadron" and omit the word "assault."
It reasoned that while the helicopter did in fact
have the initial and primary mission of assault, it
additionally had an equal "direct support" capability and responsibility in connection with missions involving observation, general utility, supply,
medical evacuation, and many more tasks once the
initial assault phase of the landing had been completed. Therefore, they commented the term
"assault" would tend to limit its employment to
the ship-to-shore phase and deny its use for the
very important other day-to-day post-assault operations.[41]

The point was taken under consideration by the
Division of Aviation and on 22 November 1950,
the Plans and Policy Division was re-informed
that henceforth the new HMR squadron designation would be "Marine Helicopter Squadron."[42] It
was short-lived, however, as in early 1951 the
Division of Aviation, referring to a CNO directive,
changed the designation again to "Marine Transport Helicopter Squadron."[43]

The Tactics and Techniques Board Reports of 1951

If the Marine Corps was to employ effectively
its anticipated six squadrons of helicopters, plans
for their employment had to be made. The first
step was contained in *Marine Corps Equipment
Policy, 1950*, which proposed a concept of future
amphibious operations based primarily on the
employment of the assault helicopter. Salient aspects of the concept were:

  1. Emphasis on tactical surprise, featuring a vertical
  envelopment by helicopter in ultimate conjunction
  with dispersed assaults capable of rapidly penetrating
  selected points in the beach defenses.
  2. Commencement of the assault proper with the
  launching of assault troops in helicopters and amphibian vehicles from ships underway in cruising or
  other dispersed formations.
  3. Landing of helicopter forces in landing zones
  from which one or more objectives might be seized.
  4. Landing of further troop components by amphibian vehicles (taking advantage of success achieved
  by the helicopter borne troops) for beach approach
  and assault at dispersed points.
  5. Early logistic support following the pattern of
  the assault itself, using helicopters to deliver supplies

to deep positions, and amphibian vehicles and trailers to transport heavy material across the beach to using units or dispersed interior units.[44]

The *Equipment Policy* recommended that development of an aircraft carrier-type ship be initiated to transport the troop elements and helicopters of the landing force. It was further proposed that the construction of helicopter platforms on other type ships involved in the amphibious operation also be studied.[45]

In view of the concept proposed in the *Marine Corps Equipment Policy, 1950*, and in particular the amphibious shipping aspects, General Cates informed the Commandant, Marine Corps Schools, that "the Navy had no firm plans at that time for providing properly configured ships for the employment of assault transport helicopters in accordance with the current concept." Therefore, it was requested that the MCS, based upon the use of both the HRS and HR2S, make separate determinations on the following for each type helicopter: [46]

1. The recommended size and composition of the helicopter landed elements of the landing force assuming the landing force consists of one Marine Division.
2. The most desirable means of embarking and transporting the troop elements and helicopters that are to execute the ship-to-shore movement in helicopters.
3. The technique of executing the ship-to-shore movement of helicopter landed troops.
4. The Marine Corps operational requirement for appropriate shipping to permit the employment of assault transport helicopters in accordance with the above [items].[47]

General Cates concluded by saying: "Due to the importance attached to this program, it is requested that this project be assigned a high priority and that the information requested . . . be submitted to this headquarters as it becomes available." [48]

The Landing Force Tactics and Techniques Board, Marine Corps Landing Force Development Center, Marine Corps Schools was tasked to conduct the study on the points delineated by the Commandant. The first interim report was submitted as early as 16 December with the final report dated 5 January 1951. The study was entitled *Employment of Assault Transport Helicopters.** The document was the first of its kind and was used extensively in conjunction with the Divi-

sion of Aviation's helicopter plan as a guide for the next five years.

The task assigned to the board was difficult as it required translating a group of general premises into material sufficiently concrete to serve as a basis for future specific guidance and computations. The board studied deeply all four areas mentioned in General Cates' letter of instruction. In determining the composition of the helicopter-landed force, the study group proposed employing one Marine division consisting of two regimental landing teams, an artillery group, and a division command group, totalling 10,000 officers and men. It was determined that this force would require 3,000 to 4,000 short tons of supplies and equipment. The most desirable means of embarking and transporting the troop elements and helicopters was that the helicopter-borne troops, equipment, supplies, and the helicopters should be transported together in aircraft carrier-type shipping.[49]

In relation to the technique of executing the ship-to-shore movement, the board recommended that control be exercised by the landing force commander who would have in his task organization a control unit capable of providing adequate control of mass flights of helicopters. A flight of 10 helicopters was considered desirable to facilitate flight control and the flights formed into waves of two or more flights to satisfy the tactical requirements. But in this area no satisfactory control organization nor guidance system existed suitable for controlling mass movements of helicopters.[50]

The solution to the problem of determining the appropriate type and number of ships required to execute the ship-to-shore movement required considerable study. Earlier in the report it had been established that the number of helicopters required to lift the main force was no less than 520 HRS-type helicopters each carrying 8- to 10-men or 208 HR2Ss carrying 20 to 25 troops each. The shipping requirements to accommodate the 8- to 10-man helicopter was established at 20 CVEs. In addition, all CVEs had to be converted to have the capability to operate at least 10 HRSs on the flight deck and store 10 on the hangar deck, plus spares. Facilities were also needed on each CVE for 500 to 600 combat troops plus approximately 200 personnel of the helicopter squadron. Turning to the larger 20- to 25-man type helicopter, the board determined that eight newly designed ships or converted CVs (fleet aircraft carriers)**

* As in so many cases where only copies of the original report are available, the names of participating members are omitted, and in some cases, the senior member's name itself does not appear. Regrettably, this is the case in this particular study.

** The length of the CV class carriers varied from 739 feet for the *Yorktown* class CV to 901 feet for the larger *Lexington* class. Both CV class ships had a top speed in excess of 30 knots.

would be required; each one having the capacity to operate 10 helicopters from its flight deck and store 10, plus spares, in its hangar deck. In this case, 1,200 to 1,500 billeting spaces would be needed for the assault troops plus the helicopter personnel. Cargo requirements were also listed as 150 to 200 short tons for the CVEs and 450 to 550 tons for each of the new or converted CVs.[51]

In replying to the questions posed by General Cates, the board found other related points which it felt should be noted. The first was derived from a comparison of the abilities and requirements for the two types of helicopters studied. There was no doubt in the minds of the board members that the larger helicopter was far superior in every way, more so in proportion than its difference in size would tend to indicate. The number of helicopters, helicopter personnel, ships, landing areas, and the complexity of the guidance system all pointed to the strong desirability of concentrating on the larger helicopter. Another point was that a time limit was suggested for making a determination upon which type of ship program to pursue. The additional remarks stated that if design and procurement of the 20- to 25-man helicopter (HR2S) was found to be less than two years, then the larger program should be undertaken. If, on the other hand, an adequate number of HR2Ss could not be procured, then the CVE conversion and the 8- to 10-man helicopter courses should be followed. Regardless of the adopted path of action, the board urged "that aggressive efforts had to be made immediately to obtain and convert a sufficient number of CVEs for use in conjunction with the first HRS squadrons for operational testing and experimentation of the entire helicopter-borne concept."[52]

The board vigorously urged that immediate action be taken on the concept so that the lessons learned and the techniques developed could be incorporated in the future production program for both the helicopter and its associated shipping. The board felt strongly that the "entire future of the helicopter-borne concept depended largely on operational testing with suitable ships and operational helicopters." It believed that "no further substantial progress could be made in the field of helicopter operations on board ship and in the technique of executing the ship-to-landing zone helicopter movement unless a ship procurement program was established."[53]

Two months after the completion of the lengthy and detailed January study, the Tactics and Techniques Board was requested to conduct another study on a closely related subject which was to deal with the more immediate problems of the Marine helicopter transport program. The requirements were "to provide a comprehensive concept for the employment of currently authorized HMR squadrons in amphibious operations." Secondly, the board was "to determine Marine Corps operational requirements for Naval amphibious shipping which could be made available to support the currently authorized helicopter strength."[54]

As stated earlier, by this date the Marine Corps was planning to equip four HMR squadrons with the interim HRS and two additional units with the HR2S. However, the authorized force structure included only the four HRS squadrons. The board apparently had advance information that the CNO tentatively planned to approve immediate formation of all six Marine squadrons. In fact the CNO's Aviation Plan 11-51, published subsequent to the Tactics and Techniques Board's report, authorized commissioning of the last two of the six helicopter squadrons sometime during February 1952 in lieu of the original 1954 date.[55] This meant that the HRS would be used to equip all six projected helicopter squadrons.

The Tactics and Techniques Board completed its second report of 28 February 1951. Dates for commissioning and the employment of all six squadrons were laid out along with a proposed initial mission assignment for each unit. The dates nearly coincided with those previously requested in the Commandant's October 1951 plan, except for the last two squadrons. A major variance existed in this latest plan wherein it envisioned all units as being commissioned on the East Coast to work with the troops of FMFLant for test and evaluation. For five of the six squadrons, the following commissioning schedule was published: *

HMR–261   1 April 1951
        (5 April 1951, MCAS Cherry Point)
HMR–162   30 June 1951
        (30 June 1951, MCAF Santa Ana)
HMR–262   1 September 1951
        (1 September 1951, MCAS Cherry Point)
HMR–163   15 November 1951
        (1 December 1951, MCAF Santa Ana)
HMR–263   1 February 1952
        (16 June 1952, MCAS Cherry Point)[56]

The first Marine transport helicopter squadron, HMR–161, had already been commissioned on 15 January 1951 at MCAS El Toro in accordance with previous planning. Lieutenant Colonel George W.

* For comparative purposes, the actual location and dates of commissioning are shown in parentheses. The major difference from the Tactics and Techniques Board recommendations was in the commissioning site.

Herring, a Georgia-born Naval Academy graduate, was the squadron's commanding officer. He had previously been assigned at HMX as its executive officer. The board recommended that HMR-161 be equipped with the HRS as rapidly as aircraft deliveries would permit and that on approximately 1 July, the squadron be deployed to Korea "for combat service evaluation with troops." The idea, due to the urgent need for helicopters in the 1st Marine Division, was that HMR-161 would serve in a dual role by operationally testing and evaluating the HRS, and the concept for its use, while concurrently supporting the 1st Marine Division. Although the squadron's primary amphibious mission would not be performed by HMR-161, it would, nevertheless, be used in a secondary role of supporting tactical elements incident to normal land warfare.[57] Later, on 15 August, HMR-161 departed for Korea, only six weeks after the recommended date established by the study group.*

The date of 1 September 1952 was established by the Tactics and Techniques Board as the target date for assembling the five squadrons on the East or West Coast to evaluate collectively the helicopter employment concept. "It is possible," the board reported, "to accomplish partial evaluation of this concept only if all five properly trained squadrons and their supporting . . . [shipping] are available at the same time and the same place." Only partial evaluation of the concept could be accomplished as the board felt that even if all five of the authorized squadrons were to be concentrated, they still would be inadequate to effect the main effort of one division in an amphibious operation. To be more exact in this respect, the board determined that all six HRS squadrons would be capable of lifting only two lightly reinforced infantry battalions, or the equivalent, within one hour. A time/distance factor of greater than one hour was considered undesirable. After completion of the operational testing, all squadrons were to be assigned individually or collectively to FMFPac or FMFLant, whichever command had an operational commitment wherein the helicopter squadrons could perform their primary or secondary missions.[58]

The shipping aspect of the study was investigated thoroughly. The erection of helicopter platforms on various types of amphibious ships revealed that on conventional transports, APA (attack transport) and AKA (attack cargo) ships, space for only one helicopter could be provided without seriously limiting the ship's normal amphibious capability. This type of ship was dismissed from further study as it would require an excessive number of vessels to operate a significant number of helicopters. The LSD (landing ship dock) was found to have the capability to transport up to 60 helicopters but it too could only launch one aircraft at a time without extensive modification resulting in the loss of its original function. The LST (Landing Ship Tank) had the capability to operate five helicopters from a modified deck or transport up to 30 and then only operate two simultaneously. However, since the LST was slow, extremely vulnerable, and was considered to be of reduced application in future operations, it also was not considered further by the board. Seaplane tenders, the board pointed out, could operate only one helicopter at a time while an oiler could handle three to five, but again it was doubtful that these ship types could be diverted from their primary mission. Therefore it was concluded that a modified CVE carrier or a helicopter transport vessel specifically designed for helicopter and troop transport was the best solution. The CVE requirement to support the approved program was determined to be a total of four ships in service by 1 September 1952, with the first ship needed by 1 November 1951.[59]

The type of CVE recommended for conversion to a helicopter carrier had been changed from the previously desired *Commencement Bay* class to that of the *Casablanca* class. The Tactics and Techniques Board's report of 5 January stated:

> . . . it had been discovered that the *Commencement Bay* (CVE-105) class aircraft carrier was being adapted to ASW missions and did not appear to be available for modification. Other class CVEs were in reserve, and as far as the board could determine, there was no immediate requirement for their use. Of these, the *Casablanca* class (CVE-55) appeared to be the best choice because of its greater speed, in addition to being available in larger numbers. In this light, the board's recommendation was for the Commandant to request the modification of the four carriers of the *Casablanca* class (CVE-55) or its equivalent.[60]

---

* Lynn J. Montross' *Cavalry of the Sky* is suggested as offering the best source of abundant detail covering the Korean operational history for both HMR-161 and VMO-6. Mr. Montross, a well-established writer and historian, was employed at HQMC for approximately 10 years, during which time he served as the Head of the Korean Histories Unit.

Activation of the 3d Marine Aircraft Wing

While the Tactics and Techniques Board was involved in laying out the future helicopter program, other planning had been underway for the mobilization of Marine forces to meet the demands of the Korean situation. Included in the overall buildup was the activation of the 3d Marine Aircraft Wing and the 3d Marine Division. The reduction of forces put into effect after World War II had left the Marine Corps with only two active Marine aircraft wings and divisions. The 1st Marine Aircraft Wing was located on the West Coast at MCAS, El Toro, California, and the 2d Wing was stationed at MCAS, Cherry Point, North Carolina, on the East Coast. For reasons of economy and availability of air base facilities and airfield complexes, the plan for the 3d Wing placed it also on the East Coast at a former naval air station at Miami, Florida. Planning called for the formation and commissioning of three additional helicopter squadrons in the 3d Wing at the Miami base.[61] Logic, however, dictated that helicopter squadrons be within reasonable flying distance of the ground FMF units which they were obliged to support. In view of the fact that the 3d Marine Division was forming at Camp Pendleton, California, the plan was changed to have the seventh through the ninth helicopter squadrons commissioned at MCAF, Santa Ana, California, in lieu of the Miami base.[62]

All previous planning had allowed the helicopter units to be formed and placed within the internal organization of the aircraft wing as special units without an intermediate command. On 15 June 1951, the Marine aircraft wing organization was reorganized to make it a balanced task organization and, for the first time, combined the helicopter units under a parent helicopter aircraft group headquarters. In addition to the headquarters squadron and the three helicopter units in the group organization, there were two supporting units: an air base squadron and an aircraft maintenance squadron. The Marine Helicopter Transport Group (MAG(HR)) structure was almost identical to the organization of fixed-wing groups. The new Marine aircraft wing, with its fixed wing and helicopter assets, was thus organized to support independently a Marine division.[63]

On 23 October 1951, the Commandant released Marine Aviation Plan 1–52 for Fiscal Year 1952. A cross-section of affected commanding generals and commanding officers of forces, units, and stations within the Continental United States were ordered to HQMC during November 1951 and briefed in detail on its aspects. As a result of monetary shortages, however, it was not until the next calendar year that implementation finally began.[64] As a consequence, changes were made which varied from the plan outlined in the November meeting and, as a result, a revision was published on 11 January 1952. Contained within its provisions were proposed commissioning dates and locations for the three helicopter aircraft groups. MAG(HR)–16 was scheduled for commissioning during February with MAG(HR)–26 and –36 dates set for the following June. Also, the helicopter groups (headquarters squadrons) had a proposed allowance of four aircraft; two fixed-wing transports and two utility helicopters. The four group aircraft were in addition to the number and types in custody of the subordinate three tactical squadrons. In this connection, aviation plans for both 1951 and 1952 indicated that each tactical squadron was also to have two utility helicopters besides the 15 transport helicopters.[65] On 31 January 1952 the Commandant announced that the revision to Aviation Plan 1–5 had been approved by the CNO and that it represented the official guideline for the expansion of Marine aviation.[66]

During the past year, 1951, the transport squadrons had been commissioned very near the date recommended by the Tactics and Techniques Board. Under the revised Aviation Plan 1–52, the three new helicopter squadrons of MAG(HR)–36 and HMR–263 of MAG(HR)–26 were designated for commissioning during 1952 as follows: *

HMR–361	February 1952	(25 February 1952)
HMR–362	April 1952	(30 April 1952)
HMR–363	May 1952	(2 June 1952)
HMR–263	June 1952	(16 June 1952)

The planned and actual dates for commissioning of each group headquarters squadron along with its air base and maintenance squadrons took place on: [67]

MAG(HR)–16	1 March 1952
MAG(HR)–36	2 June 1952
MAG(HR)–26	16 June 1952

Thus on 30 June 1952, Marine aviation was comprised of three aircraft wings, each composed of three fixed-wing aircraft groups and a helicopter group of three tactical squadrons. In addition, each wing had a fixed-wing transport group of two squadrons, plus a photographic, a com-

---

* For comparative purposes the actual dates of commissioning are indicated in parentheses.

MARINE AIRCRAFT WING (MAW)
USMC 1180 458 9112
USN 68 144
TOTAL A/C 480

MAG (HR)
USMC 127 33 891
USN 8 19

H & MS
USMC 13 12 194
A/C 4

MABS
USMC 6 12 328
USN 8 19

HMR
USMC 36 3 123
A/C 15

MAG (VF/VA)
USMC 241 57 1569
USN 12 25

H & MS
USMC 20 16 282
A/C 10

MABS
USMC 9 16 449
USN 12 25

VMF
USMC 53 6 199
A/C 24

MWSG
USMC 43 52 1187
USN 10 22

H & HS
USMC 7 31 340

MABS
USMC 9 16 543
USN 10 22

MARS
USMC 27 5 304
A/C 15

MAG (VR)
USMC 104 23 602

H & MS
USMC 14 13 206
A/C 2

VMR (ML)
USMC 45 5 198
A/C 15

MACG
USMC 46 100 849
USN 5 17

H & HS
USMC 7 12 124
USN 5 6

MACS
USMC 8 23 205
USN 3

MASS
USMC 15 19 110
USN 2

H & HS, MAW
USMC 44 54 329
USN 6 3

VMC
USMC 30 15 213
USN 1 3
A/C 24

VMJ
USMC 27 6 191
USN 1 3
A/C 18

VMO
USMC 36 4 143
USN 1 2
A/C 24

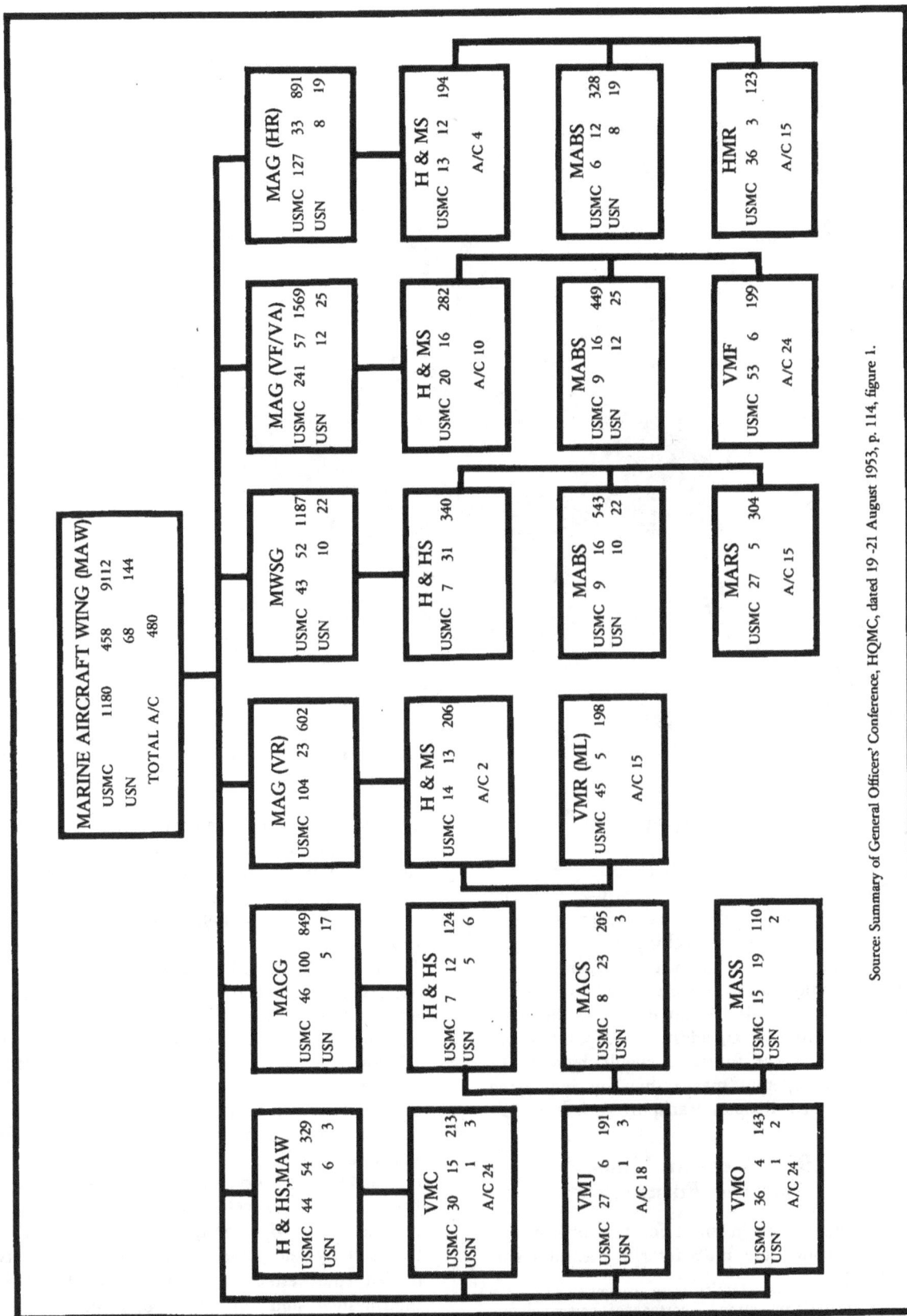

Source: Summary of General Officers' Conference, HQMC, dated 19-21 August 1953, p. 114, figure 1.

The K–225 was the first turbine-powered helicopter. Built by Kaman, it was powered by a Boeing 502-2 free turbine (Kaman Aerospace Corp. Photo 115–1).

posite, and an observation squadron.* [68] (Figure I).

The formation of the last helicopter group and squadron, MAG(HR)–26 and HMR–263, meant the planned growth of the helicopter program had been achieved. However, reaching the goal of nine tactical units did not mean that Marine Corps planners would relent in their effort to increase the maximum assault lift capability of the three helicopter groups. If an additional capability was desired in the near future, it would have to be achieved by different means than by increasing the number of helicopter transport squadrons.

1952 Aircraft Plans for the Future

While plans were in effect for the forthcoming HR2S to replace the HRS interim assault trans-

* Even though these units were commissioned, they still experienced an extreme shortage of personnel and equipment.

port helicopter, procurement of utility (HU) and observation (HO) aircraft was not quite as definite. Nevertheless, plans were being made to obtain both types. The evaluation of the Kaman K–225 observation helicopter—the model purchased by BuAer in lieu of the earlier K–190—found the design to be superior in its flight characteristics, particularly in stability, control, and ease of flying. Since Sikorsky's HO5S–1 was not meeting its expected performance ratings due to the low horsepower output of its engine, BuAer awarded a production contract during 1952 to Kaman Aircraft Company for 46 K–225s as an eventual replacement for the HO5S–1. The Kaman machine would be designated as the HOK–1 (H-helicopter, O-observation, K-Kaman) with the first of them expected to be delivered to the Marine Corps during 1954.[69] The HOK–1 had two side-by-side main rotor shafts with a two-bladed rotor attached to each shaft. The blades intermeshed and turned in opposite directions. Four people could be carried: pilot, copilot, and two passengers. The Pratt and Whitney R–1340–48 engine was installed behind the cockpit/cabin and produced 600 horsepower. The left side of the cockpit plexiglass bubble opened to allow loading of two litters one above the other, fore and aft in the cockpit; however, the copilot's seat and flight controls had to be removed. The actual weights, as the aircraft eventually evolved, amounted to 4,334 pounds empty with a maximum allowable of 5,995 pounds. Maximum sea level airspeed was restricted to 88 knots.[70]

The selection of a utility helicopter was extremely important as the Marine Corps desperately needed an all-around utility aircraft. It was not recognized at the time, but the choice would eventually have a definite influence upon the entire Marine helicopter program. The small HO3Ss and the HTLs were being used in a utility role since there were no other helicopters available. The Marine Corps desired to assign two new and larger utility aircraft to each helicopter MAG headquarters squadron for carrying cargo and bulky aircraft replacement parts. Also, two utility helicopters were to be assigned to each Marine aircraft wing headquarters squadron, each major air station, and air facility.[71] Then, as a secondary mission, the utility aircraft could be used to transport combat troops and evacuate wounded personnel.[72]

On 5 December 1952, the CNO informed BuAer of the Marine Corps' utility helicopter requirement. It was explained that in order to meet the specification, it appeared that modification to an existing Navy program would be desirable in the interest of economy rather than initiate a new design. In this respect, the CNO was referring to a new Navy ASW model, one being developed by the Sikorsky Aircraft Company.[73]

The origin of the new Sikorsky design began

The HOK–1 was the production version of the K–225. It was also known as an OH–43D (Marine Corps Photo A35013).

in 1951 when the Navy was searching for an ASW helicopter capable of operating from battleships and cruisers. The Bell-manufactured XHSL–1 helicopter was chosen originally in lieu of a Sikorsky aircraft in 1950 to meet this requirement, but had been in the developmental stage for well over a year. Many problems arose during the XHSL–1's construction which resulted in an increase in weight and size to the point where it became completely unacceptable to the Navy. At this point Sikorsky submitted its design to BuAer as a solution to the Navy's waning ASW program. The helicopter was described as a HRS–4; a modified HRS with a larger engine and cabin in addition to a differently designed tail cone and landing gear. But as the design evolved, so many changes were made to the basic HRS that it could not be considered a modification, but rather a completely different helicopter.

Basically, the Navy's requirement for an ASW helicopter specified that it be capable of carrying a pilot, copilot, sonar equipment and ordnance, and two crewmen. It was to have a three-hour flight duration and be compatible for storage in, and operating from, the same class of ships (battleships and cruisers) as the XHSL.*

By February 1952, the CNO had become convinced that the Bell XHSL–1 would not meet the ASW specifications nor be ready for delivery within an acceptable length of time. On the 27th, he directed BuAer "to proceed without delay with a program for the development of the Sikorsky HRS aircraft with the large engine—ASW configured." The first flight of Sikorsky's HRS–4 was predicted to occur in November 1953 with the delivery of the first production aircraft scheduled for January 1955.[74]

The HRS–4 had to be modified to meet the utility requirements of the Marine Corps which consisted largely of rearranging the interior of the cabin. The necessary changes involved removal of the ASW equipment, installation of a cargo deck with tie-down rings, provisions for carrying 8 litters or 12 combat equipped troops, a 400-pound rescue hoist, and a 5,000-pound external cargo hook.[75] The basic weight of the utility version was 8,598 pounds with a maximum take-off weight eventually approved at 13,300 pounds. This allowed for a payload of approximately 4,000 pounds without fuel. The forward air speed was restricted to 123 knots. The 65-foot diameter 4-bladed main rotor was driven by a

---

* According to Navy plans, a much larger twin-engine helicopter was to perform the ASW mission from aircraft carriers.

A HOK–1 from VMO–2 during Operation SEAHAWK at Pohang, Korea, 1960. The HOK–1 was used for reconnaissance (Marine Corps Photo A182678).

1,525-horsepower Wright engine where the smaller HRS had a 600-horsepower engine propelling only 3 main rotor blades. The Navy's official designation for the HRS–4 later became the HSS–1 and the Marine version the HUS–1 (H-helicopter, U-utility, S-Sikorsky). Sikorsky designation was the S–58.[76]

When the CNO instructed BuAer to develop the HUS–1 for the Marine Corps in December 1952, he also defined its procurement status. Fortunately in this respect, the Fiscal Year 1954 aircraft procurement list was revised by the CNO to allow for the modification of 33 HSS–1s to HUS–1s. This meant only that money would be available for beginning its fabrication. Delivery of the first production HUS–1 to the Marine Corps was initially estimated as occurring sometime during 1955.[77]

Initial planning documents defining aircraft requirements for the fiscal year 1954 and 1955 also were submitted to the CNO during 1952. Both documents indicated a Marine Corps requirement for nine HR squadrons, each with 15 transport helicopters for a total tactical inventory of 135 aircraft. The VMOs were to stay at 12 fixed-wing and 12 observation helicopters, and HMX–1 was to operate 12 transports and six observation aircraft. The total Marine helicopter requirements planned through 30 June 1955 were: 147 transport (HR), 36 utility (HU), and 48 observation helicopters (HO).[78] In the fall of 1953, the helicopter procurement program was slightly modified by the CNO in order to stay within the Marine Corps total operating limit of 1,425 aircraft. HMX–1 was reduced to an inventory of nine HR and three HO aircraft and each group headquarters

The HUS–1 by Sikorsky was the first major Marine utility helicopter. Its forerunner was the HRS–1 (background) (Marine Corps Photo 529979).

squadron was denied its two utility helicopters. Subject to budgetary, production, and engineering restrictions, 144 HRs, 39 HOs, and 36 HUs were approved for the Marine Corps by the end of June 1955.[79]

In the interim between submission and approval of plans for these requirements, the Division of Aviation was reviewing its tactical assignment of the forthcoming HUSs. On 18 September 1953, Colonel Edward C. Dyer, who was now assigned as deputy assistant director of the Division of Aviation after graduating from the National War College, prepared a memorandum for the Commandant concerning the helicopter program. "The HUS-1," the memorandum read, "is being procured to meet utility helicopter requirements. Initially, however, it will be used as a transport helicopter. Upon replacement by the HR2S, the HUS will revert to utility billets."[80]

Internal documents of the Division of Aviation indicated that changing the role of the HUS from utility to troop transport had been under consideration since the early part of the year. A graphic presentation of the desired complement for nine helicopter squadrons was prepared on 7 April 1953 and depicted how the progression from all HRS squadrons to an all HR2S program was anticipated. Figure 2 also illustrates chronologically where the HUSs were intended to be used.[81]

Yet amidst all the planning for future years, the Marine Corps had by this time substantially increased its helicopter inventory. Although near the end of 1952 the operating squadrons were not up to their authorized strengths, the total number of helicopters, including those assigned to

short activities (non-FMF), had reached 166. The types reflected in the total were 106 HRs, 39 HOs, 18 trainers (HT), and 3 tired HRPs. By the end of 1953, and with the Korean War over, the number of helicopters on hand had steadily increased to a total of 202 with models of the HRS accounting for 141 of the total.[82]

Peripheral Aspects of the Period

During this period, the helicopter program had grown at an unprecedented rate compared to the painfully slow pre-Korean War pace. In this same period, a few helicopter programs met with failure. These unsuccessful ventures cannot be ignored since many of them were viewed as being equally essential to the Marine Corps' amphibious mission as were those which eventually proved to be worthwhile.

One of the more notable projects was the re-

Squadrons	1954	1955	1956	1957	1958
HMR–1	HRS	HUS	HUS	HR2S———	
HMR–2	HRS	HUS	HUS	HR2S———	
HMR–3	HRS	HR2S———			
HMR–4	HRS———	HR2S———			
HMR–5	HRS———	HR2S———			
HMR–6	HRS———	HR2S———			
HMR–7	HRS———	HR2S———			
HMR–8	HRS———	HR2S———			
HMR–9	HRS———————	HR2S———			

Figure 2

quirement and subsequent development of a one-
man helicopter. It was viewed as a machine for
use within infantry units and one which could
be piloted by an average combat Marine after
minimal training. The potential of the light-weight
device made it extremely attractive for performing
missions of observation, liaison, rescue, and the
most promising of all, maneuvering of small
tactical units.

Although the experimental one-man helicopter
project survived for many years, others were not
so successful. The McDonnell XHRH–1 was one in
particular. Its short life was attributed to an economy move which required the diversion of its funds
to a similar and equally unsucecssful helicopter, the Navy's XHCH–1 (H-helicopter, C-cargo,
H-heavy). The XHCH was designed to carry loads
for very short distances as a flying crane with
the capability of operating off aircraft carriers
and being used for replenishment operations,
lifting unflyable aircraft, and in general support
of amphibious operations. Its payload was expected to be 15,000 pounds lifted over a distance
of 20 miles, and in an "overload" condition,
capable of carrying 25,000 pounds.[83] Its demise,
like that of the XHRH–1, eventually came as a
result of insufficient funds to carry out development of the power plants, rotor head, and rotor
blades.

During the developmental period of the
XHRH–1, General Cates had made repeated requests to CNO for the continuance of development
funds as the helicopter appeared to offer the
Marine Corps a greater assault lift capability than
the HR2S. Nevertheless, the CNO had remained
impervious to the Commandant's requests and
pinned all hopes for success of a heavy helicopter
on the XHCH.

Throughout the past years, Piasecki had continued the development of its XH–16, originally
the Marine Corps' hope for a large assault transport helicopter. However, it too—although still
under construction during this period—would soon
join the list of unsuccessful ventures.

Disregarding the unfruitful endeavors, the fact

must be recognized that the Marine Corps accepted the "successful" helicopters of less than
desired performance and aptly applied them, while
never giving up hope for obtaining those ex-
periencing developmental difficulties. The problem
which Marine planners had encountered, and
would continue to face in future planning, was
that the Marine Corps helicopter concept, for the
most part, was based on the aircraft meeting the
specifications listed in the operational requirements and not on the resultant flight article. A
marked difference is revealed when comparing
the original requirement against the finished
product. Of course, the planners had no idea how
a certain helicopter would vary from its proposed
design. The difference can be explained somewhat
by examining a CNO policy statement, wherein he
recognized that modifications would exist between the original design and the production
model:

> In all material developments, the Chief of Naval
> Operations considers timely availability and suit-
> ability of first importance. The performance factors
> given in [the] requirement are goals, except where
> specifically noted as minimums. During the course of
> preliminary design or development it may be found
> that in meeting these goals a large and complex
> article will result; whereas it may be possible to
> develop a much simpler and therefore, more readily
> available and suitable equipment short of the ultimate
> specified, but which nevertheless will constitute a
> considerable advance over presently available equip-
> ment. When this situation arises, the developing agency
> shall so inform the Chief of Naval Operations in
> order that consideration may be given to making an
> appropriate modification of the operational require-
> ment.[84]

The next major step taken by the Marine Corps
in developing its helicopter program would be
derived from the products of a study group at
Quantico called the Advanced Research Group.
The material produced by the assemblance of 10
Marine colonels, most of whom were destined for
the rank of brigadier general, would have a pro-
found impact upon the helicopter program, and in
general, the future course of the entire Marine
Corps amphibious concept.

CHAPTER 5

SEEKING A NEW ORDER OF
MOBILITY

A Concept for
Future Amphibious Operations

On 17 July 1951, the Commandant proposed to the CNO a Marine Corps concept for future amphibious operations. Certain conceptual aspects had appeared in both *Equipment Policy 1950* and in the studies submitted by the 1951 Tactics and Techniques Board. The Commandant declared that the time had come to settle on a fairly definite concept for employing helicopters in amphibious operations. He recommended the initiation of a program to develop the detailed techniques for large-scale ship-to-shore movement, one which would provide the fleets with some measure of ability to exploit the growing helicopter capability. In this respect, General Cates remarked to the CNO that it would be "prudent, practical, and timely to provide within the fleets the capability to land by helicopter the assault elements of one Marine division in continuous echelons." In accepting the optimistic troop-carrying capacity of the HR2S–1, as predicted by Sikorsky, General Cates also mentioned that the helicopter industry would soon produce a 36-man helicopter and that 144 of these aircraft could land the desired number of troops in execution of the concept. "Studies and past experience," he continued, "indicate that the most desirable type of assault shipping for such a force will be ships which can accommodate the necessary embarked troops, the helicopters to land them, and the crews to operate and maintain the helicopters." General Cates concluded: "It is becoming increasingly urgent to commence a ship conversion or building program that will parallel the availability of . . . the 36-man helicopter." [1]

The Commandant's letter also defined the specifications for transport shipping, an essential element of his future doctrine. From the landing force viewpoint, the most effective tactical landing would consist of a helicopter-borne attack mounted from a transport ship capable of embarking approximately 1,500 assault troops and operating at least 18 of the 36-man transport helicopters from the same ship. A ship with a minimum flight deck capacity of 10 such helicopters was considered to be acceptable. [2]

In a letter to the Commandant on 13 August 1951, the Acting Chief of Naval Operations, Admiral Donald B. "Wu" Duncan, approved the Marine Corps' concept of landing one division by helicopter. He questioned, however, whether the state of development of transport helicopters justified settling, at that time, on a definite method for conducting such operations and beginning a ship conversion or building program. He feared acceptance of the Marine Corps' concept of transporting troops, equipment, stores, and helicopters all in the same ship would automatically require radical changes to existing types of ships or the construction of specially designed new types. Either course would involve a large expenditure of funds. The decision rendered by the Acting CNO was that further experimentation and investigation should be conducted into the matter. Laying aside the Commandant's shipping request, Admiral Duncan declared, "The CNO will determine whether it is feasible, within the limits of ships and funds available, to commence . . . the program during the current fiscal year [1952]." [3]

Initial Determination of
the Marine Corps' Helicopter
Aircraft Carrier Requirements

Long before July 1951, the Commandant had made Marine Corps shipping requirements known to the CNO. As early as February, General Cates had recommended that one helicopter aircraft carrier of new construction, or one converted from a CV or CVL, be included in the Navy's shipbuilding program for the next fiscal year, *i.e.*, 1952. The Commandant pointed out that development of amphibious ships of all types had lagged in recent years and the time had arrived when constructive progress in this area was becoming necessary. In April 1951, the Director of Marine Aviation, General Jerome, told the Deputy Chief of Naval Operations for Air (Op–5B), that the Marine Corps needed a prototype amphibious troop/helicopter transport ship and that it was essential that such a ship be developed from the keel up. That part of the Marine Corps concept which required troops, equipment, helicopters, and reasonable maintenance and operational facilities be combined in one type of ship was also pointed out. Four days later, the Commandant submitted to the CNO a request for the use of a CV or a CVE in evaluating the employment of assault transport helicopters. Unfortunately, all requests appeared to have been made in vain as the Ships Requirements Board failed to provide funds for the construction of a new ship or the conversion of a CVE in the shipbuilding programs for Fiscal Years '52 and '53.[4]

On 12 October 1951, the CNO initiated action to settle the questions raised by the Commandant's concept of future amphibious operations. Although there had been general agreement that in an assault elements of one Marine division would be landed by helicopter, yet to be determined was the type of platform the assault would be launched from. To this end, the CNO directed the Commander in Chief, United States Atlantic Fleet "to evaluate the capabilities of transport helicopters and to develop doctrine, techniques and procedures for ship-to-shore movement of helicopter transported troops."[5]

Representing the Marine Corps in the conduct of this evaluation was General Graves B. Erskine, Commanding General, Fleet Marine Force, Atlantic, a much-decorated veteran of World War I and a pioneer in the development of amphibious warfare doctrine. In the early years of World War II he had been Chief of Staff, V Amphibious Corps and later commanded the 3d Marine Division on Iwo Jima.

To develop the assault helicopter concept in FMFLant, on 20 December 1951 General Erskine convened a board with Major General Field Harris, the Commanding General, Aircraft, FMFLant as the senior member. General Harris' board met on 2 January 1952 and decided that the best method for obtaining a solution to the problem was to hold a series of ship-to-shore exercises during the early part of the year. As a result, HELEX I and II took place between 20 January and 28 February. Participating in both exercises were the newly formed helicopter squadrons HMR–261 and –262. Operating from the

deck of the USS *Siboney* (CVE–122), the two squadrons lifted troops of the 1st Battalion, 8th Marines into landing zones at Camp Lejeune. In addition, the squadrons airlifted their own personnel and equipment ashore after the tactical portion of the exercise had been completed.[6]

General Harris' board made two major determinations from the results of HELEX I and II. The first conclusion was that the CVE–105 class carrier could adequately handle aircraft, personnel, and logistically support a vertical envelopment from the sea. Secondly, the board evaluated the employment of a mix of two different types of ships, *i.e.*, a helicopter transport and a troop transport with a helicopter deck, and concluded that such combination of ships was tactically unsound. The factors militating against the use of separate ships were found in the limited troop-carrying capacity of the HRS and the additional time required for the aircraft to land, load with troops, and relaunch from the troop transport.[7]

On 5 March 1952, shortly after the termination of HELEX I and II, General Cates requested that General Erskine make additional recommendation on three related items which could be derived from the recent tests. Two of the subjects had not been addressed in prior reports but the third had been treated by the Tactics and Techniques Board in February 1951. The three areas to be considered were:

> 1. The suitability of the CVE class carrier and any modifications necessary to make it more suitable for assault helicopter operations.
> 2. The general characteristics required for a helicopter transport vessel for future construction.
> 3. Based upon 1. and 2. above, the shipping requirements to support helicopter operations involving the assault elements of one Marine division.[8]

General Harris' board responded to the Commandant's request on 29 March 1952. It determined that the CVE–55 class carrier, with a few modifications, appeared to be suitable for assault helicopter operations with the HRS. For operations with the HR2S, additional modifications would be necessary. In this connection it was recommended that a design study be conducted in order to determine the extent of the alterations needed to make the ship compatible for HR2S operations.

No determination was made on the second objective as the board believed that additional helicopter assault exercises should be held prior to settling on the general characteristics for such a ship. The estimated shipping requirements for transporting the assault elements of one Marine division (12,000 to 14,000 troops and related helicopter personnel) were given as 20 CVE–55s if the HRS was the only type helicopter used. If the HR2S was to be employed in lieu of the HRS, then 13 CVEs would be necessary. However, as an immediate course of action, since there were not enough HRSs available to land the divisional assault elements, General Harris recommended that only four CVE–55s be modified for helicopter operations and suggested that only a minimum modification be accomplished. In any case each ship should be modified to accommodate at least 20 HRSs, 850 troops, and 75 tons of supplies.[9]

General Harris' report was forwarded through appropriate headquarters to the CNO. General Cates concurred with the recommendations and stated in his endorsement on 28 April that modification of four CVE–55 class aircraft carriers was considered satisfactory as an inaugural step in implementing the development of the helicopter assault capability. He mentioned that additional conversions would be necessary at an early date to fill the desired requirements. General Cates concluded by stating that the ship modification measures "are viewed as essential in maintaining the momentum of the helicopter program [and] to insure early availability of a Fleet Marine Force helicopter assault capability in connection with fleet amphibious operations." [10]

Following the Commandant's request, the CNO, on 8 September 1952, directed the Chief, Bureau of Ships, to undertake a study to determine the feasibility of modifying a CVE–55 class aircraft carrier. Two months later, the CNO was advised by BuShips that the feasibility study had been completed and the CVE–55 class appeared to be an excellent ship for such use and the suggested conversion to rotary-wing operation was recommended to permit service evaluation.[11]

Unfortunately, by the time BuShips had completed the study it was too late to have the modification included in the 1954 Fiscal Year budget. To ensure incorporation of the four Landing Platforms for Helicopters (LPHs) in the 1955 budget, the Commandant, on 26 November, repeated his request for the conversions of the CVE–55s. Soon thereafter, on 5 February 1953, General Cates revised his shipping requirements. He informed the CNO that the Marine Corps now had a specific need for a total of 16 LPHs instead of 12; four modified CVE–105s and 12 CVE–55s. These requirements were taken from a study completed earlier by the Tactics and Techniques Board at Quantico. The 16 helicopter aircraft carriers

were the minimum number of ships which the Tactics and Techniques Board felt could accommodate the assault elements of one Marine division.

Therefore by early 1953 the CNO had not only been appraised in general terms of the Marine Corps' shipping requirements—that of paralleling helicopter production but also of the specific types and numbers needed to make the vertical assault concept an effective tool of amphibious warfare. In short, while certain preliminary steps had now been taken by the Commandant to obtain helicopter platforms from which to expand the helicopter concept, the Marine Corps, in actuality, had no ship in sight from which to operate and no ship scheduled for either construction or conversion.[12]

The Advanced Research Group

Among the functions for which the Marine Corps was responsible, according to the amended National Security Act of 1947, was the development of those phases of amphibious operations that pertain to the tactics, techniques, and equipment used by landing forces. This responsibility was of paramount concern to senior Marine officers at both Headquarters Marine Corps and the Marine Corps Schools, especially in those agencies involved with development, planning, and programming.

Although Marines were still fighting in Korea, there was an obvious requirement to determine the shape and posture of the post-Korean War Marine Corps. Equally obvious was the fact that helicopters were to play a major role in the composition of the postwar Corps and in the amphibious warfare techniques employed by the Marines.

When he assumed the Commandancy on 1 January 1952, General Lemuel C. Shepherd, Jr., who relieved General Cates, touched in his inaugural address on the successes achieved by the helicopter and the role it played in the Korean War when he said:

> Seven years have passed since the development of the helicopter as a troop carrier was begun, but in the fall of 1951, in the bleak Korean countryside, the worth of the ungainly looking craft was finally proved. Just as the amphibian tractor came to the fore as a troop carrier over the reefs of Pacific atolls during World War II, so the helicopter became the greatest single innovation during the Korean conflict as a tactical and humanitarian medium of transportation. . . .

The fact that we have a suitable helicopter transport now in sight, . . . [leaves us] with a sense of confidence. I believe that the Marine Corps, with our skilled close air support and our own helicopters to pave the way for the amphibious landing, is capable of following up an atomic attack with the most powerful assault punch possessed by any nation in the world today.[13]

General Shepherd had good reason to sound confident in his statement. By late 1953 the helicopter program had expanded to the point where the Marine Corps was capable of undertaking a more positive step in developing further its helicopter concept. In this respect, the Marine Corps had more experience in helicopter operations, possessed more helicopters, trained pilots, and crewmen than any other military organization in the world. Brigadier General Noah C. New recalled:

Even as early as 1951, HMX–1 had experimented with mounting machine guns and 2.75 inch rockets on the HTL–4, but there was little interest in developing a helicopter for the close air support role. Many pilots with Korean combat experience were definitely against arming the helicopters. Also the ceiling limit of 1425 aircraft mitigated against procuring a lightly armed and vulnerable helicopter to substitute in the place of a fixed wing close air support aircraft.[14]

The combination of these factors led General Shepherd to form a special study group of highly experienced Marine officers to expand upon the 1951 concept. As one of its main tasks, the group would have the objective of deriving an ultimate concept for the conduct of future amphibious operations.

There was also another reason for forming such a group. On 19 January 1953, General Shepherd informed General Cates, who was now at Quantico as the Commandant of Marine Corps Schools, that within the Marine Corps educational structure there were no provisions beyond the Senior Course for intellectual development of Marine officers in matters relating specifically to special problems of the Marine Corps. He believed that the deficiency did not permit formalized advanced study in the field of amphibious operations, nor did it ensure the adequate and uniform indoctrination of senior Marine officers in considerations affecting formulation of Marine Corps policy. In order to correct this situation the Commandant stated:

[I] desire to establish a Marine Corps Advanced Research Group . . . [which] will comprise a small group of officers performing original research in the interest of their own professional development and for the purpose of achieving solutions to certain of the Marine Corps' basic problems.[15]

The Commandant's directive defined the mission of the Advanced Research Group as "to provide opportunity for advanced study and original research for Marine Corps officers of the rank of colonel." * [16] One major item under the outline of study for the Advanced Research Group (ARG) was the "advancement of theories and practices related to landing operations." As a matter of policy, however, the basic project problems were to be selected by the Commandant. Each nine-month session of the group was to correspond with the academic year of the Marine Corps Schools.[17]

Accordingly, the group met at Quantico in the fall of 1953. In the original outline of study for the group, the Commandant assigned three specific research projects, all of which were to be solved during the academic year. General Shepherd further directed that a fourth project be selected by the group, which could be on any subject so long as it was a matter of significant concern to the Marine Corps. As the first of the three projects, General Shepherd directed the 10 colonels to:

Develop a concept of future amphibious operations that will require maximum utilization of the Fleet Marine Force as a mobile force in readiness. Based upon this concept determine the validity and adequacy of the current tactical doctrines, organization, equipment development policies and training programs within the Marine Corps.[18]

The Advanced Research Group stated that the solution to this problem had to be based on the realities of the day, and on such developments as could reasonably be expected during the next decade. A challenging objective had to be established; a definite long-range target towards which the Marine Corps could strive in the following years. This was of paramount importance because all areas involved in future amphibious operations had to be easily discernible and provide a common approach to the problem. The concept arrived at by the group consisted principally of the following:

1. The high speed movement of helicopter assault forces to the objective area, in company with a fast carrier task force.
2. The use of nuclear weapons to destroy hostile air within tactical aircraft range of the objective area, and to neutralize the landing area.

---

* One of the prerequisites stated that members could not be within four years of selection to brigadier general. The group of 10 relatively junior colonels chosen for the session during 1953-1954 were: Thomas J. Colley, John P. Condon, August Larson, Joseph N. Renner, Carson A. Roberts, Samuel R. Shaw, George R. E. Shell, Eustace R. Smoak, William J. Van Ryzin, and Richard G. Weede. It is interesting to note that eight of the 10 officers retired as general officers.

3. The rapid exploitation of atomic preparatory fires by helicopter assault forces, from the sea, seizing key terrain features within the objective area.

4. Maneuver by helicopter troops, with the use of atomic support, to extend the area of amphibious troop control within the objective area.

5. Use of helicopter forces, teamed with combat air and atomic and conventional support, and intensive air reconnaissance combined with vigorous patrolling, to maintain, consolidate and extend the area.

6. Use of helicopters for logistic support during the assault phase.[19]

These objectives had several promising features which, if exploited to the fullest, would provide a Fleet Marine Force with a force-in-readiness capability far beyond that previously envisioned. The "all-helicopter" assault would give the landing force mobility, flexibility, and speed which would permit the commander to mass, reinforce, or redeploy task forces of division size. It was considered that even if tactical nuclear weapons were not used, or in Marine operations short of all-out war, the concept would still result in a much more powerful amphibious assault than was possible at the time.

While the ARG proposals could not be achieved immediately, they were ones which the Marine Corps could attain in the foreseeable future. The Commandant approved, on 27 April 1954, the basic proposals realizing that progressive steps had to be taken for the development of the techniques and procedures to be employed in an "all-helicopter assault." In doing so, General Shepherd directed that these new concepts now represented the long-range objective of the Marine Corps.[20]

The approval of ARG Project I led to a consideration of fields in which long-range orientation programs would be required. The areas of organization, equipment, training and techniques, and procedures would be affected. The Marine division would be required to segregate, or remove from its organic structure, those elements whose normal functions were not compatible with the new concept. In the area of equipment, emphasis had to be shifted to development of amphibious shipping which could support an all-helicopter assault.

Further, Marine Corps techniques and procedures for the conduct of amphibious operations as well as the training program which refined them did not meet the requirements of the atomic era. Atomic weapon systems had to be made available and become organic to the ground units and made totally helicopter transportable. The logistical supply system needed equal attention and revision if it was to be responsive to needs of the division.

During the forthcoming years, therefore, a series of programs had to be promulgated by the Marine Corps in order to reorient and accelerate development in these fields.

As the result of these considerations, Marine Corps Test Unit No. 1 (MCTU #1) was activated at Camp Pendleton, California, on 1 July 1954. Colonel Edward N. Rydalch was designated commanding officer of the regimental-size unit and later officially took command on 2 September.[21] The statement of missions assigned to Colonel Rydalch required the test unit to delve into practically all aspects of the major areas of concern brought about by the adoption of the new concept.

One of the core areas in which MCTU #1 would be active was in the determination of the feasibility of conducting amphibious operations with atomic weapon support. In order to prove these techniques, the test unit would participate with troops and helicopters in a series of atomic tests to be conducted at the Nevada Proving Grounds.

The first test of this nature, however, had already taken place the previous year, 1953, involving the 2d Marine Corps Provisional Atomic Exercise Brigade, at about the same time as the ARG's Project I was being conceived. Brigadier General Wilburt S. "Bigfoot" Brown, Commanding General, Force Troops, FMFPac, a combat veteran of both World Wars, the Nicaraguan campaign, and Korea, was assigned additional duty as commanding general of the Camp Pendleton-based brigade.

Helicopter support was provided by HMRs–361, –162, and –163 of Colonel Harold J. Mitchener's MAG(HR)–16. A total of 39 HRSs participated in the exercise with a few aircraft augmenting from MAG(HR)–36. Code named DESERT ROCK V, the exercise solidly proved that helicopter-borne forces could be used to support the main effort of an amphibious assault in relatively close proximity to a nuclear explosion. In the forthcoming years, MCTU #1's participation in subsequent DESERT ROCK exercises would substantially expand the data obtained during DESERT ROCK V.[22]

Advanced Research Group Project IV

Throughout the academic year of 1953–1954, the ARG generated many possible subjects for Project IV. The original solution to Project I opened a number of areas which required further detailed study before the concept could be effectively implemented. Some of the problems brought to light were:

> 1. The tactics and techniques of helicopter operations ashore.
> 2. The Marine Corps helicopter requirements.
> 3. The development of tactics and techniques of fighter escort and close support of transport helicopters.
> 4. Shipping requirements.

After careful consideration of all the subjects for Project IV, the group chose to study the one relating to helicopter requirements. They realized that combat helicopter requirements, in terms of number and type, were not now clearly defined inasmuch as the Commandant had only recently approved the new concept presented in Project I. It became apparent that Project IV had to deal with helicopter requirements, with emphasis placed on a transition period—if the Marine Corps was to meet the long-range objective of an "all helicopter" assault capability. The Advanced Research Group, therefore, identified its fourth project as "Marine Corps Transport Helicopter Requirements for the Immediate Future." [23]

The statement of the problem as written by the group was to "develop the Marine Corps' transport helicopter requirements for the immediate future as a step toward achieving the ultimate objective of the concept of future amphibious operations." The initial goal was to achieve the capability of lifting the assault elements of one Marine division and the related elements of one Marine aircraft wing. Thereafter, as conditions would permit, and as requirements dictated, the Marine Corps would expand its capability to meet its potential under the concept.

The group appreciated fully that, as in landing craft, several types of helicopters would be required to execute effectively the several operations of lifting cargo, vehicles, and personnel. Also helicopters would be needed for reconnaissance, casualty evacuation, pathfinding, and the exercise of command and control. For these operations there was seen a definite requirement for a "family" consisting of HR2Ss for heavy equipment and large personnel loads and a need for the HUSs and HRSs in lifting lighter loads of equipment and troops. While the Marine Corps had considerable numbers of the lighter helicopters, the shortcoming was in the quantity of the heavier transport helicopter—the one most essential to any significant landing operation. For this reason the colonels devoted their study to consideration of the larger transport helicopter only. [24]

A comparison was made between the existing helicopter lifting capability and that which was programmed for 1957—the time when all nine Marine transport helicopter squadrons would be equipped with the HR2S. It was figured that it would take seven hours in 1954 to land the assault elements of one battalion landing team (BLT) with one MAG (HR) consisting of three 15-plane HRS squadrons. By 1957, the increased lifting capability of the HR2S would permit the same size MAG to land a complete Marine division in approximately 15 hours. The comparison was made using the "K" series Table of Organization (T/O) with supplies sufficient for three days' operations. The radius of assault for the HRS helicopter group was 15–20 miles whereas the HR2S MAG was figured at a radius of 50 miles. An average load for the HRS was computed at 1,300 pounds and at an amazing 8,000 pounds for the HR2S. [25]

In a close analysis of the HR2S–landed division, however, it was determined that the number of helicopters was still inadequate. It was felt that the minimum assault force should consist of four battalion landing teams landed simultaneously with additional support provided on the second wave. Also, it was calculated that sufficient helicopters would not be available for providing support for tactical operations ashore while concurrently executing the ship-to-shore movement. These deficiencies could be remedied, the group stated, "by increasing Marine Corps transport helicopter units to a total of 12 squadrons with a combined strength of 180 aircraft." In addition, it would be necessary for the helicopters to be capable of carrying "an emergency payload of 35 passengers or 12,500 pounds for the initial assault and for heavy lifts." The increase of 45 HR2Ss, the group believed, would meet the initial lift requirement and provide tactical support ashore during the early phases of the assault. In the case where helicopters were needed in operations ashore during the early phase, the overall time to land the complete division would then be on the order of 12 to 14 hours. [26]

Resupply requirements of the division, combined with the total requirements necessary for lifting a Marine aircraft wing, were examined next with the view of determining the capability for landing a division-wing team with the 180 HR2Ss. By allowing 217 trips per day for resupply of the division, the wing could be moved ashore with 30 days supply in a period of 50 hours, provided the wing equipment was helicopter transportable. This period would be increased to 70 hours should one MAG of HR2Ss be employed to support operations ashore after the initial landing.[27]

As a matter of false optimism, the Advanced Research Group members had been led to believe that the HR2S could be modified to have the capability to lift 12,500 pounds. The only change to their planned field trips during their session was the addition of a visit to the Sikorsky Aircraft Company.[28] Considering this, it can be inferred from studying their report that during the course of their visit to Sikorsky a means had been proposed to them by which the lifting ability of the helicopter could be increased.* [29] The group listed in its report three ways this could be done: "By installing engines of sufficient power . . . by increasing the rating of the present engines to 2,500 horsepower . . . or by installing rotor tip jets." [30] The group knew that the importance of obtaining a payload of 12,500 pounds could not be over-emphasized as it would then be possible to helicopter-lift the most crucial heavy pieces of division property: the 155mm howitzer and the two and one-half ton truck.

The board's Project IV report to the Commandant concluded that 180 HR2S–1 helicopters were needed to meet the interim transport helicopter requirements. After reviewing the study, General Shepherd gave his approval on 22 July 1954 but directed that "a new study be initiated immediately to determine the feasibility of achieving the helicopter-landed wing" portion of the division-wing team.[31] It had been indicated in the Division of Aviation's comments on the study that in the initial stage of the concept it might not be necessary, nor desirable, to helicopter transport all the elements of a Marine aircraft wing to a shore base during an amphibious operation.

Following his approval of Project IV, General Shepherd submitted his request to the CNO for the additional number of helicopters on 23 October 1954. "The validity of the concept outlined in [the letter of 17 July 1951]," he stated, "has been borne out by events which have since transpired. It now appears that we are ready for —in fact, obliged to take—the next step in logical

progression toward development of our helicopter capabilities. . . ." The general continued, "I propose that each of the nine Marine helicopter transport squadrons be provided with 20 HR2S aircraft ** at the earliest practicable time." He further pointed out to the CNO that this would represent an increase from 135 helicopters in the present program to a total of 180.[32]

Landing Force Bulletin Number 17

Following the Commandant's approval of the Advanced Research Group's Project I, action was taken to obtain a Navy Department policy statement supporting the concept. Although this was not forthcoming until late in 1955, the Commandant, in the meantime, had been guaranteed Navy Department support. In a letter to the Commandant of Marine Corps Schools, General Shepherd stated that in this matter, "the CNO has already assured us of Navy support of the concept, and has so instructed his staff and the bureau chiefs." [33] The CNO, Admiral Arleigh A. Burke, gave his formal concurrence to the new concept on 8 December 1955. He concurred with the Marine Corps' ultimate goal of conducting future amphibious operations by the means of vertical envelopment utilizing ship-based helicopters, although he realized that complete achievement of the goal was not readily apparent in the immediate future. Admiral Burke agreed that "plans must be laid for a gradual transition from World War II concepts of landing entirely over the beaches to the ultimate goal of landing all the assault elements by VTOL *** type [helicopter] transport aircraft." [34]

The CNO outlined the areas which were regarded as intermediate goals and attainable within 5 to 10 years:

1. Preliminary softening up and isolation of the area by fast carrier task force and long-range shore-based aircraft and guided missiles.
2. Elimination or reduction to a minimum of advance force operations to increase the element of surprise. Reconnaissance of landing areas to be accomplished by photo planes and personnel operating from submerged submarines.
3. Seizure of all initial objectives, including beach defenses, by troops landed in helicopters and supported by naval gunfire and carrier-based aircraft.
4. Clearance of obstacles from beaches and beach

---

* This assumption is supported by a statement contained in a memorandum from the Director of Aviation to the Chief of Staff on 8 April 1954. Although commenting on ARG Project I, the Director of Aviation mentions:
  This T–56 [gas turbine engine] growth potential of the HR2S would provide an aircraft capable of the performance noted on page 13, Part II: 12,000 pound payload, 100 nautical mile radius, 130-150 knot speed. However, that would be about the growth limit of the HR2S.

** Adding five additional HR2Ss to each of the nine helicopter squadrons would be equal to forming one additional MAG (HR) with three 15-plane squadrons.
*** Vertical takeoff and landing.

approaches and preparation of beaches to receive
landing ships and landing craft by:

   a. Personnel landed by helicopter.

   b. Minesweepers.

  5. Landing of supporting troops, heavy equipment
and supplies over the beaches.

  6. Continued employment of assault helicopters to
land reinforcements and to provide tactical mobility
and logistic support to troops engaged in expanding
the beachhead.

  7. Use of the sea echelon concept to eliminate con-
centration of shipping in the vicinity of beaches.

  8. Adherence to principles of dispersion of ships,
landing beaches and troop elements to provide maximum practicable passive defense against enemy atomic
attack.[35]

Admiral Burke concluded his letter to General
Shepherd by mentioning that the rate of progress
towards achievement of the ultimate goal would
depend on many factors. "One of the most important," he stated "is the amount of money
which is made available by the Congress for implementation of the Navy's annual shipbuilding
and conversion program. Therefore, it is believed
that a reappraisal of the goal outlined above . . .
should be made at least annually." [36]

In the meantime, Marine Corps Schools had
prepared a landing force bulletin outlining the
concept which had been proposed in the ARG's
Project I. The school had been tasked with the
project in mid-1954 and had submitted a proposed
bulletin to HQMC during December. After undergoing extensive revision, the Marine Corps officially published its concept of future amphibious
operations on 13 December 1955 in *Landing
Force Bulletin Number 17*, only nine days after
formal recognition of the concept by the CNO.

Landing Force Bulletin Number 17 (LFB–17)
elaborated on the CNO's position and paralleled
the concept delineated in Project I. The last paragraph summarized in the following manner:

> This concept has as its ultimate goal an all-heli-
> copter assault which will endow the amphibious attack
> with maximum impact and maximum freedom of
> action. We have already progressed to a point at
> which our doctrine embraces a powerful two-pronged
> attack, one prong a vertical envelopment * by heli-
> copter, the other a surface assault across the beach
> by conventional means, with the latter constituting
> the main effort. In the future, while improving our
> still-essential beach-assault ability, we must adapt our
> organization and equipment, and our tactics, tech-
> niques, and training, so as to place major stress on
> the helicopter assault. Later, as new amphibious ships
> join the fleet, and as helicopters with greater load

---

* This appears to be the first case where the term
"Vertical Envelopment" appears in an official Marine
Corps document. It had appeared earlier in the MCS's
draft copy of LFB–17 to CMC in December 1954.

capacity become available in quantity, the beach assault can be reduced still further. Eventually, when
the concept is fully realized, the beach assault can be
eliminated altogether, leaving only follow-up troops
and supplies, exploitation forces, and base-develop-
ment units and material to be landed over beaches or
through ports in the beachhead area.[37]

The latest improvements in amphibious tactics
and techniques had been promulgated in two other
Marine Corps documents during the period, both
of which complemented the concept outlined in
LFB–17; *Landing Force Bulletin Number 2*
("Interim Doctrine for the Conduct of Tactical
Atomic Warfare") and *Landing Force Manual 24*
("Helicopter Operations"). These two documents
gave wide circulation to the most important specific elements of the new concept and made
possible the inclusion of new material in local
training programs. Operating forces were thus
enabled and encouraged to participate more actively in the development and refinement of new
ideas and to augment the efforts of the Advanced
Research Group, Marine Corps Test Unit Number 1, and the Marine Corps Development Center.

The Smith Board

The requirements for a medium helicopter,
which were intentionally omitted from the ARG's
Project IV, were taken up by a board which convened later at HQMC in January 1955. General
Shepherd had directed, on 23 December 1954, that
a board of general officers be appointed to study
the composition and functions of Marine aviation in order that a determination could be made
on the relative apportionment of personnel
strengths between ground and aviation organizations. Lieutenant General Oliver P. Smith was
appointed as the senior member. Major Generals
Robert O. Bare, Director of the Marine Corps
Education Center, Homer L. Litzenberg, Inspector
General of the Marine Corps, and Brigadier General John C. Munn, who was on duty at the time
with General Smith as Assistant Commanding
General, FMFLant, were the additional board
members.[38]

General Smith was fully familiar with the helicopter program as he was one of three generals
on the Commandant's special board which drew
up the original helicopter program in 1946. Between 1948 and 1950, General Smith had been
Assistant Commandant and Chief of Staff, HQMC.
He took command of the 1st Marine Division in
June 1950 and during the Korean War he led his

division in its epic breakout from the Chosin Reservoir. After his return to the U. S. in May 1951, he commanded the Marine Corps Base at Camp Pendleton and in July 1953 became Commanding General, FMFLant.

General Smith's board reported, in relation to the smaller helicopters, that it was concerned with the emphasis being placed on the large transport helicopters at the expense of the medium types, such as those being operated by the nine transport squadrons. The HR2S–1, the board said, was a large aircraft which would require a much larger, level landing area than the HRS. Open level areas capable of receiving a squadron of HR2Ss were comparatively rare in many types of terrain. They felt that one of the advantages of the medium size helicopter was its ability to land in almost any type of terrain. An organization with only large helicopter transports would not have the flexibility in the selection of landing zones that was enjoyed by the HRS squadrons. In stating its position in this matter, the board said, "we foresee a definite and continuing requirement for medium size helicopter transports (HRS, HUS, or equivalent) and believe that one squadron per wing is an absolute minimum." [39]

General Smith's board, in making its recommendation stated that "each Marine aircraft wing [should] contain one group of three squadrons of 20 large [HR2S] rotary-winged transports, and one squadron of 15 medium [HRS/HUS] rotary-wing transports." The total number of 180 HR2Ss was reaffirmed by the board as the appropriate number of heavy transport helicopters. [40]

On 24 May 1955, the Commandant officially announced his decisions on the recommendations made by the Smith Board. In matters relating to the helicopter program, General Shepherd not only approved the idea of adding medium helicopters to the aircraft wing organization, but increased the number from one medium squadron to two such units per aircraft group. By his action General Shepherd thereby approved for planning purposes the first additional expansion to the helicopter program since its initial massive enlargement in 1951. [41]

Although the May 24th letter officially published General Shepherd's position, the CNO had been apprised of his decision nine weeks earlier. On 1 April 1955 the Commandant requested that "the need for a vehicle to rapidly shuttle supplies to the forward elements, to execute tactical movements of small units, and to evacuate battle casualties points to the use of a utility helicopter such as the HUS." General Shepherd pointed out that

the problem had been closely studied by the Marine Corps and "that it had been determined that two squadrons of 15 HUS helicopters each will be required to support each Marine division, or a total of six squadrons and 90 HUS helicopters to support the three Marine divisions. I cannot overemphasize," the Commandant continued:

. . . the importance I attach to the helicopter for the employment by the Fleet Marine Force in the future. I strongly urge that every means be taken to increase the Marine Corps helicopter lift capability as rapidly as possible. The favorable prospects of additional production capacity becoming available at the Sikorsky's plant makes feasible the procurement of additional HUS helicopters in the Fiscal Year 1957. The requirements of the Marine Corps for the HR2S aircraft are in no way altered by this letter. A recent study of the entire Marine Corps aviation by a board of Marine Corps generals, is still under review, however, preliminary analysis indicated that the addition of 90 HUS helicopters . . . can be achieved within the present aircraft ceiling *assigned* to the Marine Corps. [42]

On 2 May the Division of Aviation had alerted the Vice Chief of Naval Operations as to the proposed aircraft group organization envisioned for accommodating the new utility helicopter squadron. "Relative to the commissioning of HMR units equipped with the HUSs," the memo stated, "it is intended to designate the new groups as MAG (HR) Light, and the squadrons as HMR (L). Upon transitioning from HRSs to HR2Ss, it is intended to redesignate the existing groups as MAG (HR) Medium, and the squadrons as HMR (M)." [43]

The three light helicopter groups, each composed of two HUS squadrons, a headquarters and maintenance squadron (H&MS), and a Marine air base squadron (MABS), were programmed for commissioning between 1 April 1956 and 1 July 1958. The three medium helicopter groups were similar to the existing MAG structure with each group having three HR2S squadrons, a H&MS, and a MABS. The dates set for commissioning ranged from November 1956 through August 1959. [44]

On 16 June 1955 the CNO replied to General Shepherd's previous requests for 180 HR2Ss and 90 HUSs. The CNO's answer presented a less desirable program than the Commandant had hoped to obtain. It approved an increase in the total number of helicopters, although on the other hand it made a compensatory reduction in the number of Marine fixed-wing aircraft. He approved an operating program for Fiscal Year 1959 of 180 HR2S helicopters and 45 HUSs. [45]

On 19 August the Commandant appealed to the

CNO requesting that the original number of 90 HUS helicopters be purchased and no reduction be made in the total number of fixed-wing aircraft. The CNO answered General Shepherd on 11 October 1955 declaring that his letter had not been received in sufficient time to have the request for the additional 45 HUSs included in the Fiscal Year 1959 budget. The CNO stated that "it is requested that the Commandant of the Marine Corps submit justification for the increase of forty-five (45) helicopters in the 1959 operating program. This should encompass the present helicopter program and any changes in numbers or organization that are contemplated." [46]

A Reduced HR2S Program

As correspondence relating to procurement of the HR2S continued between the Commandant and the CNO, the program underwent drastic revisions. The first action taken by the Commandant occurred on 19 October 1955 when he informed the CNO that information then available to him indicated that actually there were two versions of the HR2S being considered for initial production, and that both fell considerably short of meeting the specifications set forth by BuAer. Three problem areas in particular were of concern: the combat radius had been reduced two-thirds and the ability to hover out of ground effect * had decreased to approximately half the altitude specified. While the two foregoing problems were directly related to an excess in weight, the third difficulty involved the inability of the helicopter to automatically fold its blades. These shortcomings severely restricted its operational use.

In view of these problems, the Commandant recommended that the CNO restrict deliveries of the HR2S to 15 aircraft and that production and delivery of the HUS-1 be accelerated to the extent necessary to provide the Marine Corps with an

---

* Ground effect is encountered when a helicopter is hovering at a height above the ground of less than its rotor diameter.

operating inventory of 90 HUSs by the end of 1957. These two recommendations of General Shepherd were made to afford a longer interval of time for the development of the HR2S. In the interim, the HUS would partially fulfill the urgent lift requirements of the Marine Corps. [47]

Shortly thereafter, on 23 November 1955, the Commandant again modified his recommendations concerning the desired operating strengths for both the HR2S and the HUS. In his correspondence with the CNO, General Shepherd mentioned it had been discovered through informal discussions with BuAer and Sikorsky Aircraft, that two of the factors affecting the actions which he recommended the previous month had changed considerably. Mainly, these factors centered around the fact the turbine version of the HR2S had now been delayed two years and that the results of a recent weight reduction conference on the HR2S revealed it was possible to accomplish sufficient reductions in weight to provide improved performance of the first production models. In view of this, General Shepherd requested that the recently curtailed delivery rate of the HR2S be increased from 15 to 60 helicopters by the end of 1958. He also favored an increase in the numbers of HUSs, since both the Army and Navy versions of the S-58 (H-34 and HSS-1) were proving to be a highly satisfactory aircraft. [48] In fact, it had been reported to the Commandant that the Army was increasing the number of seats in its H-34s from 12 to 18 and that the Army aircraft was consistently carrying loads ranging from 3,750 pounds to 4,000 pounds with over an hour's fuel on board. [49] Realizing 60 HR2Ss was far from the original number of 180, General Shepherd desired that the CNO make a further compensatory acceleration in the HUS procurement which would provide for an operating strength of 140 helicopters by the end of 1958. [50]

In reply, a review of the procurement program for the HR2S was made by the CNO and presented to the Commandant on 12 April 1956. Tabulated in Figure 3 was the CNO's summary as it related to

Figure 3

FY 1957 Budget Cycle		Fiscal Year Procurement Programs					
Step	Date	1953	1954	1955	1956	1957	TOTAL
1	Jun 1955	7	12	43	36	30	158
2	Oct 1955	7	12	43	36	30	128
3	Oct 1955	7	12	43	0	0	62
4	Nov 1955	7	12	15	0	0	34

the Fiscal Year 1957 budget cycle and to overall procurement of the HR2S–1. It is interesting to note that the total number of HR2Ss had declined in a series of actions from a total of 158 aircraft in June 1955 to only 34 by November the same year. The drastic reduction was explained in the following manner:

> In June 1955 the FY 1957 HR2S–1 procurement submitted to OB&R [Office of Budget and Review] consisted of sixty (60)—[see Step 1.] OB&R review, and as agreed to by BuAer because of deficiencies . . . uncovered in the HR2S–1, resulted in reducing the quantity to thirty (30) [for FY 57]. This quantity (30) was submitted to OSD [Office of the Secretary of Defense] for review—Step 2. OSD review, again as a result of [the helicopter's] mechanical deficiencies, resulted in eliminating both the thirty (30) HR2S–1 in the FY 1957 program and the thirty-six (36) in the FY 1956 program—Step 3. In late October [the Marine Corps] requested that the number of HR2Ss . . . be held to a maximum of fifteen (15). . . . Accordingly, total procurement was further reduced—Step 4—and this procurement program, as thereby finalized, was incorporated in the President's budget. Subsequently, [in November, the Marine Corps requirement] for an operating strength of sixty (60) was received. However, it was impossible to incorporate this revision in the Budget at that late date.[51]

Also in the reply, signed by Vice Admiral Thomas S. Combs, Deputy Chief of Naval Operations, was the statement of views relative to future procurements of the HR2S–1. He indicated that present planning contemplated the purchase of 12 additional helicopters, thereby increasing the overall HR2S–1 total to 46. The last 12 were necessary in order to provide for sufficient FY 1958 "follow-on re-order lead time." It was felt that if and when the HR2S–1 demonstrated, by actual test, it could satisfactorily meet BuAer specifications, the pro-

curement program would be accelerated and would be designed to meet the Marine Corps operating requirements. However, Admiral Combs stressed, "until this circumstance occurs it is considered only prudent to restrict procurement to that level which will provide an adequate test quantity and a minimum production line which can be accelerated." It was pointed out that irrespective of procurement planning, Marine Corps requirements would never be met until the HR2S–1 actually proved its capability to perform its designed mission. In conclusion Admiral Combs said, "It is therefore considered that present HR2S–1 procurement is sound as present conditions permit. The CNO is fully aware of the Marine Corps' need for the HR2S type helicopter and will take action to meet this need as soon as possible."[52]

Admiral Combs' letter firmly placed the number of HR2Ss at approximately one-fourth of the desired 180. Disappointing as it was, the Marine Corps' overall helicopter program was far from bankrupt. This turn of events did, however, establish a trend in which the Marine Corps began to adopt the light, but more trouble-free, helicopter as its main assault transport. The prospects of obtaining the smaller HUS–1 appeared to be brighter at this time due to the developmental problems in the HR2S program and the fact the HUS was a much less expensive aircraft. Resistance to the reduction in quantity of the HR2S was only a natural reaction since Marine Corps planning for the execution of its new concept was based on using the larger helicopters as the main assault transport. Although the numbing agent to this stinging blow had been provided earlier in the year in the form of CNO approval for procurement of nearly 140 HUSs, it did, nevertheless, subsequently require the reorientation of the entire helicopter program.

CHAPTER 6

A PERIOD OF REEVALUATION—A MODERATE CAPABILITY

Following the CNO's action in 1956 limiting the procurement of the HR2S helicopters, the Marine Corps made three studies which significantly influenced the course of the entire helicopter program. The first study was prepared by the G–3 Division, HQMC. Completed in May 1956, it dealt with the employment of helicopters within the Fleet Marine Force during the years of 1956 to 1960. The G–3 report was followed by the publication of the Marine Corps Aviation Program for the Fiscal Years 1957 to 1962. The third report, that of the Hogaboom Board, was completed in 1957 and addressed the organization of the FMF. Although it affected the ground FMF to a larger degree than FMF aviation, it was the most detailed report of the three pertaining to the overall Marine aviation structure.

HQMC G–3 Study Number 3—1956

G–3 Study Number 3, a Memorandum for the Commandant, was completed in late April 1956 and approved by the Assistant Commandant for Air, Lieutenant General Vernon M. Megee, on 8 May. The report, "Employment of Helicopters Within the FMF During the Period of 1956 to 1960," concentrated on the distribution of all Marine Corps tactical helicopter squadrons. The primary point addressed was the question of whether the majority of helicopters would be assigned to lift one division to attain a maximum

divisional lift capability, or whether they would be apportioned among each of the three divisions.

As a guideline to estimating the future availability of helicopters by type and proposed squadron organization for the period under study, the G–3 study group used a series of charts prepared by the Division of Aviation. The DivAvn helicopter estimates included the years 1956 through 1960 and reflected a gradual growth from 9 to 15 helicopter squadrons. The G–3 Study projected the anticipated growth rate of the helicopter force over the five-year period as presented in Figure 4. It was a complete reversal from the Smith Board and prior boards' reports as the total number of HR2Ss was reduced from 180 to only 45— three squadrons of 15 aircraft each. The existing nine HRS squadrons would continue to operate with the HRS and later change to the HUS when it became operational. Three additional HUS units were to be formed later. This study reflected for the first time the fact that the Navy budget had allowed for only 45 HR2Ss to be constructed by the end of 1960 and that the additional HUSs would most likely have to compensate for the lost troop lift capability of the HR2S.[1]

In view of the five-year projection, the group made recommendations ranging from the deployment of helicopter squadrons to the desired size of assault force which should be lifted simultaneously. In relation to the assault force, the study group stated that the BLT organizational structure possessed the minimal requirements for communi-

Figure 4

	Existing					
	1956	1957	1958	1959	1960	1961
Squadrons By Type Helicopter	9 HRS	7 HRS 2 HUS 1 HR2S	5 HRS 4 HUS 2 HR2S	5 HRS 6 HUS 2 HR2S	4 HRS 8 HUS 3 HR2S	3 HRS 9 HUS 3 HR2S
Total Squadrons	9	10	11	13	15	15
Total Light Helicopter	180	180	180	220	240	240
Total Medium Helicopter	0	15	30	30	45	45
Grand Total Helicopter	180	185	210	250	285	285

cations, control, and support needed to execute a combat helicopter assault and sustain operations for a limited time. A regiment, it felt, or a comparable organization, would probably be better organized, staffed, and equipped for the mission, but a corresponding large increase in helicopters, would be required. Although the final number of aircraft by number and type would evolve as the concept developed, the planners stressed that interim specific figures had to be determined. These would facilitate development of the concept and provide the aviation establishment with guidance in relation to helicopter deployment and HMR squadron distribution. In this connection, the group's recommendation was that initially each Marine division should provide for a minimum simultaneous (one-wave) lift of assault elements of one BLT consisting of approximately 500 troops, i.e., two rifle companies and a command group. A combat radius of 25 miles was established as the minimum capability required to implement the vertical lift concept. This represented a drastically reduced initial assault force from the four BLT one-wave assault recommended three years earlier in ARG's Project IV. It should be pointed out that while the ARG was trying to helicopter-land the assault elements of a division-wing team, the G–3 study was interested in landing the minimum effective number of troops towards the eventual goal of lifting one and one-half divisions.[2] *

The study group's planning for FMF helicopter employment was reflected in two recommendations, both of which tended to support the existing program. The group endorsed the contention of the Smith Board that the Marine Corps needed different types, or families of helicopters. Secondly, the group believed that helicopter procurement programs for 1956 through 1960 would provide a significant increase in helicopter availability for the FMF to the extent that a substantial helicopter assault capability could be achieved. The current distribution policy of providing one HR MAG to support one division was concurred in with the proviso that the initial division helicopter assault capability should be achieved through selective deployment of newly procured helicopters rather than redistribution of the presently deployed helicopters. The concept behind the study group's

recommendation was that as the Marine Corps received its new helicopters during the 1956–1960 period, they would be used to expand gradually one MAG at a time until each reached the capability to provide the single-wave BLT lift. Priority for helicopter assignment was given to the helicopter MAG supporting the 1st Division. Afterwards, the MAGs supporting the 2d and 3d Divisions would be built up to meet the minimum assault capability.[4]

General Randolph McC. Pate, Commandant since January 1956, took action on the G–3 Study in the form of letters to CG FMFPac and CG FMFLant on 4 September 1956. In addition to reiterating the essential elements of the study, the Commandant told his two FMF commanders that the new concept ultimately required sufficient helicopters to support, in combat and training operations, all Marine divisions and aircraft wings available for such operations. "This capability," he said, "will not be achieved until after 1960, but the attainment of lesser lift capabilities is an essential intermediate objective." The reason for limiting the combat radius for helicopter assaults to 25 or 35 miles, General Pate explained, was to enable Marine Corps planners to compute the future required number of helicopters. His final

General Randolph McC. Pate, 21st Commandant (Marine Corps Photo A402599).

---

* General Shepherd had indicated in 1955 when commenting on the recommendations of the Smith Board that in relation to the minimum helicopter lift that "[I] approve all recommendations except the phrase 'in order that Marine Corps Aviation, as a whole, have the capacity of lifting one division.' I consider that the Marine Corps must achieve a helicopter capability sufficient to lift 1½ divisions at the earliest possible time."[3]

statement directed that both FMFs provide for early attainment of a proficient, though limited, helicopter assault capability for lifting one BLT in each division.[5]

Marine Corps Aviation Five-Year Program 1957–1962

In early 1956, before the results of the G–3 study were out, General Pate had forwarded to the CNO, Admiral Burke, a basic Marine Corps aviation objective plan for pre-mobilization for each Fiscal Year 1956 through 1961. It represented the Marine Corps' requirements for the support of three divisions in combat short of general war. The plan was based upon information available at the time and reflected the requirements for attainment of the objectives to support the Commandant's new concept.

Admiral Burke replied to General Pate in May 1956 stating he favored the plan, however, based upon the projected budgetary and personnel limitations which had been imposed upon the Navy, approval of General Pate's Five-Year Plan could not be given without having adverse effect on other essential functions of the Navy. The CNO enclosed a proposed force operating level for Marine aviation for General Pate's consideration. The Commandant then directed that a comprehensive review be made of the original plan in order to develop a program that would provide for a reasonable chance of approval by the CNO. The fundamental guidance was the projected budgetary and personnel limitations which were expected to be imposed upon the Navy and Marine Corps for the foreseeable future. The main consideration in developing a revised program was that the currently authorized Marine Corps operating level of 1,424 aircraft would remain through the period. An increase in the number of aircraft could not be accommodated and any changes reflecting new helicopter requirements would have to be accom-

panied by a compensatory reduction in fixed-wing aircraft. This was necessary in order to maintain procurement and operating costs at approximately a constant level through the next five years.[6]

As the revised plan was being developed, it was obvious that the ultimate objective of the new concept could not be achieved, although a limited vertical assault capability appeared attainable by the end of Fiscal Year 1962. The expansion of the helicopter program during the five-year period provided for an operating inventory of 180 HUS, or light helicopters. The activation of new units would take place as the aircraft became available. It was anticipated that the Marine helicopter aviation force, as depicted in Figure 5, would have nine squadrons of 20 HRS/HUSs each and six squadrons of 15 HR2Ss each by the end of the period. The build-up to the maximum number of HR2S helicopters was to be dependent upon improved performance of the helicopter and therefore considered to be highly subject to change.[7]

The total number of helicopter squadrons in the helicopter program remained at 15 in both the G–3 Study and DivAvn's Five-Year Plan. The significant difference was that the five-year plan proposed the formation of six HR2S squadrons instead of three, and retained the nine HRS/HUS squadrons at their existing level. The more optimistic Five-Year Plan gave the CNO an estimate of what the Marine Corps desired, whereas the G–3 Study was a memorandum for General Pate and reflected a realistic projection of the program's growth in consonance with the approved budget.

Another logical planning change occurred after the CNO reduced the procurement of the HR2S. This development reflected the reversal of designations of the light (L) and medium (M) aircraft groups. In view of the small "buy" of medium helicopters, new plans were made to assign the HR2Ss to the two-squadron utility (L) groups and to redesignate them as MAG (HR(M)) and to retain the three HRS/HUS groups as light. This

Figure 5

	FY '57	'58	'59	'60	'61	'62	Total Aircraft
No. of HMR(L)s	9	9	10	9	9	9	
A/C per Sqdn	20	20	20	20	20	20	180
No. of HMR(M)s	1	2	3	6	6	6	
A/C per Sqdn	15	15	15	15	15	15	90
No. of VMOs	3	3	3	3	3	3	
A/C per Sqdn	24	21	18	18	18	18	54

was a completely opposite plan from the one proposed by the Smith Board. Essentially then, according to the revised Five-Year Plan, each Marine aircraft wing would still retain two helicopter groups within its structure with the MAG (HR(M)) having two HR2S squadrons of 15 planes each and three 20-plane light squadrons in the MAG (HR(L)). Another decision also rendered during this period placed the VMO squadrons in the light helicopter group structure. Their complement of aircraft was to be eventually reduced from 12 fixed-wing and 12 helicopters to only nine of each type.

The Hogaboom Board of 1956

In order for the Marine Corps to achieve its new concept as rapidly as possible, while still preserving its past and present capabilities, it had to undertake a vast reorganization of its forces. It had kept the organization of the FMF under constant review with the latest change made in 1955 by the Smith Board which undertook an examination of the entire aviation structure. Later on 4 June 1956, the Commandant appointed Major General Robert E. Hogaboom as president of a 16-man board* to conduct a thorough and comprehensive study of the entire FMF, including aviation, with the purpose of making recommendations for the optimum organization, composition, and equipment of the FMF. The results of this organization and composition study were to set the pattern for all major organizational changes within the FMF during the remaining part of the decade.

General Hogaboom's permanent assignment was Deputy Chief of Staff (Plans), HQMC, a post he had held since his return from Korea in 1955. In 1949 he had attended the National War College, and from 1951 to 1952 he had been the Marine

---

* A total of 16 officers was appointed to the 1956 FMF Organiation and Composition Board. Those named in addition to the president, Major General Robert E. Hogaboom, were:

BGen Ronald D. Salmon (Relieved on 16Jul56)
BGen Edward C. Dyer (Joined on 16Jul56)
Col Bruce T. Hemphill
Col Frederick P. Henderson
Col Odell M. Conoley
Col Herbert H. Williamson
Col Cliff Atkinson, Jr.
Col Henry H. Crockett
Col David W. Stonecliffe
Col Lewis W. Walt
Col William R. Campbell
Col Norman J. Anderson
Col Keith B. McCutcheon
Col Allan Sutter
Col William K. Jones
Maj Frank R. Young (Recorder)

Corps liaison officer in the office of the CNO. In July 1952 General Hogaboom became the assistant commander of the 2d Marine Division, and later, during 1954 and 1955, he served in Korea as assistant commander and later as commanding general of the 1st Marine Division.

General Pate provided General Hogaboom's board with a six-paragraph letter of concepts and criteria. In relation to the helicopter, he explained that the helicopter would become the principal means of achieving tactical surprise and flexibility. He mentioned that surface landing craft and land vehicles would continue to be the principal means of mobility at the objective until sufficient helicopters of improved capabilities were available to permit the landing, tactical maneuver, and logistical support of all assault elements of a Marine division. It was considered that as the helicopter capability increased, the need for surface landing craft and land vehicles would decrease.[8]

The primary purpose of the Hogaboom Board was to determine what the FMF needed to meet the initial requirements for achieving the new concept for amphibious warfare, beginning with Fiscal Year 1958. Additionally, the study was to determine the phase objectives of the FMF in organization and composition for the foreseeable future.[9]

In preparing its study, the board interviewed and gave careful consideration to a large body of Marine officers. The staffs of the Education Center, Development Center, Marine Corps Test Unit Number 1, and HQMC were the source of many highly competent and experienced officers who appeared before the board. Also the board conducted a thorough and comprehensive examination into the tactical concepts of the FMF and took due cognizance of such documents as *LFB-2* (Interim Doctrine for the Conduct of Tactical Atomic Warfare) and *LFM-24* (Helicopter Operations).

In arriving at its conclusions, General Hogaboom's board had relatively little difficulty in dealing with its recommendations for equipment and armament for Fiscal Year 1958. In many cases the members felt there was little choice in this matter as they had to take that which was currently developed and available. The basic and most difficult problem then was to find the soundest possible balance of units and equipment for the FMF organization. With respect to the phased objectives, the board projected itself as far into the future as research and development reasonably would allow.[10]

The board then proceeded in a detailed examination of the "current organizations, the organizational thinking, and in the thinking of the Marine Corps in general." This was considered necessary in order to isolate those parts of the organizational structure which were incompatible with the essential requirements of the helicopter assault concept. It very soon became apparent to the board that some of the prevailing thoughts as to how these requirements were to be met were far from conclusive, and, in some cases, erroneous.[11] The board stated:

> An area which the board believes particularly requires clarification is the subject of just how the landing force as a whole is to be projected onto the hostile shore. There appears to be a considerable body of opinion in the Marine Corps today which holds that in the foreseeable future all movement from ship-to-shore will be by helicopter. Thus the "all helicopter assault" concept has somehow become the "all helicopter concept." This idea the board believes to be invalid and should be corrected immediately. It leads among other things to requirements being stated specifying helicopter transportability for all the arms and equipment of the Fleet Marine Force. This requirement is in fact written into the current issue of the Equipment Development Policy and Guide as an ultimate goal.
>
> The board believes that this line of thinking has perhaps obscured the continuing importance of crossing the beach operations in our modern concept. We believe that for the foreseeable future a substantial portion of the men and materiel required in effecting a lodgement on a hostile shore must still cross the beach in a "conventional" fashion. This is not in our opinion inconsistent with the "all helicopter assault" concept, or with the requirement for the projection of seapower ashore without the necessity of direct assault on the shoreline. Reduced to its simplest terms the board visualizes an operation wherein the flexibility of the helicopter-borne assault forces would be exploited to uncover and secure the beaches and to seize critical areas which will be required to enable us to phase in the additional means to maintain the momentum of the assault and secure the objective area.
>
> The board considers that helicopters will be employed initially to displace the assault elements of the landing force from ships at sea to attack positions ashore from which they can seize the critical terrain features.
>
> In subsequent operations ashore helicopters will be employed to maneuver disengaged units into attack positions from which they can launch an attack against critical objectives at a decisive time.[12]

In the end, the reorganizational changes recommended by the board resulted in a reduction of about 2,000 personnel in each division. A few of the more significant changes in the organization of the Marine division, although not accounting for the major reductions, may be summarized as:

1. Addition of a fourth rifle company in the infantry battalion.

2. The division tank battalion transferred to Force Troops.

3. Expansion of the division reconnaisance company into a reconnaissance battalion.

4. Addition of an antitank battalion equipped with 45 ONTOS.

Changes were also made in the Force Troop structure which affected the areas of command and communication, artillery, antiaircraft, tanks, amphibian units, and reconnaissance.[13]

In reviewing the overall structure of FMF aviation, an assumption was made that short of a general war, not more than two Marine divisions and two Marine aircraft wings would be deployed. Based upon this assumption, the board determined that the best functional balance attainable within the authorized 27 attack and interceptor squadrons was to set the ratio at 9 fighter, 6 all-weather fighter, and 12 attack squadrons. It was also determined that the wing, being primarily a task organization rather than a T/O organization such as the division, could not be categorically structured except in functional groups. The aircraft wing had to be organized, the board felt, to perform the essential air support tasks in the overall missions assigned. As shown in Figure 6 the board presented a typical Marine aircraft wing, recognizing that a structure identical in all respects to the one presented would be the exception rather than the rule.[14]

Although there were no substantial changes made in the organization or composition of the nine fixed-wing aircraft groups, it was suggested that the light helicopter group structure be modified to fulfill the transportation requirements visualized by the concept for employment of the division's reconnaissance battalion. In addition, it was considered necessary that helicopter crews be intimately familiar with the tactics and techniques of the reconnaissance battalion and be available to the battalion for training and combat operations. More specifically, operational concepts for the reconnaissance battalion envisioned continued requirements for helicopters to perform missions of observation, utility, and transportation. To accomplish this, one squadron in each MAG (HR(L)) was to be designated as a "Helicopter Reconnaissance Squadron," HMR(C), (C-Composite) and assigned an aircraft complement of 12 HRSs and the 12 HOKs. The HOKs were to be transferred from the VMO squadron. The other two HMRs within the group would retain their designation but would have the number of aircraft increased from 20 to 24. This reorganization, as shown in Figure 7 was made to insure vigor-

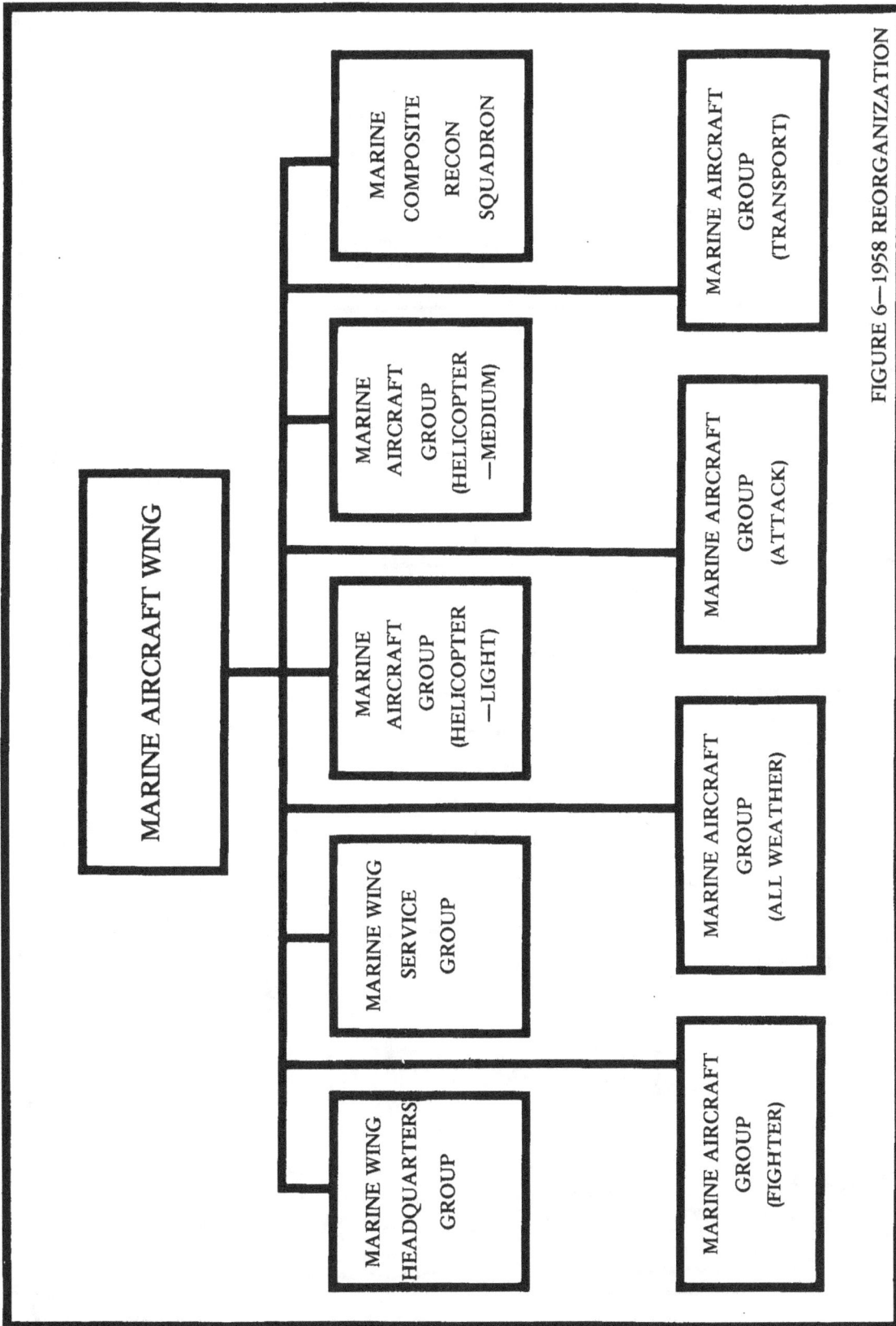

FIGURE 6—1958 REORGANIZATION

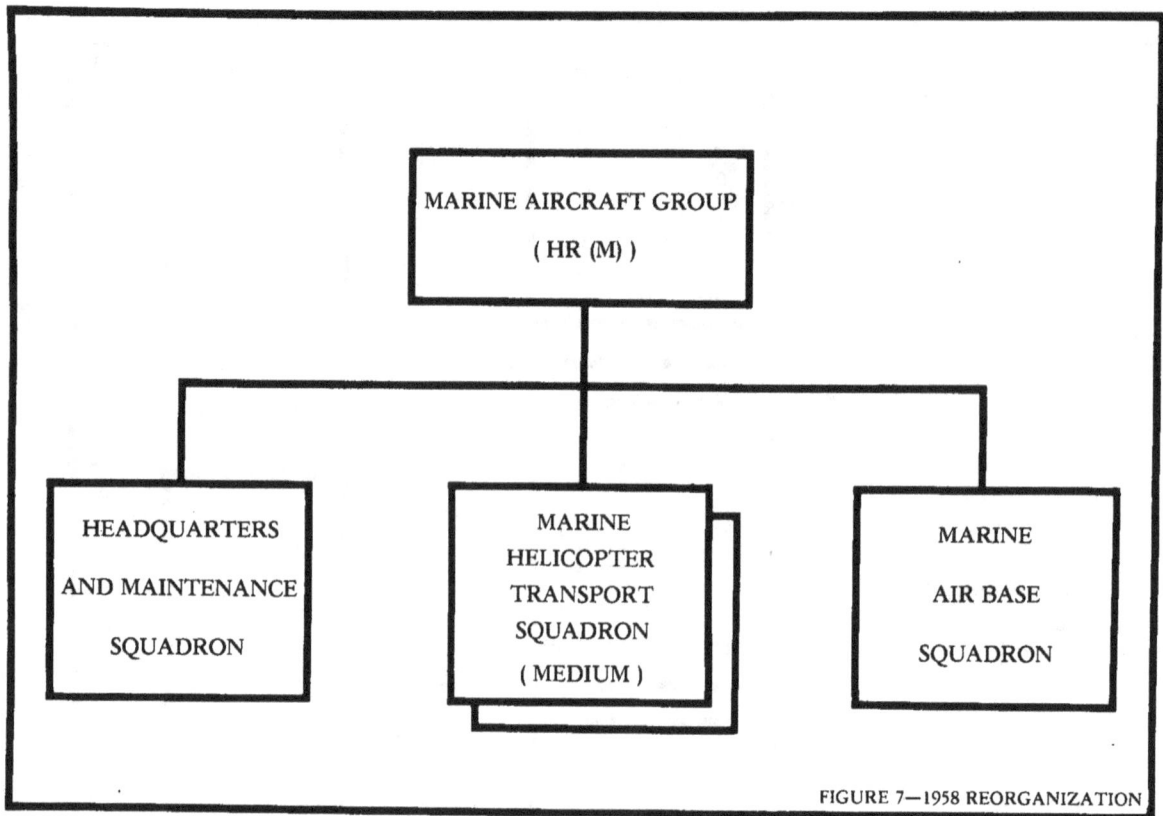

FIGURE 7—1958 REORGANIZATION

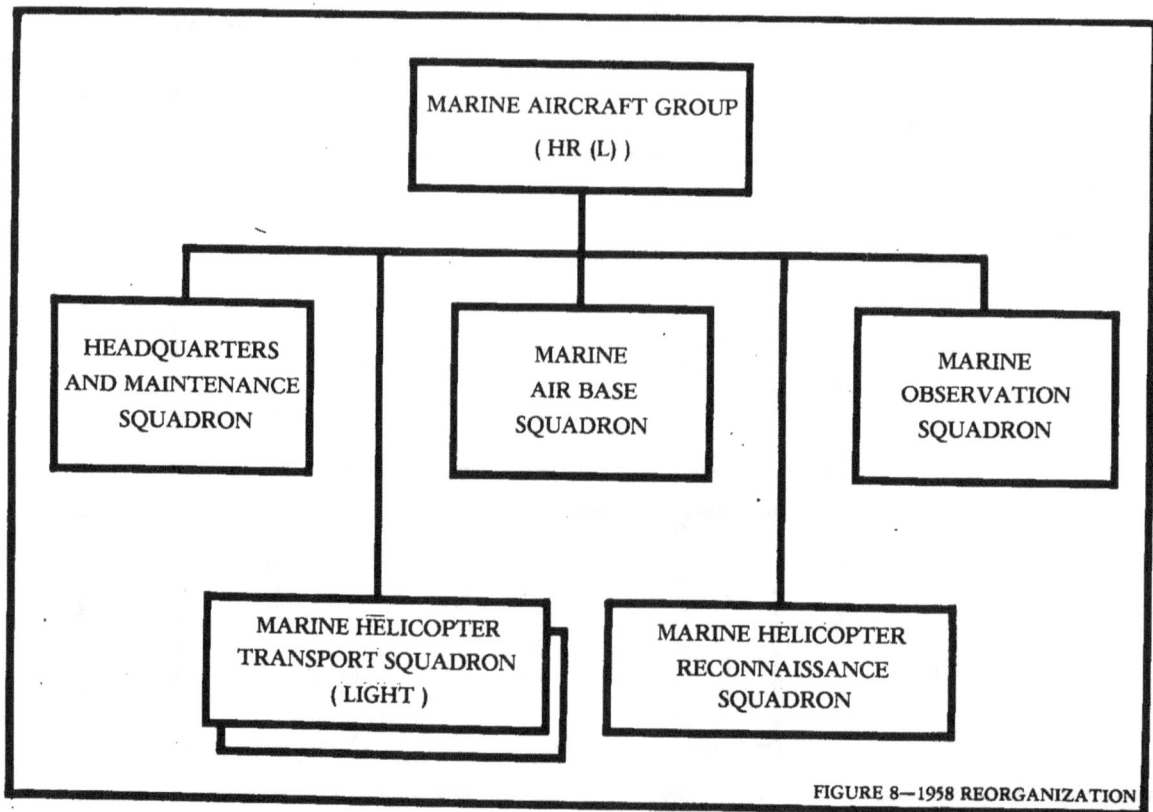

FIGURE 8—1958 REORGANIZATION

ous development of the reconnaissance aspect for this type of air support. As for the VMO squadrons, they had been assigned earlier in the year to the MAG (HR(L)) as a supported unit, one squadron to each group. The board established the VMO complement at 12 fixed-wing aircraft. The structure of the two-squadron medium MAGs in Figure 8 were not changed by the organization and composition board.[15]

The board declared that reorganization of the ground and aviation units was a practical first phase objective in light of existing equipment and tactical concepts under which the Marine Corps had to operate. It was further decided that certain areas needed immediate emphasis in order to increase the Marine Corps' capability to operate under the modern concept. Among those seen as pertaining to the helicopter were the need for additional helicopters of improved performance, more adequate and efficient amphibious shipping with emphasis on the LPH type, and assault weapons and equipment which would be helicopter transportable—particularly the antitank and close support weapons. The board emphasized the need for a gradual reduction and simplification in the number of different types of all weapons and equipment, in addition to maintaining continued emphasis on decreasing the weight and bulk of FMF equipment. This requirement paralleled the central theme of the study which was to make the entire assault force helicopter-transportable and the division all air-transportable.

From a consideration of the several factors which would influence the speed and extent of attaining a full capability to operate under the modern concept, the board recommended, in relation to the helicopter program, that the following objectives be established:

1. Phase I; 1957–1958
   a. The phasing in of sufficient helicopters of improved performance to attain a capability to land and support one BLT in each Marine division.
2. Phase II; 1958–1961
   a. The phasing in of sufficient additional helicopters of improved performance to attain a capability to land and support one RLT in each Marine division.
   b. The attainment of three additional LPH ships in the amphibious forces of the fleet.
3. Phase III, 1961–1965
   a. The improvement of the helicopter lift capability developed during Phase II.
   b. The attainment of seven additional LPH ships in the amphibious force of the fleet.[16]

As shown in Figure 9, the board recommended a graduated expansion of both the light and medium MAGs to a structure of 15 helicopter squadrons. The board failed to mention, however, the flying distance involved in the execution of the lift and whether or not the lifting of the assault elements of the BLT during the Phase I period, and the RLT in Phase II, was to be performed in one simultaneous lift. The plan closely resembled the Division of Aviation's schedule in the Aviation Five-Year Plan published earlier in July. Additionally, the phased build-up suggested a gradual increase in the number of LPH type ships to a maximum of 12; six on each coast.[17]

General Hogaboom's board completed its report and made a presentation to the Commandant and his staff late in December with the written report distributed on 7 January 1957. General Pate's

Figure 9

	FY58		FY59		FY60		FY61		FY62	
	No. Units	No. A/C	No. Units	No. A/C	No. Units	No. A/C	No. Units	No. A/C	No. Units	No. A/C
MAG (HR-L)	3	—	3	—	3	—	3	—	3	—
H&MS	3	6	3	6	3	9	3	11	3	11
MABS	3	—	3	—	3	—	3	—	3	—
HMR (L) (24 a/c)	6	144	7	164 *	6	144	6	144	6	144
HMR (c) (24 a/c)	3	72	3	72	3	72	3	72	3	72
VMO	3	36	3	36	3	36	3	36	3	36
MAG (HR-M)	1	—	1	—	2	—	3	—	3	—
H&MS	1	3	1	3	2	4	3	6	3	6
MABS	1	—	1	—	2	—	3	—	3	—
HMR (M) (15 a/c)	2	30	3	45	6	90	6	90	6	90

* One squadron (20 a/c) HMR(L).

immediate action subjected the newly proposed structure to field testing which was completed by 30 June. The recommendations from the various FMF testing units were consolidated with comments from the HQMC staff sections into one package which the Commandant subsequently reviewed and approved for implementation. The provisional "M" series of tables of organization (T/O) and Tables of Equipment (T/E) were also prepared and sent to all FMF organizations and by September 1958 all elements of the FMF had been reorganized. General Pate, reflecting back on the reorganization at the General Officers' Conference in 1959, said:

> The idea of the helicopter-borne assault first appeared in 1946. It was subjected to a quite thorough theoretical examination in the late 40s and early 50s. By 1956 we knew the concept was valid. Our responsibility, then, was to put it to work—to develop the ability for applying the theory to practical situations . . . [Reorganization of the FMF] was a long step forward, and an important one. Taking it broke a log jam of resistance based on the traditions of earlier days. I am not unmindful of the trauma the change visited upon some of our people—but it was something that had to be done.[18]

Forced Reduction

While the FMF was being reorganized, the entire Marine Corps had to undergo a severe reduction in personnel and aircraft due to drastic military-wide budget cuts. On 12 August 1957, the Secretary of the Navy directed that certain force level reductions be made in both the Navy and Marine Corps during the forthcoming Fiscal Years 1958 and 1959. As an indication of the magnitude of this reduction, the total officer and enlisted strength had to drop from over 200,000 on 30 June 1957 to approximately 175,000 by midyear 1959 and was to continue near the lower level until 1962.

Working with the new guidance provided by the Secretary of the Navy, the Division of Aviation revised its Five-Year Plan. The revision was published on 23 September 1957 as the Marine Corps Aviation Program Changes for Fiscal Years 1958 to 1962. One of the guidelines used in achieving the necessary changes was that no alterations would be made which might decrease the progress toward the goal of vertical envelopment. This was a difficult task as the total number of Marine aircraft had to be reduced from 1,425 to approximately 1,200 by 1 July 1959, approximately a 15 percent loss, and still further to about 1,000 by

mid-1962, for a total 30 percent loss.* Three Marine aircraft wings were kept in force; however, the aircraft complement of some units was, by necessity, lowered. In addition, some units were completely eliminated and those which remained were manned at approximately 80 percent of their T/O strength. The basic structure of Marine aviation at full T/O strength as defined by the Hogaboom Board and approved by the Commandant was based on an operating program of 1,424 aircraft.[19]

Despite the austerity move, the existing helicopter structure fared considerably well, although some of the expansion called for in the Five-Year Plan had been cancelled. The medium helicopter squadrons were placed within the MAG "light" structure, one medium unit to each MAG. This arrangement eliminated the need for the establishment of the three two-squadron medium groups. In all, the greatest loss suffered by the helicopter program occurred in the medium helicopter groups as only sufficient funds remained available for commissioning three of the programmed six medium squadrons.[20]

In addition to the budget cuts, mechanical troubles still plagued the HR2S, thereby justifying the reduction in numbers from 90 to 60—three squadrons of 20 each. Another factor influencing the reduction of HR2Ss was that a new type aircraft, a VTOL (non-helicopter), appeared to be a desirable future replacement. To compensate for the loss of the fourth, fifth, and sixth medium squadrons, the number of HUSs were adjusted upward from the previous total of 180 to 210, with the latter figure to be reached by 1959 and maintained through 1962.** [21]

The reduction of the budget not only affected personnel and aircraft programs but also hampered the Navy's shipbuilding schedule. Of major concern to the Marine Corps was the serious shortage of amphibious shipping, and, in particular, the lack of helicopter aircraft carriers. This had been

---

*As a comparison the Navy suffered a 25 percent loss of its operating aircraft through the forced reduction move.

**There were many suggestions on how to distribute the last 30 aircraft of the 210 light helicopters. DivAvn's revised program, 1959–1962, indicated a structure of six light squadrons of 24 each and three composite squadrons of 12 each; making a total of 180. Obviously, the increase of 30 light helicopters was to compensate equally for the difference in the reduced number of medium helicopters (90 to 60). Although two additional light squadrons were subsequently formed during the period, one in 1959 and the other in 1962, which absorbed the extra 30 helicopters, they were apparently omitted altogether from this five-year plan.

a continuing area of concern since the end of the Korean War and with the recent congressional budget reduction, the existing shortage of money for shipbuilding purposes was compounded.

Tightening of the fiscal purse strings did not mean that the Marine Corps was without a helicopter aircraft carrier. The first results of the Commandant's request for LPHs in early 1953 were realized on 20 July 1956 when the USS *Thetis Bay* (CVE–90) was commissioned after undergoing a conversion in the San Francisco Naval Shipyard. Redesignated as the CVHA–1 (Assault Helicopter Aircraft Carrier), the *Thetis Bay* was designed to afford the Marine Corps the opportunity to evaluate the vertical assault concept. Although it was not intended that the converted ship be the prototype for future LPH (CVE) conversions, it did provide the Marine Corps with the opportunity to evaluate some features desirable in new construction.[22] Later reclassified in 1959 to LPH–6, the CVHA–1 had an overall length of 512 feet, a beam of 108 feet, a displacement of 11,000 tons full load, and a maximum speed of 19½ knots. Approximately 1,000 combat troops and 20 HRS helicopters could be accommodated.[23]

The Fiscal Year 1955 budget called for two such conversions, but due to monetary shortage the second CVHA, the USS *Block Island* (CVE–106), was not started until January 1958. The conversion of the *Block Island* was never completed though, mainly as the result of an austerity move. By late 1958, the Marine Corps had gained valuable operational experience with the *Thetis Bay* and the Commandant had determined that the best solution for meeting assault helicopter aircraft carrier requirements was through new construction or by modifying other type World War II carriers. The *Block Island* was classified as the LPH–1 on 22 December 1957 although it was never used as an amphibious assault ship.

Growth and Changes Under Austere Conditions, 1956–1962

The structure of the helicopter groups remained constant from 1952 until the latter half of 1956 when changes began to appear. Some of these changes were the transfer of VMO–1 and –6 to MAG (HR(L))–16 and –36, respectively. Previously they had been attached to a Marine Wing Headquarters Group (MWHG).* Another change implemented during 1956 was the addition of the designator "light" to the transport groups and squadrons titles as envisioned in the program plans. Most of the redesignations were effective on 31 December 1956, since a distinction was now necessary as the Commandant desired to commission the first HR2S squadron in January 1957 under the "medium" designation.** [24] [25]

Following the title changes in December 1956, the Marine Corps began forming its first medium helicopter squadrons. In January 1957, HMR(M)–461, under the command of Lieutenant Colonel Griffith B. Doyle, was commissioned at MCAF, New River. The new squadron received the Marine Corps' most sought after helicopter, the HR2S–1, during March.*** [26] On the west coast, in November of the same year, HMR (M)–462 was formed within MAG (HR(L))–36 with Lieutenant Colonel Alton W. McCully as the commanding officer. The following year the third medium squadron, HMR(M)–463, was commissioned in September in MAG (HR(L))–16 under Major Kenneth L. Moos. The squadron was short lived, however, due to the scarcity of HR2Ss, and nine months later it was deactivated.[27]

The replacement helicopter for the HRS was received shortly before the HR2S. In February 1957, both HMR(L)–261 and –363 began exchanging their HRSs for the larger and faster HUS–1. Since the HUS–1 was essentially the same aircraft as the Navy's HSS–1 except for the cabin's interior arrangement, flight evaluation at Patuxent River was waived, thereby expediting its availability to the operating units. During 1957, the extent of modernization of the helicopter program can be seen by comparing its composition on 1 January 1957, in Figure 10, with that of 30 December 1957.[28]

---

* VMO–2 had previously been attached to MAG (HR(L)–16.

** In spite of the forced reduction in 1957, the existing three HMR MAGs retained their "light" designation even though there were no medium groups commissioned. In 1959, however, the MAG (HR) designation was changed again to Marine Aircraft Group (MAG), dropping the "Helicopter Transport" (HR) portion of its title.

*** Although the first HR2S had been accepted in April 1956, it had been used for test purposes at the Naval Air Test Center, Patuxent River, Maryland. Also HMX–1 had been operating the HR2S on a similar research and development basis during the same year. The March 1957 date represented its initial assignment to a tactical squadron.

Figure 10

Type Aircraft	1957 Helicopter Totals and Locations						
	FMFPac		FMFLant		HMX–1		Total
	Jan–Dec		Jan–Dec		Jan–Dec		Jan–Dec
HR2S	0	0	0	12	2	2	2	14
HUS	0	22	0	21	0	6	0	49
HRS	83	79	47	44	10	8	140	131
HOK	22	20	3	18	3	3	28	41

Implementation of the Hogaboom Board Recommendations

In June 1958, as the result of the Hogaboom Board recommendations and the subsequent implementation of the "M" Series T/O, the helicopter group structure underwent the recommended modification. The major alterations involved the reassignment of aircraft within the group. It reduced VMO to 12 light fixed-wing observation models and created a composite squadron of 12 HOKs and 12 HRSs. The trading of aircraft did not involve the creation of a new unit within the group, only the redesignation of one HMR(L) to Marine Helicopter Reconnaissance Squadron (HMR(C)). The remaining two light units had their helicopter strength increased from 20 to 24 aircraft each. The change of aircraft between units was made in MAG(HR(L))–26 and –36 involving HMR–263 and –363, leaving the Oppama, Japan-based MAG(HR(L))–16 under an all light HMR arrangement.* [29]

The composite structure was tested in MAG–26 for slightly less than 10 months. The New River helicopter group was then under the command of Colonel Keith B. McCutcheon, an officer who had been active in the helicopter program for many years and who had served as recorder to the Smith Board.

Colonel McCutcheon had received a Master of Science degree in aeronautical engineering from the Massachusetts Institute of Technology in 1944 as a lieutenant colonel, and later participated in air operations with MAG–24 at Bougainville, Luzon, and Mindanao. In World War II he earned the Distinguished Flying Cross and six Air Medals in the Solomons, New Guinea, and Philippine Islands combat areas. After the war, Colonel McCutcheon instructed in the Aviation Section, Marine Corps Schools, and from 1946 to 1949 served in the Pilotless Aircraft Division of BuAer.

In 1950 he was ordered to Quantico where he assumed command of HMX–1. From December 1951 to October 1952 he commanded HMR–161 in Korea. Leaving the Korean area, and after a two year tour in Europe, he again returned to Quantico in 1954 to assume the duties as Chief, Air Section, Marine Corps Equipment Board. Then in June 1957, Colonel McCutcheon moved to Jacksonville, North Carolina where he assumed command of MAG–26.

The group commander gave his appraisal to the Commandant concerning the problem of operating under the new "M" Series T/O. "The greatest single deficiency," Colonel McCutcheon stated, "occurs at the group level. This is the loss of

Major General Keith B. McCutcheon, one of the leaders of the Marine helicopter program (Marine Corps Photo A413009).

* Since there were only two HMR(L)s in MAG–16, no redesignation to HMR(C) was made. The third squadron (HMR(C)–161) was Hawaii-based under MAG–13.

flexibility in carrying out assigned missions due to the reduction of light transport squadrons from three to two." He made four recommendations to General Pate:

1. Disband the HMR(C) squadron.
2. Reform three HMR(L) squadrons with 20 aircraft each.
3. Reform VMO with 12 HOKs and 12 OEs.
4. Assign HUS helicopters to all light transport squadrons as expeditiously as possible.[30]

On 31 July 1959, General Pate replied to McCutcheon's recommendations. Although no definite decision was rendered, the Commandant assured the group commander that the contents of his letter were under study along with other aviation program changes. The final results were soon forthcoming as both HMR(C)–263 and –363 were directed to revert to their prior HMR(L) designations during February 1960 and the VMOs reconstituted to their original 12 fixed-wing and 12 helicopter complement. The reconnaissance mission of the division was to be absorbed by VMOs or the HMR(L)s.[31]

By this time, however, the Division of Aviation had made plans for increasing the helicopter lift capability as proposed in Phase II and III of General Hogaboom's Organization and Composition Board Report. This action resulted in the commissioning of HMR(L)–264 in MAG–26 on 30 June 1959 under the command of Lieutenant Colonel Edwin O. Reed, a future commanding officer of HMX–1.[32] In further expanding the program, the Division of Aviation published its Program Changes for Fiscal Years 1961–1964, which allowed for the graduated increase in the light structure from 10 to 15 squadrons. The number of helicopters assigned to each of the 15 units was to vary from 18 to a maximum of 24 depending upon the total number of aircraft available in the Marine Corps inventory, and the mission of the squadron. Only two medium units were programmed to be in existence throughout the entire period due to further reductions in HR2S procurement.[33] The last squadron to be commissioned prior to 1962 was HMR–364 in MAG–36 on 1 September 1961. The relationship between the numbers of helicopters in the Marine Corps and the number projected by the Division of Aviation for the years 1960 to 1962 is presented in Figure 11.

Figure 11

Recapitulation of Helicopter Program 1960–1962

Sqd.	FY 1960 Acft Planned	On Hand	Sqd.	FY 1961 Acft Planned	On Hand	Sqd.	FY 1962 Acft Planned	On Hand
VMO	72	63	3	66	89	3	63	73
HMR(L)	208	245	10	228	255	11	246	308
HMR(M)	35	27	2	26	28	2	28	31

The number of aircraft in the on hand column includes all helicopters assigned to FMF, HMX, and shore activities.[34]

CHAPTER 7

BEGINNING THE TRANSITION
TO TURBINE-POWERED HELICOPTERS

Selection of the CH–46

Military planners are faced continually with the problem of obsolescence of combat equipment. This is particularly true of aircraft. In the late 1950s when the Marine Corps was faced with the problem of maintaining three combat ready divisions and aircraft wings under a severely restricted budget, it had to prepare for the replacement of the aircraft being introduced into service. General McCutcheon touched on this subject and although his remarks were made almost a decade later, they were just as appropriate for this period as they were then. He said, "Aviation is a dynamic profession. The rate of obsolescence of equipment is high and new aircraft have to be placed in the inventory periodically in order to stay abreast of the requirements of modern war." In relation to the helicopter program, this involved suitable replacements for the piston-engine-powered HR2S, HUS, and HOK models.[1]

Despite the tightening budget, the Commandant on 9 January 1958 informed the CNO that the Marine Corps required a replacement for its light (HUS) helicopter fleet. General Pate noted the inadequacy of the HUS–1 to fulfill future assault requirements and requested that 210 troop and cargo versions of the Navy's newest ASW helicopter, the twin-jet engine HSS–2, be procured during the 1962–1966 time frame. At the time, there appeared to be no other helicopter available which was competitive with the Sikorsky-built aircraft from either a cost or technical viewpoint. The recommended designation for the transport version of the HSS–2 was HR3S–1.[2]

It was not until 16 March 1959 that the CNO published Operational Requirement Number AO–17501, the second revision of the new transport. One year later, on 7 March 1960, he issued Developmental Characteristic Number AO–17501–2, VTOL Assault Transport Helicopter, as Appendix II to the 1959 operational requirement. This second revision spelled out a requirement for a helicopter capable of carrying a payload of 4,000 pounds, or 17 combat-equipped troops, over a 100-nautical mile radius. Additional requirements specified that it have multi-engines, a rear loading ramp, automatic blade-folding capability, carry a crew of three, and cruise at a speed of not less than 125 knots. It further stated that the specifications listed in the developmental characteristics had to be met by a modification of a helicopter already developed and that it must be ready for operational evaluation by 1963.[3]

While detailed specifications for the HR3S–1 were being developed by BuAer, Sikorsky discovered that in order to modify the HSS–2 to a rear-ramp-loading transport, an extension to the forward fuselage would be necessary.

Due to the delay caused by this problem, the HR3S was now being compared to another aircraft. The Vertol Corporation had developed the YHC–1A transport for the Army and the commercial version of this helicopter, the 107M, offered a high degree of competition to the Sikorsky HR3S. As a result, BuWeps * representatives in June 1960 gave a presentation in which the capabilities of both helicopters were outlined. In the proceedings, the HR3S–1 was shown to be a significantly cheaper aircraft and to have obvious logistics and training advantages; however, the Vertol 107 was presented as being fully as adequate, technically, as the HR3S–1 to accomplish the assault mission.[4]

On 1 July 1960, the Director of the Marine Corps Landing Force Development Center at Quantico, Brigadier General William R. Collins, (and a former president of the Tactics and Techniques Board), informed General David M. Shoup, the Marine Corps' 22d Commandant, that the Development Center was monitoring closely the progress of both helicopters and that the data given at the BuWeps briefing differed considerably from

---

* On 1 December 1959 the Bureau of Naval Weapons was established and absorbed the functions of the abolished Bureau of Aeronautics and Bureau of Ordnance.

that available at the development center. General Collins pointed out that "there was a considerable divergence which, if valid, shows the Vertol 107 in a much more favorable light. It appears to be in the best interest of the Marine Corps to make a more comprehensive evaluation of the two aircraft." Accordingly, the general recommended that a comparative flight evaluation be conducted between the Vertol 107 and the Sikorsky HR3S–1.[5]

As a result of the pressure generated at Quantico for an objective comparison between the two competing designs, BuWeps assured the Commandant on 8 September that proposals from both Vertol and Sikorsky would be obtained. The next month BuWeps sent invitations for bids to the two companies. The following February, BuWeps announced its decision, declaring Vertol's design as the winner of the competition. Subsequently, the first flight of the HRB–1 was scheduled by Boeing-Vertol for June 1962 with delivery to FMF units projected for early 1964.[6]

The official military designation of HRB–1 (H-Helicopter, R-Transport, B-Boeing) was given the 107 along with the nickname of Sea Knight. The HRB–1 followed the typical Vertol design having two rotors in tandem. Two General Electric T-58 shaft turbine engines, exactly the same as those in the HSS–2, were mounted in the rear and on top of the 46-foot-long fuselage and powered the 51-foot diameter rotors. For the primary assault mission, the empty weight was listed as 11,641

A CH-46A Sea Knight lands on board the U.S.S. Guadalcanal. The Sea Knight carried 17 combat troops at a speed of 137 knots and became the mainstay of the Marine helicopter force (Marine Corps Photo A411783).

pounds and a maximum gross weight limited to 18,621 pounds. The cabin section of the fuselage measured approximately 24 feet long, 6 feet high, and 6½ feet wide allowing for 17 combat-equipped troops or 15 litter patients. The helicopter was manned by a crew of three with the maximum sea level airspeed limited to 137 knots. The overall length of the prospective assault aircraft was quite long, 84½ feet. A hydraulically operated ramp was incorporated in the rear of the cabin in order to facilitate loading and unloading of troops and large pieces of cargo.[7]

Choosing a Heavy Helicopter

In early 1958, in response to a request from the Office of the Secretary of Defense, BuAer conducted a study of the feasibility for a single VTOL aircraft development to satisfy the requirements of the Navy, Marine Corps, Air Force, and Army. When the study had been completed it showed conclusively that it was feasible and practical to develop a pressure-jet convertiplane/compound helicopter which would meet the requirements of all services. At the time, however, each service had their own ideas on the issue. The Army indicated that it wanted to proceed unilaterally with the development of a 6,000-pound payload, gear-driven, tandem helicopter being produced by Vertol as they felt that a pressure-jet convertiplane, as proposed by BuAer, would not be suitable for its mission. Later, the Air Force indicated an unwillingness to pursue such a development as it needed an aircraft with an extensive range capability for search and rescue purposes. The Department of Defense (DOD) reluctantly authorized the Army to proceed with its program but agreed that the Navy-Marine Corps' position of developing a pressure-jet convertiplane was feasible and technically sound and authorized the Navy to proceed with its research and development.[8]

The existing operational requirement (AO–17501) under which the HR2S had been developed, was revised by the Marine Corps to reflect the desired characteristics for such an aircraft to replace the HR2S which was scheduled to be phased out in the 1964–1965 period. The Commandant submitted the document to the CNO on 26 November 1958. On 16 March 1959, it was promulgated as Operational Requirement Number AO–17501–2, with Developmental Characteristic Number AO–17501–1 (VTOL Assault Transport) as Appendix Number One. The operational requirement stated that the VTOL aircraft should be capable of carrying a payload of 8,000 pounds outbound to a distance of 100 miles at a cruising speed of 200 knots and return with a 4,000-pound payload. A maximum airspeed of 250 knots was also specified.[9]

By 27 January 1961, the Air Force and Army had shown a renewed interest in a VTOL aircraft and through a series of DOD actions an agreement had been reached wherein all services consented to participate in the development of a prototype VTOL transport. BuWeps, the DOD-appointed manager for the tri-service aircraft, then issued a revised statement of requirements which specified the same payload but extended the aircraft's radius to approximately 250 miles and increased the cruising airspeed to 250–300 knots and the maximum airspeed to 300–400 knots. However, for the Marine Corps mission, the requirement stated that the fuel load could be reduced so that the maximum gross weight would not exceed 35,000 pounds so long as a 100-mile nautical radius of action could be flown.[10]

By August 1961, the Navy recognized that the four-engine tilt-wing aircraft, the design which had now been selected for the tri-service evaluation instead of the compound helicopter, would be unsuitable for Navy or Marine Corps use and withdrew from the program. Long before this time, however, the CMC and CNO had recognized that any production aircraft resulting from the high-speed VTOL program would not reach the fleet in time to replace the HR2S. In view of this, and at the Commandant's urging, the CNO issued on 27 March 1961 a revised developmental characteristic (AO–17501–3) for a medium assault transport helicopter with essentially the same requirements as the convertiplane (AO–17501–2) but with a cruising airspeed of only 150 knots. The gross weight was also to be limited to a maximum of 35,000 pounds.[11]

Since it had been determined that such a short time existed before the new helicopter was needed in the fleet, a replacement aircraft would again have to be a development of an existing model. The initial competition was therefore between three major helicopter manufacturers; Kaman, Sikorsky, and Boeing-Vertol. The Kaman Aircraft Company had shown an interest in competing for the contract but dropped out before submitting a formal bid.[12]

Vertol proposed that it could meet the requirements of AO–17501–3 by modifying its Army HC–1B Chinook, an enlarged version of its 107, or HRB–1. Sikorsky, on the other hand, based its design for the large helicopter on a revision of its jet-powered S–64 Flying Crane, an aircraft being built completely from company funds for future sale to West Germany. The general description of the proposed transport helicopter revealed that it was to utilize a sixbladed single main rotor and a 16-foot diameter tail rotor. The cabin measured 30 feet long, 6½ feet high, and 7½ feet wide with a rear loading ramp. It featured a watertight hull, seats for 30 combat equipped troops, tricycle retractable landing gear, twin turbine engines, automatic blade folding, and required a crew of two pilots and a crew chief. The aircraft had an overall length of 88 feet, a gross weight of 32,000 pounds, and an empty weight of approximately 19,000 pounds. The cruising speed at the designed gross weight was listed at 150 knots with a maximum airspeed of 171 knots at sea level.* [13] [14]

Request for proposals on the large transport helicopter were sent to the competing manufacturers by BuWeps on 7 March 1962. Sikorsky and Vertol replied in May, and on 24 August 1962 BuWeps announced the Sikorsky Aircraft design as the winner. Not only had Sikorsky submitted the lowest bid, but there was a decided preference based on technical, production, and maintenance aspects of the Sikorsky proposal.[15]

The first aircraft was to be delivered during May 1964 with fleet deliveries beginning the following year. The original designation of H-H(X) was given the assault helicopter (H-Helicopter, H-Heavy, (X)-Experimental). It was later designated by Sikorsky as its S-65 and by the Navy as the CH–53A.[16]

During September 1962 the designation for all Navy-Marine Corps aircraft changed. Class HO (helicopter observation) became HL (helicopter-light); Helicopter Light (HL) was changed to Helicopter Medium (HM) and Helicopter Medium (HM) became Helicopter Heavy (HH). Squadron designations were also changed during the same year: HMR(L) became HMM, HMR (M) became HMH. The VMOs retained their designation. In addition, the Department of Defense changed the helicopter designations for the HRS to CH–19, HOK to OH–43D, HUS–1 to UH–34D, and the HR2S–1 to CH–37A.[17]

---

* Mr. Lee S. Johnson, President of Sikorsky Aircraft mentioned to BuWeps that the company had not, as of 14 August 1961, received a formal request for proposal. Therefore, the details of his letter (proposal) for the heavy helicopter were based on a limited knowledge of the Marine Corps detailed requirements for such an aircraft.

The CH–53A was developed during 1962 and placed in service in 1964. It is a heavy assault transport with a cruising speed of 172 knots and a troop capacity of 38 (Marine Corps Photo A412901).

The Selection of an Assault Support Helicopter (ASH)

At the same time the Marine Corps was working on the development of its heavy and medium helicopters, it also was attempting to obtain a replacement for its light helicopter fleet. A forerunner in this category was the proposed Hiller Aircraft Company turbine-powered CAMEL (Collapsible Airborne Military Equipment Lifter). This type of light helicopter received considerable support from the Development Center and was seen as an essential element of strategic and tactical mobility during the later 1950s. It was to have the capability of being disassembled for transport by air or in any class of amphibious shipping to a combat area where it would be reassembled later and made ready for flight. It was not until 1960, though, that the Marine Corps began to see results of its efforts to obtain a replacement for its HOK and OE aircraft, both of which were to be completely phased out by 1965. In the past, vain attempts had been made to obtain funding for a single VTOL observation aircraft, or an ASH. It became apparent that to offset a forthcoming inventory shortage in these aircraft, immediate funding of a new program would be required.

The decision to pursue a program to provide a single rotary-wing type aircraft was the fruit of lengthy staffing at HQMC. As a result, the Division of Aviation submitted Developmental Characteristic Number AO–17503–3 to the CNO during late April 1960 for approval and promulgation. The desired characteristics for the ASH listed the gross weight at 3,500 pounds, a payload capability of 800 pounds or three troops, and a cruising airspeed of 85 knots.[18]

The Developmental Characteristic was published by the CNO on 9 August 1960. Concurrently, however, the Army had also stated a requirement for a light observation aircraft (LOA) which was very similar to that of the ASH. The Army placed emphasis on volume procurement of such a machine as a replacement for its fixed-wing and helicopter observation aircraft. An opportunity thereby existed for the Marine Corps to establish a joint services procurement program which would greatly reduce the unit cost for both services. This was also an advantage to the Marine Corps as there was now insufficient time to embark on a new development program unilaterally.[19]

The Coordinator, Marine Corps Landing Force Development Activities (CMCLFDA), Lieutenant General Edward W. Snedeker, took a different view toward the headquarters proposal for the ASH. Snedeker, a veteran officer who had commanded both the 1st and 2d Marine Divisions and served as Assistant Chief of Staff, G–3 at HQMC, reiterated the position developed at Quantico. In November 1960, a proposed developmental characteristic had been sent to CMC specifying a helicopter with a 100-knot, 1,000 pound payload and

100-mile radius of action, which the Hiller's CAMEL was capable of meeting. The same specifications had been submitted earlier by the Development Center but it was now officially submitted as a proposed developmental characteristic since it was felt that AO-17503-3 (ASH) did not measure up to the requirements stated in either the Marine Corps Landing Force Development Center or HQMC research and development plans for that type of aircraft. A lengthy rebuttal to the concept of using one type aircraft as a replacement for the HOK and OE was also included. The letter pointed out that the Army's LOA requirement was within the framework of an aircraft "family" completely different than that envisioned for the Marine Corps. General Snedeker emphasized that the Marine Corps needed a separate replacement for each, a 100-knot ASH for the HOK and an STOL (short takeoff and landing) light attack-reconnaissance aircraft to replace and expand the mission of the OE aircraft.[20]

In March, the following year, the CNO suggested to BuWeps that a limited competition be conducted to select an aircraft to fulfill the Marine Corps ASH mission. He stated that once a satisfactory selection and model evaluation had been made, every effort would be expended to effect necessary programming of funds within the FY 1962 budget to permit the accelerated purchase of operational aircraft. Soon thereafter, BuWeps conducted a study of those helicopters under consideration for selection as an ASH. The results revealed that each prospective model failed to qualify because of one or more deficiencies in size, cost, capability, or simply lack of overall qualification. It became apparent that a compromise had to be made in regard to selection of an aircraft prototype.[21]

Time was now an important factor since the HOKs were programmed for replacement in less than two years as they had been in the VMO squadrons continuously since May 1956. The Deputy CNO (Air), Vice Admiral Robert B. Pirie, had stated earlier that it would be in the best interest of the Marine Corps to accept the burden of increased size and cost of an operationally qualified model rather than gamble on a reduced capability or a possible protracted and costly developmental program such as the Hiller CAMEL or Army's LOH. He mentioned that the potential of an existing trainer, or light utility aircraft, might well be considered by the Marine Corps planners as its ASH. The Deputy CNO also recommended to BuWeps that a request for proposal be issued as soon as possible with reasonable latitude in con-

sideration of helicopter capability of performing the ASH mission. "The imperativeness," Admiral Pirie said "of positive action leading to a selection of this increasingly critical subject cannot be overemphasized."[22]

BuWeps acted promptly to Admiral Pirie's directive. On 16 October 1961, requests for bids went to 10 helicopter manufacturers and by 27 November seven companies responded with their proposals.* [23] After considering all the factors of each proposed design, BuWeps decided on 2 March 1962 that an existing Bell-manufactured helicopter, the Army-designated HU-1B, could fill the Marine Corps' ASH role.[24]

A number of elements entered into the decision which led to the choice of the Bell HU-1B. The paramount consideration was the time factor. The Army's LOH was not programmed for production until 1965 where the Marine Corps' ASH was needed by 1963. Additionally, the LOH was to be equipped with a smaller engine than the Marine Corps deemed necessary and provisions were not made in the LOH for carrying litters internally. The Marine Corps version (UH-IE) differed from the standard Army HU-1B in that it was necessary to remove most of the Army communication and electronics and install standard USMC/USN equipment. Other changes included the incorporation of a rotor brake for shipboard operations, a rescue hoist, and replacement of magnesium skin with aluminum to reduce salt water corrosion problems.[25]

Although the UH-1E utility helicopter was a fairly large and heavy aircraft, it met or exceeded the specifications of AO-17503-3 in all categories. The performance summary listed the empty weight at 4,734 pounds, maximum gross takeoff of 8,600 pounds, and the payload at approximately 1,300 pounds with a full fuel load. A combat radius of 100 miles was given along with a cruising speed near 100 knots and a maximum airspeed of 140 knots. The single-turbine engine, two-bladed helicopter had a rotor diameter of 44 feet and an overall length of 53 feet. The cabin had large sliding doors on each side allowing straight-through loading. A total of three litters could be accommodated and they could be loaded from either side or from both sides simultaneously. Seats for five passengers were provided. Only one pilot was needed, although provisions were incorporated for a copilot.

---

* The seven aircraft companies submitting bids to BuWeps were: Bell, Hiller, Kaman, Lockheed, Piasecki, Republic, and Sikorsky. Cessna, Gyrodyne, and Doman were the three companies which failed to respond to BuWeps request for bids.

The UH–1E was designed in 1962 and placed into service in 1964. It is the smallest and lightest aircraft in the modern Marine helicopter service.

The first flight of the UH–1E was scheduled for February 1963 with delivery to the fleet the following month. The selection of the UH–1E was viewed as a wise choice from the developmental point of view since by the time the Marine Corps would get its first –1E more than 400 –1Bs would be in Army service.[26]

The Essex Class Carrier as an Interim LPH

While preparation and negotiation had been underway for the transition to an all-turbine-powered helicopter fleet, major changes had been made in the Navy shipbuilding program. The disappointing factor in this case was the unavailability of helicopter aircraft carriers (Amphibious Assault Ships—LPHs). Although the *Thetis Bay* was providing the Marine Corps with a floating helicopter platform for training and evaluation purposes, it was inadequate as a full-fledged assault helicopter carrier. The Marine Corps had been hopeful, however, that by the late 1950s it would have the desired numbers of LPHs but the Navy had placed a priority on other types of ships thus delaying the LPH development.

Originally the amphibious assault ship program

called for conversion of CVA–55 and –105 class aircraft carriers. Knowing that converted CVEs could not accommodate fully the larger types of helicopters and that they would have a limited service life expectancy, the Commandant reversed his prior position and recommended that all such ships be built from the keel up as LPHs. In May 1956, after strong urging by the Navy and after considerable compromise on the part of the Marine Corps, General Pate agreed to a program which would provide one new LPH and one converted CVE–105 each year through the period of 1958 through 1962.[27]

With the approved five-year program to commence in 1958 and the LPH conversion and construction periods requiring two and three years respectively, an equal number of years would lapse during which the Marine Corps would be without the services of properly designed shipping from which to conduct an amphibious vertical assault. At the earliest, it would be 1960 before the first converted LPH would be operational, therefore another solution was needed. The relief came in the form of a suggestion from Rear Admiral Frederick N. Kivette, a member of the Navy's Standing Committee, Long Range Shipbuilding and Conversion.* At a meeting of the

* The Marine Corps was represented by one officer on this committee after mid-1956.

committee on 29 July 1957, he introduced the subject of utilizing *Essex*-class CVSs (ASW support aircraft carrier) as interim LPHs since some carriers of this type were scheduled for retirement.

Actually this thought had been presented as early as 1954 in a proposed CMC letter to the CNO recommending the use of CVSs or CVAs for helicopter operations. However, it is believed that the letter was never sent. Colonel James C. Murray, Head, Policy Analysis Division, HQMC, when commenting on the proposed letter, stated to the Chief of Staff on 28 April 1954:

> While this letter (the use of CVS and CVA carriers for helicopter operations) was prepared prior to the approval of the New Marine Corps concept (that proposed in LFB–17), it can now be associated with that concept.
>
> So far as I can determine, no formal discussion had been held which would provide assurance that this request will be approved.
>
> I do not feel that we should risk a formal disapproval on what might be regarded as an element of the new concept until we have attempted to gain Navy acceptance to the concept itself. . . .
>
> In summary, in the absence of any informal prior indication that this recommendation will be approved, its submission at this time may result in a disapproval which would tend to crystallize CNO opposition to the concept itself. It is recommended that: (a) the letter be delayed until the new concept has been presented to the Navy or (b) if time is pressing, that the matter be taken up on an informal basis to assure approval prior to the submission of a formal recommendation.[28]

The suggestion emphasized economy since the necessary modifications needed to make the *Essex*-class carrier into an acceptable LPH were estimated to be minimal. Additionally, the Navy could make the CVSs available to the Marine Corps within a relatively short period of time.

The outcome of Admiral Kivette's proposal was not known until 2 May 1958 at which time General Pate officially informed the CNO of the Marine Corps decision. In a memorandum to Admiral Burke the Commandant remarked:

> . . . [on] 15 March 1958 I stated that I would advise you of my views concerning the use of the CVS as an interim LPH following a report of their use during LANTPHIBEX 1–58.* [29] This report has

---

* LANTPHIBEX 1–58 took place in early 1958 off the coast of Onslow Beach, North Carolina. In addition to evaluating the feasibility of using the CVS as an interim LPH, it was the largest test up to this time of the vertical envelopment doctrine. Helicopters from Colonel McCutcheon's MAG–26 lifted in the ship-to-shore movement a complete RLT of the 2d Marine Division. Operating from the USS *Tarawa* (CVS–40), *Valley Forge* (CVS–45), and the *Forrestal* (CVA–59), the aircraft group demonstrated the soundness of the portion of the doctrine which envisioned the simultaneous use of more than one LPH.

been very gratifying and indicates that the CVS with limited modification will be a suitable type to meet existing needs until new LPH[s] are available in the fleet. . . . I recommend for your consideration that a least two CVS's which are scheduled to be deactivated in the near future, be modified to meet landing force requirements and made available for deployment with the amphibious forces as soon as possible.[30]

The *Essex*-class aircraft carrier had characteristics which made it quite compatible for helicopter operations and suitable as a platform from which to launch a ship-to-shore movement, but yet it also had some drawbacks. The shortcomings were mainly in its poor cargo-handling and combat troop-billeting facilities. Another undesirable condition, one imposed by the Navy, was the Marine Corps' obligation to provide Marine officers and enlisted men to augment the Navy crew. Those features which made the ship appealing, however, were its 889-foot flight deck, three aircraft elevators between the hangar and flight deck, 14 or more HUS launching locations, and a top speed in excess of 30 knots. Additionally, it was figured that a total of 30 HR2Ss or up to 60 HUSs could be transported when utilizing all available space. In wartime situations, an *Essex*-class ship had a complement of personnel, both ship's company and air group, that often reached as many as 2,800, a far greater capability than that of the *Thetis Bay*.[31]

Comparing the features of the *Essex*-class carriers against the newly constructed LPHs, the older CVSs appear, in many respects, superior. The newly constructed LPHs would have a 590-foot flight deck with deck spots for only eight HUS helicopters, two elevators, and a top speed of about 20 knots. The maximum number of transported helicopters would vary from 20 to 40 depending on their type and the method of storage. However, the modern command facilities, latest type cargo and material handling system, plus adequate space for the movement and berthing of combat troops would made the new ships more desirable in these areas. The new LPHs were not intended to compete with the larger aircraft carriers but rather they were designed particularly to combat load, transport, and land a Marine BLT of up to 2,000 personnel with an embarked Marine transport helicopter squadron.[32]

Accordingly, the USS *Boxer* (CVS–21) was reclassified as the LPH–4 on 30 January 1959 and the USS *Princeton* (CVS–37) reclassified as LPH 5 on 2 March. A third ship, the USS *Valley Forge*, (CVS–45) joined the ranks of amphibious assault ships on 1 July 1961 as the LPH–8.[33]

The three converted CVSs "filled the gap" as interim LPHs until sufficient number of new con-

Figure 12

LPH*	Name	New Construction LPH Auth in FY	Commissioned
2	*Iwo Jima* _____	58	26 August 1961
3	*Okinawa* _____	59	14 April 1962
7	*Guadalcanal* _____	60	July 1963 **
9	*Guam* _____	62	January 1965 **
10	*Tripoli* _____	63 **	August 1966 **
11	*New Orleans* _____	65 **	November 1968 **
12	*Inchon* _____	66 **	June 1970 **

* LPH–1 *Block Island*; LPH–4 *Boxer*; LPH–5 *Princeton*; LPH–6 *Thetis Bay*; LPH–8 *Valley Forge*.
** Projected dates.

struction LPHs were in service, with the plans for converting the five CVEs subsequently being dropped. Figure 12 gives the data on the new ships as it was planned at the time.[34]

One-Man Helicopters * [35]

Other projects, not as successful as those which have been mentioned, were subjected to lengthy and detailed evaluation. The Marine Corps sought a wide range of helicopters capable of fulfilling nearly every requirement of the ground commander.

The smallest size helicopter to undergo Marine Corps evaluation was the one-man helicopter. It was this project the Marine Corps actively pursued for over an eight-year period and was seen originally as some sort of "pinwheel" which could be strapped to a man's back and would be capable of transporting him short distances. The concept was translated in 1952 into an operational requirement (AO-17503), when the Commandant apprised the Chief of Naval Operations of the Marine Corps' need for a one-man helicopter. General characteristics of this device were:

1. Capacity—One man with combat equipment (240 lbs)
2. Operating Range—10 to 15 miles
3. Weight—50 to 75 lbs (one man portable)
4. Endurance—15 minutes
5. Speed—30 mph
6. Capable of autorotative landings
7. Require minimum training by nonpilots
8. Inexpensive
9. Packaged in a one-man load and capable of being readied for flight by one man in not more than five minutes.

---

* The contents of the following subsections were condensed and taken exclusively from a study on Marine Corps helicopter requirements prepared by the T&T Board, MCLFDC, Quantico, dated 2 May 1961.

In order to keep one-man helicopters from becoming an aircraft inventory item, in 1954 the CNO redesignated the one-man portable helicopter as an item of equipment, called the "Rotorcycle." In 1956 the CNO published a revised Operational Requirement AO–17505 reflecting a few changes to the original requirement which subsequently became the basis for testing several other experimental air vehicles.

Of the several types tested, none proved capable of satisfying the Marine Corps requirements. Two mandatory requirements were that it be light enough for one man to carry and simple to operate so that no specialized training for the "driver" would be necessary. The Gyrodyne RON–1 and the Hiller ROE–1 were the most promising models but they weighed in excess of 300 pounds empty, and were tricky "aircraft" which required the skills of an experienced helicopter pilot. Other models, such as Rotorcraft's "Pinwheel," Kellet's "Stable Mable," DeLackner's "Aerocycle," or Hiller's "Flying Platform," while easy to fly and maintain,

The dream of a one-man, portable, flying machine never materialized. The closest operational device was this Rotocycle (Navy Photo Np/45/5834).

proved unacceptable because of size, a requirement for exotic fuel, or the inability to autorotate to a safe landing after an in-flight power failure.

It appeared that while a valid requirement existed for some sort of small, inexpensive vehicle (not an aircraft) which would be available to the unit commander as his personal "jeep" and free him from the limitations of terrain-mobility, construction of such a vehicle would have to depend on some new technological development. Marine Corps exploration in the field of simple, lightweight aerial vehicles was cancelled by the Commandant in October 1960 and the satisfaction of this unfilled requirement, therefore, would have to rely on overland transportation or the use of a utility-type helicopter.

The Flying Crane Helicopter

A flying crane was generally visualized as a sort of heavy cargo unloader consisting of a skeleton fuselage, lift and power systems, and a pilot cab containing the flight and power controls. The flying crane's use would be to transport heavy pieces of materiel, rolling stock, engineer equipment, or large tonnages of bulk supplies. Initially, the first Marine Corps requirement for a flying crane helicopter was submitted to the CNO on 21 November 1950. The primary mission envisioned was to transfer aircraft from replenishment class 55 or 105 carriers to the *Midway* class CVLs and smaller *Independence* class CVBs. Soon thereafter, on 27 December, the CNO published a letter to all his departments setting up a requirement for the flying crane helicopter with the specification that it be capable of lifting a payload of 25,000 pounds over a radius of 10 miles.

Later in 1954, a Marine Corps Development Center study on helicopter requirements saw a need for a 20,000-pound payload XHCH-1 (Cargo Unloader Helicopter) to land the ONTOS (anti-tank weapon system) and 2½-ton cargo trucks. The XHCH was then an experimental helicopter being built by McDonnell Aircraft Corporation in accordance with the CNO's 1950 requirement, but it was never produced. In 1956 the Marine Corps Equipment Development Policy and Guide also saw a requirement for a cargo unloader helicopter, again with a 25,000-pound payload capability.

In 1959, the Director, Marine Corps Development Center stated a requirement for a crane helicopter. He specified in a letter to the Commandant:

> One of the most serious deficiencies in our vertical assault capability that exists today is the inability to lift heavy equipment essential to the landing force . . . It is considered that the number of pieces of equipment requiring heavy lift in support of a landing force would not be great . . . It now appears that developmental advances in rotor design and gas turbine engines is such that with proper direction, support and guidance, a helicopter capable of lifts up to 25,000 pounds could be obtained in a few years. It is, therefore, recommended that Headquarters, U. S. Marine Corps:
>
> a. State an operational requirement for a crane type helicopter capable of carrying a payload of 12,000 pounds with a minimum combat radius of 50 nautical miles. Encourage and support the aircraft industry to develop on an expeditious basis a crane type helicopter to meet this requirement.
>
> b. Program continued development of a crane type helicopter capable of carrying a payload of 20,000 pounds with a minimum combat radius of 50 nautical miles but with a greater combat radius if it can be achieved.
>
> c. Procure at an early date at least two prototypes of the most promising "Flying Crane" type helicopter for user test.

In March 1960, the Coordinator, MCLFDA submitted to CMC a "Proposed Operational Requirement for Landing Force VTOL Aircraft." Included therein was a "VTOL Cargo Unloader Aircraft (Flying Crane)" with a lift capability of 25,000 pounds. One significant fact concerning these views was that they were an expression of the "All helicopter concept" philosophy of LFB–17.

Why not a flying crane helicopter before 1960? Basically, the manufacturers could not produce one capable of lifting the desired weight. The first model of Piasecki's XH–16 was truly a flying crane as it was designed to carry its load in detachable "pods." Piasecki's second XH–16 had a large cabin and was the type which had interested the Marine Corps as an assault transport. Both aircraft failed primarily because the state of power plant and transmission development had not advanced sufficiently to match the demand. Also the Navy-funded McDonnell's XHCH–1 failed due to the same shortcomings. During 1956–1958, the U. S. Army Transportation Research and Engineering Command (TRECOM) actively studied the technical aspects of flying crane helicopters. Research contracts to conduct design and cost analysis were let to leading aircraft manufacturers. TRECOM examined the flying crane concept and evaluated the conclusions reached by the several manufacturers. Two of the most significant conclusions were: 1. The flying crane had singular requirements and design considerations which were not inherent in helicopters then in operation, and was very sensitive to changes in design, operating radius, and payload. For each payload and range combination there was an optimum power plant (shaft drive/tip-jet drive) and rotor (single, tandem, quad) combination. 2. Flying cranes were very large, very heavy aircraft. Rotor diameters on the order of 120 feet and empty weights in excess of 30,000 pounds were representative of flying cranes designed for payloads of 12 tons and operating radii of 50 nautical miles. A pure flying crane helicopter would have been of little value to the Marine Corps as there was only a limited opportunity for its useful employment in combat and, because of its size, it was difficult to load in amphibious shipping.

To satisfy the requirement for heavy lifts without a true flying crane, it was envisioned that a heavy cargo helicopter could be stripped of its auxiliary power unit, communications/navigation equipment, and other removable equipment and operate with a reduced fuel load and minimum crew. It then could become a flying crane, of sorts, capable of lifting five or six tons of external cargo for a tactically significant distance.

Handicapped by not having a flying crane, the Marine Corps' course of action would be to continue to make up light loads, and sectionalize heavy items of equipment, and employ the future CH–53 8,000-pound payload helicopters in a limited flying crane role until technology could produce a smaller, more versatile, and efficient crane helicopter.

Robot (Remotely Controlled) Helicopters

The Marine Corps for several years had been interested in the feasibility of employing pilotless helicopters. Basically, they were viewed as being a replacement for manned vehicles on missions where survival probability would be unacceptably low and also on missions which would not necessarily require the decision-making capability of a pilot.

In April 1954, the Marine Corps Development Center, at the direction of the CMC, submitted a brief research paper entitled "Study of Marine Corps Requirements for Remotely Controlled Rotary Wing Aircraft." This study recommended the acquisition of a limited number of remotely controlled helicopters for service use in order to evaluate their effectiveness in the following roles:

(1) As an atomic weapons close support delivery system remotely controlled and positioned by radar.
(2) As a remotely controlled platform for television cameras, airborne early warning or other intelligence gathering devices.

(3) As an "umbrella" of atomic aerial mines for defense against enemy aircraft and missiles.
(4) As a transporter of battlefield illumination devices.
(5) As a vehicle utilized for the routine shuttling of supplies.

In May, after reviewing the study, the Commandant established with the Chief of Naval Operations a tentative requirement for a few robot helicopters for test and evaluation purposes.

The next year a proposal was submitted by Kaman for "The Kaman Drone Helicopter System." This proposal saw the advantages of a drone helicopter as:

(1) The possibility of operating under hazardous conditions without endangering lives of pilot and crew.
(2) The possibility of operating under all-weather conditions using relatively unskilled operators because the helicopter is, at all times, completely stabilized and locked to a remote electronic control system.
(3) The possibility of lifting very small useful loads with a proportionately small vehicle because of the absence of pilot and attendant weight items.
(4) A considerable reduction in aircraft weight to accomplish any given mission.

Similar to the 1954 Marine Corps Development Center study, the Kaman proposal saw the drone helicopter applicable to a number of Navy-Marine missions, including: ASW, battlefield illumination, troop logistical support, minefield clearance, and, by installation of drone controls, as an all-weather navigation system for manned transport and utility helicopters.

Continuing to pursue the requirement, the 1956 Marine Corps Equipment Development Policy and Guide contained a statement expressing a need for

Research in drone helicopters has continued from the days of the autogyro. HTK–1 testing in 1958 lead to the conclusion that the major use of drone helicopters would be for cargo transport (Kaman Aircraft Corp. Photo 2570-1).

remotely controlled helicopters answering the following description:

> A family of helicopters, remotely controlled by sur-
> face or airborne devices, capable of transporting sup-
> plies and equipment, in weight categories of 100,
> 1,000 and 3,000 pounds, for use by the landing force
> during all phases of amphibious operations. These
> helicopters will operate from vessels of the amphib-
> ious task force on scheduled or programmed routes
> to specific or selectable landing areas. Operators will
> control landing and take-off operations. Provisions for
> command and control during all phases of operations
> are mandatory.

In 1959 the Operations Research Analysis
Branch at Headquarters, Marine Corps, under the
direction of Dr. Alexander L. Slafkosky, made a
detailed study which proceeded on the assumption
that:

> If a robot cargo carrying helicopter could be de-
> veloped which would be capable of handling a part
> of the logistical load of the manned helicopter, the
> limited number of manned helicopters and trained
> helicopter pilots might be utilized more effectively
> for tactical operations.

The report concluded with a recommendation that
the Marine Corps pursue the development of robots
in order to achieve an adequate vertical lift capability over a radius of 25 nautical miles or more.

Meanwhile, the Kaman Aircraft Corporation and
the Bell Helicopter Company had been actively
engaged in research and development of remotely
controlled helicopters, primarily in pursuit of
Office of Naval Research and BuWeps projects.
They had made numerous proposals and had
demonstrated successfully robot versions of their
HTK and HUL models.

During early 1959, the Marine Corps Landing
Force Development Center and HMX–1, at the
direction of Headquarters Marine Corps, sought
to determine Marine Corps requirements for robot
helicopters and at the same time to evaluate the
Kaman HTK–1 Drone, a trainer version of the
HOK–1. Three test objectives of this project were
to determine: the Marine Corps' requirements for
robot helicopters, the performance characteristics
desired in robot helicopters, and the operating
characteristics from which to develop concepts of
employment. An analysis of the report of the
MCLFDC/HMX–1 project does not indicate an
exhaustive pursuit of the extensive problem. However, those conclusions reached were worthy of
note insofar as they reflected the thinking at
Marine Corps Schools at that time.

1. The Kaman robot helicopter system was suitable
for point-to-point cargo transport utilizing enlisted
personnel as controllers. But the system was not suit-

able for performing reconnaissance, pathfinding, radio
and radar relay and radiological monitoring missions.
2. The Marine Corps had a requirement for cargo
carrying drone helicopters but did not have a requirement for drone helicopters capable of performing a
variety of missions as: reconnaissance, pathfinding,
radio and radar relay, radiological monitoring. The
availability of drone helicopters, and their use as the
primary means for resupply of tactical units, would
result in a significant increase in the mobility of
tactical elements of the Marine division.
3. The desired performance characteristics of cargo
carrying robot helicopters were listed as having a
100 mile radius of action, 90 knot cruising speed and
capable of lifting a 6,000-pound payload.

The only clear result of the 1959 MCLFDC/
HMX–1 evaluation was the demonstration that a
single helicopter could be droned and controlled in
a local area by either ground or air controllers.
Tactical or practical applications of drone employment were not evaluated.

Hopeful that the Kaman system would prove
successful, the Marine Corps Aviation Programs
for 1959–1964 were changed on 8 March 1960 to
provide for the formation of one helicopter drone
(cargo) squadron during FY 63 and two more
during FY 64. Commissioning these squadrons
was to be subject to budgeting, development, and
production variables, and not to be chargeable
against the operating aircraft inventory. The formation of a squadron with drone helicopters never
occurred since they did not prove to be inexpensive
or so reliable and easy to operate as to provide
a clear advantage over the manned helicopters.

VTOL Aircraft as They Pertain to Helicopters

Such advanced VTOL design as the compound
helicopter or convertiplane, tilt-rotor, tilt-prop, tilt-
wing, ducted fan, lift fan, and tail sitter had all
shown promise of being operational realities and
were seen by many to be a desirable replacement
for the helicopter. Also there was a stated operational requirement for a 30-passenger 250-knot
VTOL assault transport. Its characteristics were described in Operational Requirement AO–17501–2,
which said in part:

> The concept of VTOL Assault Transport systems is
> considered sound and is based on the requirement for
> significantly greater speed, range and ton mile capa-
> bility in the conduct of amphibious vertical lift
> assault operations and for reduced vulnerability in
> expected operating environment from hostile ground
> and air weapons.

The statement appearing in AO-17501-2 con-

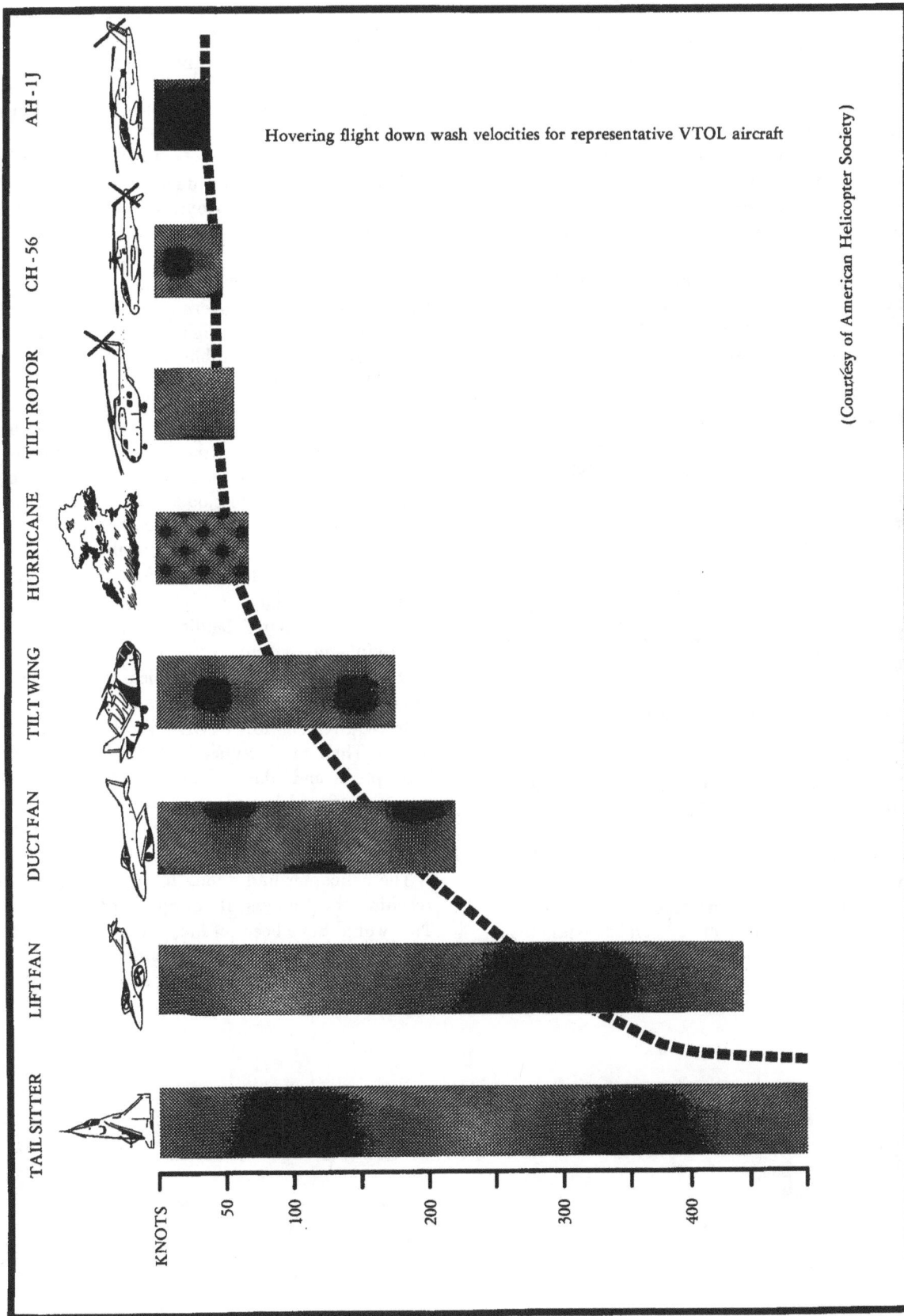

Hovering flight down wash velocities for representative VTOL aircraft

(Courtesy of American Helicopter Society)

tained the fundamental basis for replacing the helicopter with VTOL transport aircraft: "Speed with which to purchase greater combat survivability and speed with which to purchase greater aircraft productivity." Obviously, all other variables being equal, the faster an aircraft could fly the less it would be exposed to enemy fire and the probability of it being destroyed would also be reduced. However, speed was not the only element of combat survivability. Aircraft design and tactics were considered more important effects on survivability than speed. It was thought that a faster aircraft designed with exposed engines and fuel cells, or an unprotected crew may actually be more vulnerable than a slower aircraft with these essentials well protected.

Speed was, however, an essential element of productivity, and an aircraft capable of carrying the same load faster should enjoy greater productivity. Speed was not the only essential element of productivity; radius of action, logistic support needs, and Marine Corps aircraft-LPH compatibility were among the many factors which could influence aircraft productivity.

VTOL transport development did not prove to be as productive as helicopters for the short range/low altitude mission representative of Marine Corps helicopter operations. One of the most important reasons for the relatively poor short-haul/low altitude productivity of VTOL transports was found in the tremendous power-to-hover requirements for these aircraft, a requirement which renders the aircraft uneconomical to operate until it can transition into conventional flight.

Another important factor was cargo handling. High-speed aircraft would have to carry cargo internally and fly at considerable altitude at design cruising speed. Large items of combat equipment easily carried externally by conventional helicopters could not be carried at all by many VTOL designs. Others, like the convertiplane, could transport heavy items but only for short distances and with considerable loss of aircraft efficiency.

Helicopter-LPH compatibility was a factor of major importance in determining the suitability of a particular aircraft for Marine Corps use. Generally speaking, the higher the payload-size ratio, the better the aircraft. Most of the VTOL designs examined in any detail did not compare favorably with true helicopters in this respect.

Inherent in the design of any advanced VTOL aircraft was the problem of "downwash," the hypervelocity winds directed at the ground during landing, take-off, and hovering flight. Conventional helicopters generated high velocity downwash winds, often uncomfortable and a nuisance, but still tolerable. As an example, the most severe downwash generated from a helicopter came from the HR2S which had a "disc-loading" of 7.5 lbs/sq. ft. The downwash of the HR2S helicopter was strong enough to blow men and equipment about a ship's deck or create clouds of sand and dirt at unprepared landing sites. The convertiplane type VTOL "disc-loading" would probably have been on the order of 10 lbs/sq ft, while those of more sophisticated designs as high as 35-50 lbs/sq ft, making well-prepared landing sites a prerequisite for useful employment.

It appeared that for the typical Marine short-range/low altitude troop support mission there was little requirement for VTOL aircraft of advanced design. Their productivity could not compete with helicopters and the enhanced combat survival potential offered by speeds in excess of 200 knots was offset by poorer productivity and logistic support problems.

The helicopter had a long infancy and was now reaching the fullness of its operational potential. This would have been an inopportune time for the Marine Corps to trade the new-found maturity of modern helicopters for a new design, still to be proven.

NOTES

Most of the documents cited are located in the Historical Reference Section, History and Museums Division, Headquarters, U. S. Marine Corps, Washington, D.C. Other materials may be found in the Classified Control Center, Marine Corps Development and Education Command, Quantico, Virginia; Classified Files Section, Headquarters, U. S. Marine Corps; and the U. S. Navy Operational Archives, Naval Historical Center, Washington, D.C.

INTRODUCTION

Early Helicopter Developments

1. CO Aircraft One, 1stMarBrig, FMF, Quantico, Va. Memo to Brig Comdr, dtd 16Jul36, USMC Avn A4–1 Navy Record Section, National Archives as cited in Lynn Montross, *Cavalry of the Sky* (New York: Harper, 1954).
2. Frank J. Delear, *The New World of Helicopters* (New York: Dodd, Mead and Company, 1967), p. 14.

Initial Procurements and Designs

3. Sikorsky Aircraft, *The Miracle of the Helicopter* (Stamford, Connecticut: Sikorsky Aircraft, 1961), p. 2.
4. BuAer Record of Aircraft Acceptance 1936–1946, (Aer 5013B)

HRP–1 Development

5. CNO ltr to CMC, dtd 30Jan47, Subj: Army and Navy Helicopter Developments, encl (1), p. 2, hereafter CNO ltr, Army and Navy Helicopter Developments.
6. *Ibid.*
7. BuAer–E–13–GT VV(2) Memo for Admiral Davidson, dtd 21May42, Subj: P–V Engineering Forum, Recent Experimental Helicopter Study.
8. *Ibid.*
9. *Ibid.*
10. *Ibid.*

The HJP–1 Utility and Rescue Evaluation

11. Cdr William C. Knapp, USN, "Helicopter in Naval Aviation," *Journal of the American Helicopter Society*, Vol. 1, No. 1, Jan56, p. 3, hereafter Knapp, *Helicopter in Naval Aviation*.
12. *Ibid.*

Helicopter Applications

13. CNO Planning Directive 96–A–43, dtd 18Dec43, Subj: Navy Helicopter Program.
14. Knapp, *Helicopter in Naval Aviation*, p. 13.
15. CNO Planning Directive, dtd 18Dec43, *op, cit.*
16. CNO msg 161915May56 cited in CNO ltr to Adees, dtd 6Jun46, Subj: Establishment of Helicopter Development Program.

17. CNO ltr to Adees, dtd 6Jun46, Subj: Establishment of Helicopter Development Program.
18. Marine Corps Schools, Quantico msg to Major Armond H. DeLalio, 06420, dtd 13Jul46, Subj: Reassignment, Officers Mis Correspondence and Orders Jacket, National Records Center, St. Louis, Mo., p. 698–715.
19. Montross, *Cavalry of the Sky*, p. 182.
20. CO HT–18 ltr to CMC, dtd 29Aug72, Subj: Chronological List of Qualified Helicopter Pilots, Encl (1).
21. BGen Noah C. New ltr to DirMCHist&Mus, dtd 2May75. Comment File, "Development History of the Helicopter in the USMC 1946–1962."

Early Outlook

22. Igor I. Sikorsky, "Helicopter—Today and Beyond," *Aero Digest*, Jan47, p. 85.
23. CNO ltr, Army and Navy Helicopter Developments, p. 4.

CHAPTER 1
The Advent

The Quest for an Alternative

1. CMC ltr to CNO, dtd 18Jun46, Subj: Establishment of Helicopter Development Program.
2. Capt Davis Merwin, HQMC Memo to Dir of Avn, HQMC, dtd 19Jul43.
3. LtGen Roy S. Geiger ltr to CMC, dtd 21Aug46.
4. CMC ltr to Chairman, Special Board, dtd 13Sep46, Subj: Effect of Atomic Explosion on Amphibious Warfare.
5. BGen Edward C. Dyer, Tnscrpt of intvw by Oral HistU, Hist&MusDiv, HQMC, dtd 16Feb71 (Oral HistCollection, Hist&MusDiv, HQMC), p. 199, hereafter *Dyer Interview*.
6. *Ibid.*
7. *Ibid.*
8. *Dyer Interview*, pp. 199–200.
9. *Ibid.*, p. 198.
10. Chairman, Special Board, CMC, Advanced Report of CMC, dtd 16Dec46, Encl (c) part I, cited in Montross, *Cavalry of the Sky*, p. 63.
11. CMCS ltr to CMC, dtd 10Mar47, Subj: Employment of Helicopter in Amphibious Warfare, Encl (a), Military Requirements of Helicopter for Ship-to-Shore Movement, p. 1.
12. *Ibid.*, p. 2.
13. *Ibid.*, p. 3.

A Helicopter Program for 1947

14. OP–05 Memo to OP–03, dtd 21Mar47, Subj: Future Amphibious Operations.
15. Chief of BuAer ltr to OP–5, dtd 25Feb47, Subj: Future Amphibious Operations.

16. DCNO(Ops) Memo to DCNO(Air), dtd 6May47, Subj: Employment of Helicopters in Amphibious Warfare, p. 2.

Assault Helicopter Characteristics and Design Problems

17. *Ibid.*, p. 7.
18. DCNO (Ops) Memo to DCNO(Air), dtd 6May47, Sub: Employment of Helicopters in Amphibious Warfare.
19. CMC ltr to CNO, dtd 19Dec46, Subj: Future Amphibious Operations.
20. DCNO(Air) Memo to DCNO(Ops), dtd 15Apr47.
21. *Ibid.*
22. DCNO(Ops) Memo to DCNO(Air), dtd 6May47, Subj: Employment of Helicopters in Amphibious Warfare.
23. DCNO(Air) ltr to DCNO(Ops), dtd 3Jun47, Subj: Employment of Helicopters in Amphibious Warfare.
24. CNO ltr to CMC, dtd 23Mar 47, Subj: Future Amphibious Operations.
25. *Ibid.*
26. CMC ltr to CNO, dtd 5Jun47, Subj: Future Amphibious Operations.
27. *Ibid.*
28. Div of Avn Memo for the Dir of Plans and Policy, dtd 23May47, Subj: Proposed CMC ltr Ser 003A12947, comments on.
29. Chief, Aviation Military Requirements Section (Op-55R) Memo to Op-52, dtd 3Jun47, Subj: Employment of Helicopters in Amphibious Warfare.
30. CMC ltr to CNO, dtd 9Jul47, Subj: Employment of Helicopters in Amphibious Warfare.
31. CNO ltr to BuAer, dtd 4Nov47, Subj: Assault and ASW Helicopter Program.
32. BuAer ltr to CNO, dtd 24Dec47, Subj: Amphibious Warfare Assault Helicopter Program—Joint Air Force-Navy Participation.

CHAPTER 2
Concept Development

Commissioning and Operations of HMX-1

1. *Dyer Interview*, p. 209.
2. *Ibid.*, p. 210.
3. OP-50 ltr to DCNO(Air), dtd 23Jun47, Subj: Helicopter Program, titled: Aviation Plan No. 57, with 1st end. fm DCNO(Air) to Dist, dtd 10Jul47.
4. CNO ltr to BuAer, dtd 10Sep47, Subj: Planned Employment of HO3S-1 Helicopter.
5. CNO ltr to BuAer, dtd 12Sep47, Subj: Planned Employment of HRO-1 Helicopter.
6. ACNO (Marine Aviation) memo to OP-50, dtd 4 Nov 47, Subj: Marine Helicopter Squadron.
7. CNO msg to CMC dtd 22Nov47 (DTG 221359Z).
8. OP-50 ltr to DCNO(Air), dtd 21Nov47, Subj: Helicopter Program, titled: Aviation Plan No. 57, Supplement No. 2. with 1st end. fm DCNO(Air) to Dist List, dtd 24Nov47.
9. HMX-1 Muster Roll, 1-31Dec47.
10. CO, Helicopter Training Sqdn Eight ltr to CMC, dtd 29Aug72, Subj: Certification of Marine Corps Trained Helicopter Pilots.

11. *Dyer Interview*, p. 214.
12. CMC ltr to CO MCAS Quantico, dtd 3Dec47, Subj: Marine Helicopter Squadron One, employment of.
13. *Ibid.*
14. CNO ltr to CO MCAS Quantico, dtd 28Nov47, Subj: Aircraft Complement and Allowance of HMX-1.
15. OP-50 ltr to DCNO(Air), dtd 6Apr48, Subj: Helicopter Program, titled: Aviation Plan No. 57, Supplement No. 3, with 1st end. fm DCNO(Air) to Dist List, dtd 8Apr48.
16. Navy Dept, BuAer Standard Aircraft Characteristics, NavAer, 1335, Performance Summary, Sikorsky HO3S-1, dtd 1Feb49.
17. HMX-1 SqdnHist, 1Dec47-30Jun49, p. 3.

Initial Request for an Observation Helicopter

18. CO HMX-1 ltr to CMC, dtd 28Apr48, Subj: Type HTL-2 Helicopters, procurement of.
19. CNO ltr to CMC, dtd 23May48, Subj: Aircraft Complement and Allowances of Marine Helicopter Squadron One, revision of.
20. Navy Dept, BuAer Standard Aircraft Characteristics, NavAer 1335A, Performance Summary, Bell HTL-2, dtd 1Mar50.
21. HMX-1 SqdnHist, 1Dec47-30Jun49, p. 8.
22. CMC ltr to CNO, dtd 24Nov48, Subj: Change of Complement, Marine Observation Squadron.
23. *Ibid.*
24. Montross, *Cavalry of the Sky*, p. 101.
25. ACNO (Aviation Plans) ltr to DCNO(Air), dtd 7Apr49, Subj: Helicopter Program, titled: Aviation Plan No. 21-49, with 1st end. fm (DCNO(Air)) to Dist List, dtd 18Apr49.
26. CMC ltr to CNO, dtd 1Jul49, Subj: Military Requirement for Artillery Observation Helicopters.
27. *Ibid.*
28. CNO ltr to Dist List, dtd 16Aug49, Subj: Navy Research and Development Plan; Operation Requirement No. A0-17503 (Liaison Helicopter), p. 2.
29. Navy Dept, BuAer Standard Aircraft Characteristics, NavAer 1335A, Performance Summary, Sikorsky HO5S-1, dtd 1May51.
30. Ivan A. Sikorsky, *The Technical History of Sikorsky Aircraft and its Predecessors* (Stratford, Conn., May 1966), p. 191.

Operation PACKARD II

31. *Ibid.*
32. HMX-1 Amphibious Command Post Exercise, Operation PACKARD II, 10-26May48, p. I-1.
33. *Ibid.*
34. LtGen Victor H. Krulak ltr to Dir MCHist&Mus, dtd 26Mar75. Comment File, "Developmental History of the Helicopter in the USMC, 1946-1962."
35. HMX-1, Operation PACKARD II, *op. cit.*
36. *Ibid.*, p. III-7.
37. *Ibid.*, p. VI-7.

Publication of the New Concept—PHIB-31

38. MCS *Amphibious Operations—Employment of Helicopters* (Tentative), NavMC-4544 (Quantico, 1948).
39. *Ibid.*
40. LtGen Victor H. Krulak ltr to Dir MCHist&Mus, dtd

3Aug70. Comment file, "Developmental History of the USMC, 1900–1970."

41. Krulak ltr, dtd 26Mar75, *op. cit.*
42. Krulak ltr, dtd 3Aug70, *op. cit.*
43. Krulak ltr, dtd 26Mar75, *op. cit.*

Other Significant Demonstrations and Operations by HMX–1

44. CO HMX–1 ltr to CMC, dtd 1Aug49, Subj: Progress Report Period, 1Jan–30Jun49, p. 6.
45. HMX–1 Amphibious Command Post Exercise, Operation PACKARD III, 18–24May49, p. I-1.
46. *Ibid.*, p. III-3.
47. *Ibid.*, p. III-3—III-7.
48. *Ibid.*, p. V-1.
49. HMX–1 SqdnHist, 1Dec47–30Jun49, p. 15.
50. HMX–1, Operation PACKARD III, *op. cit.*, p. V-1.
51. CMC ltr to CO HMX–1, dtd 20Jun49, Subj: Authorized Allowances of Personnel, as ref in CO HMX–1 ltr to CMC, dtd 1Aug49, Subj: HMX–1 Progress Report for Period 1Jan–30Jun49.
52. CNO Aircraft Complement and Allowances for Naval and Marine Corps Aircraft, OpNav 503C, 1003, dtd 5Jun49.
53. HMX–1 SqdnHist, 1Jul–31Dec49, p. 3.
54. HMX–1 SqdnHist, 1Jan–30Jun50, pp. 1–5.
55. *Ibid.*
56. CO HMX–1 to CMC, dtd 30Jul50, Subj: SqdnHist, Period 1Jan–30Jun50, encl (1), p. 3–4.
57. *Ibid.*, p. 5.
58. CO HMX–1 ltr to CMC, dtd 20Jul50, Subj: Progress Report for period 1Feb–30Jun50.
59. *Ibid.*

CHAPTER 3

A Revitalized Helicopter Program

The Marine Corps Board

1. Chairman, Marine Corps Board ltr to CMC, dtd 3Jun49.
2. *Ibid.*
3. *Ibid.*
4. *Ibid.*
5. *Ibid.*
6. *Ibid.*
7. *Ibid.*
8. *Ibid.*

The Second Attempt to Procure a 3,000 Pound Payload Helicopter

9. CO HMX–1 ltr to CMC, dtd 25Jun49, Subj: Transport Helicopters, development and procurement of.
10. *Ibid.*
11. *Ibid.*
12. *Ibid.*, CMCS 2d end., dtd 5Jul49.
13. BGen Edwin A. Pollock, Dir Div P&P, HQMC, memo for Dir of Avn, dtd 8Jul49, Subj: Joint DivAvn, Div P&P, Study Group for Transport Helicopter Program, formation of.
14. CMC ltr to LtCol George S. Bowman, Jr., dtd 5Aug49, Subj: Board to Study and submit recommendations on a transport helicopter program for the Marine Corps.

15. CMC ltr to CO HMX–1, dtd 19Aug49, Subj: Transport Helicopter, development and procurement of.
16. *Ibid.*
17. CO HMX–1 ltr to CMC, dtd 12Sep49, Subj: Transport Helicopters, development and procurement of.
18. CMC ltr to CO HMX–1, dtd 13Oct49, Subj: Transport Helicopters development and procurement of.
19. Senior Member, Board to Study and Submit Recommendations on a Transport Helicopter Program, Report to CMC dtd 14Oct49, Subj: Transport Helicopter Board, Report of, p. 2.
20. *Ibid.*, pp. 3–6.
21. *Ibid.*, p. 6.

The First Six Months of 1950

22. Op–52 memo to Op–501D, dtd 16Jun50, Subj: Op–50 (Marine Aviation) Historical Summary for the Period 1Oct–31Dec49, Encl (1), p. 4.
23. Maj Norman W. Hicks, *A Brief History of the United States Marine Corps* (Washington: HistBr, G–3 HQMC, 1964), p. 42.
24. CMC ltr to CNO, dtd 12Jan50, Subj: Marine Corps assault helicopter requirements.
25. CNO ltr to CMC, dtd 2Feb50, Subj: Marine Corps assault helicopter requirements.
26. DivAvn memo to Op–50, dtd 10Apr50, Subj: Conference to determine assault helicopter program.
27. *Ibid.*
28. CNO ltr to Dis List, dtd 4Apr50, Subj: Navy Research and Development Plan; Operational Requirement No. AO–17501 (AL–01502 revised), (Rotary Wing Assault Helicopter), encl (1), pp. 1–3.

Further Action by the Marine Corps Board

29. Chairman Marine Corps Board ltr to CMC, dtd 27Apr50, Subj: Report on project.
30. *Ibid.*
31. CMC ltr to CNO, dtd 12May50, Subj: Operational Requirement No. AO–17501; request for higher priority.
32. OP–52 memo for the record, dtd 24May50, Subj: Assault helicopter requirement for the Marine Corps.
33. *Ibid.*
34. *Ibid.*
35. CMC ltr to CNO dtd 31May50, Subj: Interim Helicopter.
36. CNO ltr to CMC dtd Jun50, subj: Operational Requirements No. AO–17501.

Initial Interest in the Kaman Helicopter

37. Frederick G. Swanborough, *Vertical Flight Aircraft of the World* (New York: Aero Publishers, 1964), p. 54.
38. CMC ltr to CMCS, dtd 14Sep49, Subj: Kaman Helicopter, procurement of for experimental purposes.
39. *Ibid.*
40. CMC ltr to CNO, dtd 6Oct49, Subj: Kaman Helicopter Aircraft, procurement of for experimental purposes.
41. CNO ltr to BuAer, dtd 20Oct49, Subj: Kaman Helicopter procurement of for experimental purposes.
42. BuAer ltr to CNO, dtd 23Dec49, Subj: Kaman Helicopter procurement of for Marine Corps evaluation.

The Beginning in Retrospect

43. MajGen Charles L. Bolte, USA, Asst Chief of Staff, G–3, Office of the Army Field Forces, Liaison Group, memo for the Secretary of the Army, dtd 13Dec50, Subj: Army Helicopter Transport.

CHAPTER 4
Korean War Expansion

Plans for an Accelerated Helicopter Program

1. OP–52 memo to OP–55, dtd 21Jul50, Subj: Transport Helicopter, immediate procurement of.
2. CNO ltr to BuAer, dtd 27Jul50, Subj: Marine Corps Assault Helicopter Program, with copy to CMC.
3. *Ibid.*
4. *Ibid.*
5. BGen Noah C. New ltr to DirMCHist&Mus, dtd 2May75. Comment file, "Developmental History of the Helicopter in the USMC 1946–1962."
6. Navy Dept Standard Aircraft Characteristic Performance Summary, Sikorsky HRS–1, dtd 1May50, p. 4.
7. Harry S. Pack, Vice President, Piasecki Aircraft Corp., ltr to Gen Cates, dtd 22Aug50.
8. Special Action Report, 1st Prov. Marine Brigade, 1950, extract in LtGen Edward A. Craig ltr to History and Museums Division, dtd 7Apr75. Comment file "Developmental History of the Helicopter in the USMC 1946–1962."
9. Col Vincent J. Gottschalk ltr to DirMCHist&Mus, dtd 8May75. Comment file, "Developmental History of the Helicopter in the USMC 1946–1962."
10. Special Action Report, 1st Prov. Marine Brigade, extract in Craig ltr to History and Museums Div, dtd 7Apr75, *op. cit.*
11. Cited in BGen Clayton C. Jerome memo to VAdm Cassady, RAdms Soucek, Duckworth, Pride, and Goe, dtd 19Sep50, no Subj, hereafter cited as *Jerome memo.*
12. *Jerome memo.*
13. MajGen F. H. Lamson-Scribner (Ret.) ltr to Dir MCHist&Mus, dtd 23Mar75. Comment file, "Developmental History of the Helicopter in the USMC 1946–1962."
14. CMC ltr to CNO, dtd 23Aug50, Subj: Increases in Delivery Schedule of Marine Assault Helicopter.
15. *Ibid.*
16. *Ibid.*
17. *Ibid.*
18. G–3, HQMC memo to Dir P&P, dtd 21Jun50, Subj: Procurement of an interim assault helicopter and additional liaison type helicopter.
19. *Ibid.*
20. Dir of Avn memo to Dir P&P, dtd 25Sep50, Subj: Increased Complement of Observation Type Helicopter.
21. CMC ltr to CG FMFLant, dtd 26Sep50, Subj: Replacement of OY aircraft in Marine Observation Squadron One; plan for.
22. Op–52 memo to Op–50, dtd 11Oct50, Subj: HTL–4 Helicopters for possible deployment, request for, with attached DivAvn routing sheet comments, dtd 9Oct50.
23. Navy Dept, BuAer Standard Aircraft Characteristics, Performance Summary, Bell HTL–4, dtd Nov51.

Awarding of the First Assault Transport Helicopter Contract

24. BuAer ltr to CNO, dtd 21Oct53, Subj: Assault transport and Cargo helicopters; research and development program for.
25. DivAvn route sheet comment on DA–17560, dtd 16Dec54, Subj: Model XHRX–1 Assault Transport Helicopter; info concerning.
26. Ivan A. Sikorsky, *Technical History of Sikorsky Aircraft and its Predecessors* (Stamford, Conn; May 1966), pp. 197–198.
27. *Ibid.*
28. *Ibid.*
29. *Ibid.*
30. CNO ltr to CG FMFPac, dtd 19Sep52, Subj: Amphibious Material New Development Guide, July 1951; comments and recommendations concerning, review of.
31. CNO ltr to Commander Amphibious Forces, U.S. Pacific Fleet, dtd 9Apr52, Subj: Amphibious Material New Development Program Guide.
32. BuAer Schedule of Important Flight dates, dtd 1Dec51, p. 10.
33. *Ibid.*

Related Events to the Expanded Helicopter Program

34. Head, Plans, Operations and Training Branch Memo to Dir of Avn, dtd 11Sep50, Subj: Plans for the Helicopter program.
35. Op–52 memo to OP–05, dtd 19Oct50, Subj: Marine Corps Helicopter Plans.
36. BGen New ltr, dtd 2May75, *op. cit.;* CMC ltr to Dist List, dtd 27Oct50, Subj: Helicopter Program, Implementation of.
37. Op–52 memo, dtd 19Oct50, *op. cit.*
38. *Ibid.*
39. Op–50 memo to Op–52, dtd 14Dec50, subj: Marine Corps Helicopter Plan.
40. DivAvn memo to Div P&P, dtd 17Nov50, Subj: Marine Assault Helicopter Squadron; number designation.
41. MCS memo to President, Marine Corps Board, dtd 19Sep50, Subj: Marine Corps Board's study on the mission of Marine Corps aviation and its supporting establishments.
42. DivAvn memo to Div P&P, dtd 22Nov50, Subj: Marine Corps Assault Helicopter Program.
43. DivAvn memo to Dir P&P, dtd 20Mar51, Subj: Marine Corps Transport Helicopter Program.

The Tactics and Techniques Board Reports of 1951

44. Cited in MCS, MarCor Landing Force Development Center, Landing Force Tactics and Techniques Board, Staff Study: Employment of Assault Transport Helicopter, dtd 5 Jan51, p. 2., hereafter *T&T Board Study of 5Jan51.*
45. *Ibid.*
46. CMC ltr to CMCS, dtd 22Nov50, Subj: Marine Corps Assault Helicopter Program.
47. *Ibid.*
48. *Ibid.*
49. *T&T Board Study of 5Jan51*, App. A, p. 10.

50. *Ibid.*, p. 30.
51. *Ibid.*, pp. 29–35.
52. *Ibid.*, p. 30.
53. *Ibid.*, p. 34.
54. MCS, MarCor Landing Force Development Center, Landing Force Tactics and Techniques Board, Staff Study: Marine Helicopter Transport Program, dtd 28Feb51, p. 1., hereafter *T&T Board Study of 28Feb51.*
55. CNO ltr to Dist List, dtd 12Mar51. Subj: Aviation Plan 11–51 (Planned Expansion of the Naval Aeronautical Organization during the remainder of Fiscal Year 1951 and Fiscal Year 1952).
56. *T&T Board Study of 28Feb51*, App. C, p. III. The actual commissioning dates and locations are cited from Montross, *Cavalry of the Sky*, pp. 234–239.
57. *T&T Board Study of 28Feb51*, App. C, pp. III–IV.
58. *Ibid.*
59. *Ibid.*, App F, pp. I–II.
60. *T&T Board Study of 5Jan51*, p. 24; *T&T Board Study of 28Feb51*, p. 5.

Activation of the 3d Marine Aircraft Wing

61. Op–52 memo to Op–50, dtd 1Sep50, Subj: Marine Aviation Shore Establishment and Aircraft Requirement through Fiscal Year 1953.
62. Op–53 memo to Op–50, dtd 20Nov51, Subj: Tentative Naval Aeronautical Organization.
63. CMC ltr to Dist List, dtd 27Aug51, Subj: The Current Marine Corps Aviation Organization.
64. CMC ltr to Dist List, dtd 11Jan52, Subj: Plans for expanding Marine Aviation.
65. *Ibid.*
66. CMC ltr to Dist List, dtd 31Jan52, Subj: Plans for expanding Marine Aviation, implementation of.
67. CMC ltr, dtd 11Jan52, *op. cit.* The actual commissioning dates are cited from Montross, *Cavalry of the Sky*, pp. 234–238.
68. DivAvn memo to Asst C/S G–3, dtd 25Aug52, Subj: Annual report for the CNO for FY–52, encl (1), p. 9.

1952 Aircraft Plans for the Future

69. DivAvn memo to CMC, dtd 18Sep53, Subj: Helicopter information, encl (2), p. 2.
70. Navy Dept BuAer Standard Aircraft Characteristics, Performance Summary, Kaman, OH–43D (HOK–1), dtd 1Jul67, p. 4.
71. CNO ltr to BuAer, dtd 5Dec52, Subj: Utility version of the XWSS–1 helicopter (HUS), Marine Corps requirement for.
72. CNO ltr to BuAer, dtd 27Feb52, Subj: ASM Helicopters, development of.
73. CNO ltr, dtd 5Dec52, *op. cit.*
74. *Ibid.*
75. *Ibid.*
76. Navy Dept. BuAer Standard Aircraft Characteristics, NavAer 00–110AH34–1, dtd 1Jul67, pp. 2–5.
77. CNO ltr, dtd 5Dec52, *op. cit.*
78. Op–52 memo to Op–52, dtd 24Mar52, Subj: Aircraft requirement to support FY54 program objectives; CMC ltr to CNO, dtd 15Dec52, Subj: Department of the Navy program objectives, FY–55.
79. Op–50 ltr to Op–52, dtd 4Aug53, Subj: Revised FY–55 Marine Aircraft Requirement (within 1424 operating ceiling).

80. DivAvn memo to CMC, dtd 18Sep53, Subj: Helicopter information, encl (2).
81. DivAvn routing sheet, dtd 7Apr53, Subj: Additional HRS helicopter procurement.
82. CMC ltr to Dist List, dtd 23Nov52, Subj: Marine Aviation Status Board Photograph, encl (1); CMC ltr to Dist List, dtd 29Dec53, Same Subj, encl (1).

Peripheral Aspects of the Period

83. BuAer ltr to Commander Naval Air Test Center, dtd 20Apr53, Subj: Letter of intent for contract No. 52–947: Model XHCH–1 (Cargo Unloader) helicopter.
84. Cited in MarCor Development Center, Staff Study: Employment in Marine Observation Squadrons in an Amphibious Operation, dtd Jan54, Anx D, p. 3, Operational Requirement No. CA–17505.

CHAPTER 5
Seeking a New Order of Mobility

A Concept for Future Amphibious Operations

1. CMC ltr to CNO, dtd 17Jul51, Subj: Concept for future amphibious operations.
2. *Ibid.*
3. CNO ltr to CMC, dtd 13Aug51, Subj: Concept of future amphibious operations.

Initial Determination of the Marine Corps' Helicopter Aircraft Carrier Requirements

4. BGen Albert D. Cooley ltr to BGen Frank H. Lamson-Scribner, dtd 30Jul51, no subject; Op–52 memo to Op–05B, dtd 6Apr51, Subj: Helicopter tender (prototype), requirements and development of.
5. Cited in MajGen Harris ltr to CGFMFLant, dtd 29Mar52, Subj: Development of Helicopter Concept.
6. FMFLant, Final Report in HELEX I and II, dtd 7Apr52, p. 2.
7. *Ibid.*, p. 4.
8. *Ibid.*
9. MajGen Field Harris ltr to CGFMF, dtd 29Mar52, Subj: Development of Helicopter Concept, pp. 2–4.
10. CMC 2d end., dtd 28Apr52, on CG FMFLant ltr to CNO, dtd 1Jul52, Subj: Development of Helicopter Concept.
11. CNO ltr to Chief, Bureau of Ships dtd 8Sep52, Subj: CVE–55 Class Aircraft Carrier; modification for rotary wing type aircraft operations; Chief, Bureau of Ships ltr to CNO, dtd 20Nov52, Subj: Shipbuilding and Conversion Program for Fiscal Year 1955, recommendations for.
12. CMC ltr to CNO, dtd 26Nov52, Subj: 1955 Shipbuilding and Conversion Program; CMC ltr to CNO, dtd 5Feb53, Subj: Development of Helicopter Concept, CVE–55 class conversion, cited in: DirAvn memo to CMC, dtd 27Feb53, Subj: Information for the Commandant's briefing of the Secretary of the Navy, "The Marine Helicopter Program."

The Advance Research Group

13. Montross, *Cavalry of the Sky*, p. 226.
14. BGen Noah C. New ltr to DirMCHist&Mus, dtd

2May75. Comment File, "Developmental History of the Helicopter in the USMC, 1946, 1962."

15. CMC ltr to CMCS, dtd 19Jan53, Subj: Marine Corps Advanced Group.
16. *Ibid.*
17. AC/S, G-1 memo to CMCS, dtd 7Dec61, Subj: Advanced Research Groups, roster of, years 1953–1957.
18. "A Summary of the General Officers' Conference, HQMC," dtd 14–16Jul54, p. 31.
19. *Ibid.*, p. 39.
20. *Ibid.*, p. 40.
21. H&SCo, MarCorTU#1, Unit Diary, dtd 2Sep54.
22. CG FMFPac Troops ltr to BGen Wilbert S. Brown, dtd 27Feb53, Subj: Activation of 2d Marine Corps Provisional Atomic Exercise Brigade (MCPAEB); CG MCPAEB ltr to CMC, dtd 19May53, Subj: Exercise DESERT ROCK V—MarCor, report on, p. 12.
23. 1953–1954 Advanced Research Group, Project IV, Marine Corps Transport Helicopter Requirements for the Immediate Future, p. 4.
24. *Ibid.*, pp. 6–7.
25. *Ibid.*, pp. 9–51.
26. *Ibid.*, pp. 35–37.
27. *Ibid.*
28. Col John A. Saxton, G-3, HQMC, memo to Advanced Research Group Panel, n.d., Subj: Proposed program for the 1954–55 Advanced Research Group.
29. Dir of Avn memo to C/S, dtd 8Apr54, Subj: Solution to Advanced Research Group Project I "Concept of Future Amphibious Operations," comments and recommendations regarding, p. 3.
30. 1953–54 Advanced Research Group, Project IV, *op. cit.*, p. 55.
31. CMC memo to C/S, HQMC, dtd 22Jul1954, Subj: Marine Corps Transport Helicopter Requirements.
32. CMC ltr to CNO, dtd 23Oct54, Subj: Aircraft requirements for Marine Helicopter Transport Squadrons.

Landing Force Bulletin Number 17

33. CMC ltr to CMCS, dtd 7Dec55, Subj: Program for the implementation of the Marine Corps Amphibious Concept.
34. CNO ltr to CMC, dtd 8Dec55, Subj: Concept of Future Amphibious Assault Operations.
35. *Ibid.*
36. *Ibid.*
37. HQMC, Landing Force Bulletin Number 17: Concept of Future Amphibious Operations, dtd 13Dec55.

The Smith Board

38. CMC ltr to LtGen Oliver P. Smith, dtd 23Dec54, Subj: Precept convening board to study the composition and functions of Marine Aviation.
39. HQMC Study: The Composition of and Functions of Marine Aviation, dtd Jan–Feb55, p. 21.
40. *Ibid.*, p. 51.
41. CMC memo to C/S, dtd 24May55, Subj: Board to Study the Composition and Functions of Marine Corps Aviation.
42. CMC ltr to CNO, dtd 1Mar55, Subj: Marine Corps requirements for helicopter utility aircraft.
43. Op-52 memo to Op-09M, dtd 2May55, Subj: Information on transport helicopter program.

44. *Ibid.*
45. CNO ltr to CMC, dtd 16Jun55, Subj: Marine Corps requirements for helicopters.
46. CNO ltr to CMC, dtd 11Oct55, Subj: Marine Corps requirements for helicopters.

A Reduced HR2S Program

47. CMC ltr to CNO, dtd 19Oct55, Subj: Procurement of transport helicopters for the Marine Corps; recommendation concerning.
48. CMC ltr to CNO, dtd 23Nov55, Subj: Procurement of transport helicopters for the Marine Corps, recommendations concerning.
49. MajGen Henry R. Paige ltr to Gen Randolph McC. Pate, dtd 24Jan56, no subj.
50. CMC ltr to CNO, dtd 23Nov55, *op. cit.*
51. CNO ltr to CMC, dtd 12Apr56, Subj: HR2S-1 Procurement Program.
52. *Ibid.*

CHAPTER 6
A Period of Reevaluation—A Moderate Capability

HQMC G-3 Study Number 3—1956

1. G-3, HQMC Study No. 3—1956 memo to CMC, dtd 8May56, Subj: Employment of Helicopters within the FMF during the period 1956–60.
2. *Ibid.*, pp. 2–6.
3. CMC ltr to C/S, dtd 24May55, Subj: Board to Study Composition and Functions of Marine Corps Aviation.
4. G-3, HQMC Study No. 3, dtd 8May56, *op. cit.*, pp. 7–8.
5. CMC ltr to CG FMFPac and CG FMFLant, dtd 4Sep56, Subj: Helicopter Assault Capabilities, 1957–1960.

Marine Corps Aviation Five-Year Program 1957–1962

6. A Summary of the General Officers' Conference, HQMC, dtd 12–17Jul56, pp. 37–45.
7. CMC ltr to CNO, dtd 5Jul56, Subj: Marine Corps Aviation Program, Fiscal Years 1957–1962, p. 2. to encl. 3.

The Hogaboom Board of 1956

8. HQMC, Report of the Fleet Marine Force Organization and Composition Board, dtd 7Jan57, App. C, encl. (1), p. 7, hereafter *Hogaboom Board—1956.*
9. *Hogaboom Board—1956*, part 1, p. 1.
10. *Ibid.*
11. *Ibid.*, Part II, p. 14.
12. *Ibid.*
13. *Ibid.*, Part III, pp. 2–7.
14. *Ibid.*, Part III, p. 9. Fig. 1 taken from Part VII, p. 180.
15. *Ibid.*, Part III, p. 10. Figs. 7 and 8 taken from Part VII, pp. 194 and 212.
16. *Ibid.*, Part V, p. 7.
17. *Ibid.*, Part V, p. 8.
18. A summary of the General Officers' Conference HQMC, dtd 13–15Jul59, p. 5.

Forced Reduction

19. HQMC, Marine Corps Program Summary, dtd Jan–May59, Avn Program Sec, pp. 1–7; HQMC, Summary of the General Officers' Conference, dtd 13–15Jul59, pp. 47–55.
20. Dir of Avn memo to CMC, dtd 23Sep57, Subj: Marine Corps aviation program changes Fiscal Years 1958–1962 under current guidance for force level reductions, encl. (2), p. 2.
21. *Ibid.* ,encl. (5).
22. CNO ltr to CMC, dtd 11Apr56, Subj: Amphibious Assault Ship requirements to support the mobility of the FMF.
23. *Jane's Fighting Ships 1961–1962* (London: Jane's Fighting Ships Ltd., 1962), pp. 316–319.

Growth and Changes Under Austere Conditions 1956–1962

24. CMC ltr to CG FMFPac and CG FMFLant, dtd 11May56, Subj: Assignment of Marine Observation Squadrons to Marine Helicopter Groups.
25. CNO spdltr Op–332D to CMC, dtd 18Feb59, cited in UD RUC 01074, reel 14–59, p. 99.
26. Avn UHist File, RefSec, Hist&MusDiv, HQMC.
27. CMC ltr to Dist List, dtd monthly, 1956 and 1957, Subj: Aviation Status Board Photographs, dist, of, encl (1), hereafter *CMC AvnStaBrdPho*, with relevant year.
28. *CMC AvnStaBrdPho*, Jan57–Dec57.

Implementation of the Hogaboom Board Recommendations

29. CMC ltr to CNO, dtd 14Mar58, Subj: Establishment and redesignation of certain Marine squadrons; CO, MAG–16 ltr to CMC, dtd 14Mar58, Subj: Organization of MAG–16, pp. 1–7; *CMC AvnStaBrd Pho*, 1958.
30. CO, MAG–16 ltr to CMC, dtd 22Apr59, Subj: Organization of MAG–16, pp. 1–7.
31. Avn UHist File, RefSec, Hist&MusDiv, HQMC.
32. *Ibid.*
33. CMC ltr to CNO, dtd 8Mar60, Subj: CMC ltr of 31Mar59, encl (2), Aircraft Operating Program.
34. *CMC AvnStaBrdPho*, Jan60–Dec62.

CHAPTER 7
Beginning the Transition to Turbine-Powered Helicopters

Selection of the CH–46

1. LtGen Keith B. McCutcheon, "Marine Aviation in Vietnam 1962-1970," *Naval Review 1971*, p. 134.
2. CMC ltr to CNO, dtd 9Jan58, Subj: Future procurement of a transport version of HSS-2, cited in CNO ltr to CMC, dtd 8Feb58, same subj.
3. CNO ltr to Dist List, dtd 7Mar60, Subj: Development Characteristic No. AO-17501-2 (Subj: VTOL Assault Transport Helicopter), promulgation of, encl (1), pp. 1–3.
4. BuWeps Program Report, Model HRB-1 Helicopter, dtd 8Feb62, sections A-1 to A-3 and B-1 to B-4.

5. Dir MCLFDC ltr to CMC, dtd 1Jul60, Subj: Comparison of the Vertol 107 with the HR3S.
6. BuWeps Summary Report, dtd 8Feb62, *op. cit.*
7. *Ibid.*

Choosing a Heavy Helicopter

8. Dir of Avn ltr to Dist List, dtd 25Nov59, Subj: VTOL Assault Transport Program.
9. *Ibid.*
10. BuWeps. RA2v Memo for the record, dtd 16Nov62, Subj: H-H(X) Assault Transport Helicopter Competition, Evaluation and Recommendations, encl (2), pp. 1-3, hereafter *BuWeps memo, dtd 16Nov62*.
11. *Ibid.*
12. *Ibid.*
13. Lee S. Johnson, President, Sikorsky, ltr to BuWeps, dtd 14Aug61, Subj: Four-ton Assault Helicopter for Marine Use—Proposal for.
14. *Ibid.*
15. *BuWeps Memo, dtd 16Nov62*.
16. *Ibid.*
17. *Ibid.*; Department of Defense Directive 4505.6, dtd 6Jul62, Subj: Designation, Redesignation and Naming of Military Aircraft.

The Selection of an Assault Support Helicopter (ASH)

18. DivAvn Memo to DC/S, R&D), dtd 29Sep60, Subj: Aircraft Briefs, encl (2), p. 2.
19. CMC ltr to CMCLFDA, dtd 4Feb61, Subj: Assault Support Helicopter.
20. Dir MCLFDA memo to CMC, dtd 4Nov60, Subj: Study Project 70–59–09 (Marine Corps Helicopter Requirements) Phase I, completion of.
21. CNO ltr to BuWeps, dtd 5Sep61, Subj: Assault Support Helicopter (ASH) Program.
22. *Ibid.*
23. *Ibid.*
24. *Ibid.*
25. *Ibid.*; DC/S Air Memo to C/S, HQMC, dtd 26Dec63, Subj: Hiller OH5A (entry in Army LOH Competition), Information concerning.
26. BuWeps NavAir 00-110AH1-1, Standard Aircraft Characteristics, p. 3; 1stLt Joe D. Browning, "Meet the Assault Support Helicopter," *Marine Corps Gazette*, V. 46, No. 11 (Nov62), p. 16.

The Essex Class Carrier as an Interim LPH

27. CNO ltr to CMC, dtd 11Apr56, Subj: Amphibious Assault Ship requirements to support the mobility of the FMF; CNO ltr to CMC, dtd 27Jun56, same subj; Col Samuel R. Shaw memo to Chairman, Standing Committee, Shipbuilding and conversion, dtd 14Aug57, Subj: Use of CVS (Unconverted *Essex*) Aircraft Carriers as LPH.
28. Head, Policy Analysis Division memo to the C/S, dtd 28Apr54, Subj: Proposed CMC ltr to CNO re use of CVS or CVA for helicopter operations.
29. DC/S (RD&S), HQMC memo to DirMarCorHistMus, dtd 25Nov70, in Comment File, "Developmental History of the United States Marine Corps, 1900-1970."

30. CMC memo to CNO dtd 2May58, Subj: Use of CVS Aircraft Carriers as Interim LPH.

31. *Jane's Fighting Ships 1959–1960* (London; Jane's Fighting Ships Ltd., 1960) pp. 366–371; U.S. Army Armor School, *United States Marine Corps Reference Data* (Fort Knox, Kentucky: March 1966) pp. V–3—V–7.

32. *Ibid.*

33. *Ibid.*

34. BuShips, Monthly Progress Report on Shipbuilding and Conversion, dtd monthly 1958–1967 (Naval Hist-Div, Ships HistBr., Washington, D.C.)

One-Man Helicopters

35. MCLFDC, T&T Board Report: Marine Corps Helicopter Requirements, Project #70–59–09, dtd 2May61, App A–1 to F–9 (CCC, MCB, Quantico).

APPENDIX A

ABBREVIATIONS

ACNO	Assistant Chief of Naval Operations
AKA	Attack Cargo Ship
APA	Attack Transport Ship
Asst	Assistant
BLT	Battalion Landing Team
BuAer	U.S. Navy Bureau of Aeronautics
BuWeps	U.S. Navy Bureau of Naval Weapons
CG	Commanding General
CMC	Commandant of the Marine Corps
CMCS	Commandant Marine Corps Schools
CNO	Chief of Naval Operations
CO	Commanding Officer
CV	The letters designating an aircraft carrier. The third letter is added to distinguish between the various types:
	CVA—Attack Aircraft Carrier
	CVE—Escort Aircraft Carrier
	CVHA—Escort Helicopter Aircraft Carrier
	CVL—Light Aircraft Carrier
	CVS—Support Aircraft Carrier
DCNO	Deputy Chief of Naval Operations
Div	Division
DivAir	Division of Aviation
Div P&P	Division of Plans and Policies
Encl	Enclosure
FMF	Fleet Marine Force
FMFLant	Fleet Marine Force, Atlantic
FMFPac	Fleet Marine Force, Pacific
HMR	Marine Transport Helicopter Squadron
HMX	Marine Helicopter Squadron
HQMC	Headquarters, U.S. Marine Corps
Lex	Landing Exercise
LPH	Amphibious Assault Ship
LSD	Landing Ships, Dock
LST	Landing Ships, Tank
Ltr	Letter
MAG	Marine Aircraft Group
MCAS	Marine Corps Air Station
MCDC	Marine Corps Development Center
MCEB	Marine Corps Equipment Board
MCEC	Marine Corps Educational Center
MCS	Marine Corps Schools
Memo	Memorandum
NAS	Naval Air Station
RLT	Regimental Landing Team
USA	U.S. Army
USAF	U.S. Air Force
USMC	U.S. Marine Corps
USN	U.S. Navy
VMO	Marine Observation Squadron

APPENDIX B

HELICOPTER DESIGNATIONS

The first letter *, in Navy and Marine Corps usage, denotes the type of machine, the second its primary function (mission). The third letter identifies the manufacturer. A number inserted between the function and manufacturer's letter indicates the model number of the designer's aircraft in the same class—the first model or design number "1" is always omitted. The number following the dash indicates the number of modifications to the basic model, i.e., the HR2S-1 is defined as a (H) helicopter, (R) transport, (2) second model, (S) Sikorsky, and (-1) first modification.

---

* The letter "X" or "Y" may precede the entire designation. In this case the letter "X" is used for denoting experimental aircraft. The letter "Y" is used for the more advanced experimental types and also to denote aircraft procured in limited quantities to develop the potentialities of the design.

Type letter	*Manufacturer*
H—Helicopter	B—Boeing
HO—Observation	K—Kaman
HR—Transport	L—Bell
HS—Antisubmarine	P—Piasecki (after 1952)
HT—Trainer	P—Pitcairn (before 1937)
HU—Utility	S—Sikorsky
	U—Vought–Sikorsky

APPENDIX C

CHRONOLOGY

1932

May — Marine Corps received Pitcairn OP-1 autogyro at Quantico, Virginia.

28 Jun — Evaluation of OP-1 began in Nicaragua.

1939

14 Sep — Igor I. Sikorsky test flew the VS-300, the first practical helicopter in the Western Hemisphere.

1946

18 Jun — CMC established Marine Corps helicopter program.

8 Aug — Major Armand H. DeLalio became first Marine to be designated as a helicopter pilot.

21 Aug — General Geiger, after viewing A Bomb tests, expressed concern to CMC of nuclear weapons effect on future amphibious operations.

13 Sep — CMC tasks Special Board to find solution to amphibious warfare in an atomic environment.

16 Dec — Special Board recommended development of a helicopter program as one solution for conducting amphibious operations in an atomic environment.

19 Dec — CMC directed implementation of a helicopter program and outlined concept of future amphibious operations.

1947

1 Dec — HMX-1 Commissioned.

1948

9 Feb — HMX-1 received first helicopter, Sikorsky HO3S-1 (S-51).

23 May — HMX-1 executes first vertical assault in Operation PACKARD II.

9 Aug — HMX-1 received first Bell HTL-2 (H-13).

19 Aug — HMX-1 received the HRP-1 (PU-3).

Nov — MCS publishes PHIB-31 (Amphibious Operations—Employment of Helicopters (Tentative)).

1949

3 Jun — Marine Corps Board recommended the activation of the first two 12-plane transport helicopter squadrons to commence in 1953.

6 Oct — CMC requested Kaman 190 helicopter for evaluation as an observation helicopter.

1950

12 Jan — CMC requested 13-15 man assault helicopters.

28 Mar — Informal Helicopter Conference drew up specifications for a 20-man assault transport helicopter which subsequently became Operation Requirement No. AO-17501 for the Sikorsky HR2S-1 (S-56).

22 May — Joint Helicopter Conference recommended a two-phase helicopter program: Long-range solution was AO-1750 (HR2S) and short-range the procurement of an interim helicopter to satisfy immediate requirements.

14 Jul — VMO-6 departed San Diego for Korea with four HO3S-1 helicopters.

21 Jul — CMC requested the Sikorsky HRS-1 (S-55) as an interim assault helicopter.

1951

5 Jan — Tactics and Techniques Board published its study, Employment of Assault Transport Helicopters.

15 Jan — Marine Corps commissioned HMR-161, the first Marine transport helicopter squadron.

28 Feb — Tactics and Techniques Board published its study, Marine Helicopter Transport Program.

20 Mar — Sikorsky awarded the contract to build the HR2S-1.

5 Apr — HMR-261 commissioned.

14 Jun — Marine aircraft wing reorganized. Helicopter squadrons placed under a parent aircraft group headquarters.

30 Jun — HMR-162 commissioned.

1 Jul — HMR-161 deployed to Korea.

17 Jul — CMC published concept of future amphibious operations urging CNO to provide a shipbuilding program to parallel the availability of the HR2S-1.

13 Aug — CNO approved CMC concept of future amphibious operations of landing the assault elements of one Marine division by helicopter.

1 Sep — HMR-262 commissioned.

15 Nov — HMR-163 commissioned.

1952

11 Jan — CMC published Marine Aviation Plan 1-52 which allowed for the expansion of Marine aviation with the commissioning of MAG (HR)-16, MAG(HR)-26, and MAG(HR)-36.

25 Feb — HMR-361 commissioned.

1 Mar — MAG(HR)-16 commissioned.

29 Mar — MajGen Harris submitted report on HELEX I and II outlining the suitability and requirement for CVE and CVL class carriers as modified LPHs.

28 Apr — CMC requested four converted CVE-55s be modified for helicopter assault operations.

30 Apr — HMR-362 commissioned.

2 Jun	HMR–363 commissioned.		31 Dec	HMR squadrons began changing designation to HMR(L).
2 Jun	MAG(HR)–36 commissioned.			
16 Jun	HMR–263 commissioned.			
16 Jun	MAG(HR)–26 commissioned.			**1957**
5 Dec	CNO instructed BuAer to develop the HUS–1 (S–58) for the Marine Corps.		7 Jan	Hogaboom Board report published, outlining three phase objective, 1957 to 1965, for the helicopter program.

1953

5 Feb CMC revised Marine Corps assault helicopter aircraft requirements to a total of 16 LPHs; four converted CVE–105s and 12 CVE–55s.

1954

27 Apr CMC approved the Advanced Research Groups Project I thereby establishing the concept contained therein as the long-range goal of the Marine Corps.

1 Jul Marine Corps Test Unit One activated.

22 Jul CMC approved Advanced Research Group Project IV, Marine Corps Transport Helicopter Requirements for the Immediate Future.

23 Oct CMC requested CNO authorize an increase in the number of HR2S–1 helicopters from 135 to 180, *i.e.*, nine squadrons of 20 aircraft each vice 15 each.

1955

24 May CMC announced decision on Smith Board which resulted in two medium utility helicopter squadrons being added to each aircraft wing organization.

24 May CMC established a goal of helicopter lifting the assault elements of one and one half divisions by helicopter.

16 Jun CNO approved Marine Corps helicopter program of 180 HR2S–1s and 45 HUS–1s.

13 Dec Landing Force Bulletin Number 17 approved which officially promulgated the Marine Corps concept of future amphibious operations.

1956

8 May G–3 Study Number 3 completed recommending an increase from nine to 15 transport helicopter squadrons; 245 light and 45 medium aircraft.

22 May CMC agreed to a five-year shipbuilding program producing five new construction LPHs and five converted from the CVE–105 class. One of each type per year from 1958 to 1962.

4 Jun Hogaboom Board appointed to study the organization and composition and equipment of the FMF.

5 Jul Marine Corps Aviation Five-Year Program submitted to CNO. Plan called for nine light helicopter squadrons of 20 aircraft each and six medium squadrons of 15 Aircraft each, plus three VMOs of 18 aircraft each, all by 1962.

20 Jul *Thetis Bay* (CVS–90) commissioned as CVHA–1.

1957

7 Jan Hogaboom Board report published, outlining three phase objective, 1957 to 1965, for the helicopter program.

12 Jan HMR(M)–461 commissioned.

13 Feb Marine Corps received first HUS in a tactical squadron.

3 Nov HMR(M)–462 commissioned.

1958

9 Jan CMC requested replacement for the HUS–1.

2 May CMC informed CNO that Marine Corps considered the CVS as an acceptable interim LPH.

1 Jun Helicopter groups reorganize under "M" series T/O as recommended by Hogaboom Board. Two HMR(L)s and one HMR(C) in each group.

1 Sep HMR(M)–463 commissioned.

1959

30 Jan USS *Boxer* (CVS–21) reclassified as the LPH–4.

2 Mar USS *Princeton* reclassified as the LPH–5.

16 Mar MAG(HR) designation changed to MAG.

30 Jun HMR(L)–264 commissioned.

1960

1 Feb Helicopter groups revert to "L" series T/O structure. Three HMR(L)s vice two HMR(L)s and one HMR(C).

7 Mar CNO published Developmental Characteristic Number AO–17501–1 for the CH–46A.

9 Aug CNO issued Developmental Characteristic Number AO–17503–3 for the ASH.

1961

20 Feb BuWeps announced that Boeing–Vertrol would build the replacement for the HUS–1, the CH–46A (BU–107II).

27 Mar CNO issued Developmental Characteristic Number AO–17501–3 for the CH–53A (S–65).

1 Jul USS *Valley Forge* reclassified as the LPH–8.

1 Sep HMR–364 commissioned.

1962

1 Feb HMR(L)s began changing designation to HMM and HMR(M)s to HMH.

2 Mar BuWeps announced that Bell Aircraft Company would build the Marine Corps ASH, the HU–1E (BELL–204).

24 Aug BuWeps announced Siorsky's CH–53A would replace the HR2S–1.

APPENDIX D
HELICOPTER SPECIFICATIONS

	HRP-1	HRP-2	HO3S-1	HRS-1	HRS-2	HRS-3	HO5S-1	HOK-1	HUS-1	HR2S-1	HTL-1	HUP-2
Normal Gross Weight	6,900	6,979	4,985	7,000	7,125	7,750	2,695	5,798	13,300	28,023	2,350	5,750
Empty Weight	5,193	5,205	3,788	4,697	4,832	5,193	2,100	4,160	7,435	20,075	1,570	4,120
Useful Load	1,707	1,774	1,197	2,303	2,293	2,557	595	1,638	5,865	7,948	780	1,630
Zero Range Payload	1,307	1,373	947	1,543	1,533	1,797	303	1,224	4,900	6,435	516	1,015
Maximum Fuel Load (Pounds)	580	580	580	1,050	1,050	1,050	342	619	1,578	2,400	174	950
Cruising Speed (KTS)	83 *	87 *	65	60	60	60	70	70	90	100	60	80
Power Plant	R-1340	R-1340	R-985-AN5	R-1340	R-1340	R-1300	O-425-1	R-1340-48	R-1820-84	R-2800	O-335-5	R-975-42
Total Horsepower (Take off)	600	600	450	600	600	700	245	525	1,525	4.200	200	550
Rotor Diameter (feet)	41	41	45	53	53	53	33	50.5	56	72	35	53½
Maximum Height	15'	15'	12'6"	14'	14'	14'	8'8"	16'8"	15'8"	22'	9'2"	12'6"
Maximum Length	83'4"	83'4"	57½'	62'6"	62'6"	62'6"	39'1"	47'	65'7"	88'	41'5"	75'
Number of Pay Seats (Permanently Installed)	8	8	3	10	10	10	3	3	12	23	2	5
Litter Capacity	6	6	0	3	3	3	2	2	8	16	2	2
Crew Required	2	2	1	2	2	2	1	2	2	3	1	2

* Maximum Airspeed

APPENDIX E

U.S. MARINE CORPS HELICOPTERS ON HAND 1947–1962

	1947	1948	1949	1950	1951	1952	1953	1954	1955	1956	1957	1958	1959	1960	1961	1962
HRP-1		5	6	5												
HRP-2				2	3	3	1									
HO3S-1		5	8	5	4	3	1	2	2							
HTL-1				2	2	1										
HTL-2		1	1	1	1											
HTL-3				2	2											
HTL-4				8	11	12		5								
HTL-5								1	5							
HRS-1					47	35	36	27	25	27	8	2				
HRS-2						71	60	52	11	2						
HRS-3							45	51	77	113	123	113	50	35	17	13
HO4S-1					6	3	2	2	2	1						
HO5S-1						33	57	37	26	6						
HTK						4						1				
HUP1&2								11	13		3		2			
H-13D									6							
HR2S-1										2	14	37	36	29	29	28
HOK-1										28	41	45	39	37	35	30
HUS-1											49	124	159	199	255	309
HUS-1Z														4	4	4
HUSS-2															3	5
TOTAL HELO *	0	11	15	25	76	166	202	188	167	179	238	322	286	304	343	389
OY/OE	22	24	14	17	24	43	45	41	53	41	42	37	39	34	22	25

* Figures include all aircraft on hand in Marine Corps inventory (FMF, HMX, and shore activities) as of 31 Dec for each calendar year.

INDEX

www.ingramcontent.com/pod-product-compliance
Lightning Source LLC
Chambersburg PA
CBHW080518110426

42742CB00017B/3162